AMERICA'S
ECONOMIC
RESURGENCE

AMERICA'S ECONOMIC RESURGENCE

A Bold New Strategy

RICHARD ROSECRANCE

1817

HARPER & ROW, PUBLISHERS, NEW YORK

Grand Rapids, Philadelphia, St. Louis, San Francisco
London, Singapore, Sydney, Tokyo, Toronto

For Barbara

Allen County Public Library
Ft. Wayne, Indiana

FIRST EDITION

Library of Congress Cataloging-in-Publication Data

Rosecrance, Richard N.
   America's economic resurgence : a bold new strategy / Richard
Rosecrance. — 1st ed.
       p.   cm.
   Includes bibliographical references.
   ISBN 0-06-016251-1
   1. United States—Economic policy—1981– 2. United States—
Commercial policy. 3. Competition, International. I. Title.
HC106.8.R665   1990
338.973'009'048—dc20   89-45710

90 91 92 93 94 CC/HC 10 9 8 7 6 5 4 3 2 1

Contents

Foreword

A few years ago I wrote a book, *The Rise of the Trading State,* chronicling and explaining the role of countries like Japan, which have surged to the forefront of international relations in the last forty-five years by emphasizing international trade in preference to military and territorial expansion. In comparison, the United States and the Soviet Union have done less well because they have continued to pursue outmoded territorial and imperial policies. If many nations joined the group of "trading states," the prospect of military conflict would gradually recede, perhaps ushering in a new era of general peace in world politics. In this book, I try to explain how the international system can be made stable in such a context. Broadly speaking, if the system is to regain equilibrium, the United States must prosper. But stability is important not only for America. A worldwide depression could bring great suffering among nations and perhaps also lead to a reassertion of the territorial urge, and thus to war.

The achievement of stability depends on America's taking new measures to improve its economic performance. But it also needs other countries both to carry a greater share of the international relations burden and to help reduce its amount. If they do, America will undergo a profound economic resurgence. If they do not, economic stagnation confronts the contemporary United States, imposing a restriction on world growth as well. Fortunately, the military burden will decline with the evolution of Soviet policy, and the economic burden will be lifted by Japan. This alleviation will not occur automatically. Neither American nor Japanese leadership—to say nothing of their respective populations—is ready for new policies as yet. America clings to an imperial role centered on high defense spending, while Japan continues to adhere to its export surplus and exclusionary mentality. Japan needs to be "internationalized" and America to refocus on domestic economic priorities. It will take a sudden shock, an economic and political crisis, to force both countries to reconsider their policies and adopt new remedies.

That economic shock is coming. Economic policy makers have not yet abolished the business cycle or the rise and fall of the stock market. A new crisis will encourage longer-term perspectives in the United States and shorter ones in Japan. America will regain economic strength, but in the new international context it will not need its former power. The future United States will not be a hegemonic overlord. In a more multipolar system, including the European Community and other nations, its association with Japan in a new Group of Two (G-2) will provide a mechanism for addressing major world problems.

American recovery is thus a function both of international cooperation and new domestic measures. The cooperation and assistance of close U.S. allies is the necessary, but not sufficient, condition for American economic renewal. If the United States does not use its international support to make the necessary changes in its own internal functioning, recovery will be short-lived. An economic crisis will set the stage for reform, but it will take new leadership from the President and the cooperation of the Congress to make the long-term changes needed to keep America productive and growing.

I have many to thank for their help in shaping the ideas of this work. The Woodrow Wilson International Center for Scholars provided an ideal environment to formulate and test hypotheses, and I am grateful to Jim Billington, Sam Wells, Ron Morse, Rob Litwak, and Barry Posen for their guidance. Constantine Symeonides-Tsatsos was an indefatigable research aide. At Brookings I am indebted to Tom Mann, Kent Weaver, Joe White, Alice Rivlin, and the members of the Governmental and Economic Studies faculties for their help. I learned a great deal from the Members of the House Ways and Means Committee and particularly want to thank Dan Rostenkowski and Bill Archer. At UCLA I benefited from discussions with Ron Rogowski, and Art Stein shared with me his extremely insightful criticisms. Virginia Haufler made very useful comments. Mary Colacurcio and Dave D'Lugo made the research go much faster. Greg Ginet drew my attention to the social relevance of computer games. Martin Ginsburg, while warning that a good tax lawyer could get around the most ingenious reform, nevertheless convinced me of the merits of an "integrated" tax system. Alan Alexandroff, while disagreeing with much of the argument, made extremely helpful suggestions. Cass Canfield gave me the benefit of his keen insight in reshaping an unwieldy manuscript. Bob Tabian, my agent, was of great assistance from the very inception of the project. My greatest debt, however, is to my loving Barbara, who sharpened and deepened the work at every point. The remaining failings of the work are entirely my own.

RICHARD ROSECRANCE
Brentwood, California

Preface

Two Futures

Two possible futures await the United States. In one, the oceanic world in A.D. 2010 has become a Japanese lake. The United States has been admitted to membership in the Greater World Co-Prosperity Sphere run by Nippon. Just as the Japanese sometimes benignly refer to America's second-largest western state as "California Prefecture," so the rest of America has become a kind of dependent protectorate of Japan. Economically, the United States is now an "export platform" for Japanese goods. With low wages and a low-valued dollar, American workers assemble Japanese products and ship them overseas to Japan, the Middle East, Europe, China, and the Pacific rim. Because American economic growth has declined, the U.S. economy no longer can absorb the bulk of Japanese exports produced in the home islands. Instead, America is used to fabricate Japanese-designed goods to be sold in other markets.

To be sure, there is no trade imbalance; if anything, the United States runs an export surplus, given the comparative advantage it receives from Japanese technology. America also continues and even increases her exports of food to the residents of Tokyo, Osaka, Yokohama, Kyoto, and Nagoya. Soybean exports reach a new peak, and American meat is plentiful in Japanese shops. Given the exchange value of $1 = 50$ yen, American prices are exceedingly low in Japanese terms. Even lower-middle-class Japanese can easily afford to rent suites at the Stanford Court Hotel in San Francisco, the Carlyle or the Waldorf-Astoria in New York. The few remaining rich Americans can no longer obtain reservations at the

1

Japanese-owned Bel Air Hotel in Los Angeles; it has been booked ahead for ten years by Japanese tourists.

The economic relationship between Japan and the United States works well because Japanese managers direct the two economies. They decide both the quantity and location of investment in the United States. In the year 2000, the United States ceased to generate capital in any appreciable amount as the American household savings rate fell to under 1 percent of gross national product. Thereafter, Japan provided the necessary funds for the development of American industry.

The same is true for science. American universities ran out of research funds in 2005 because the Federal Government's National Science Foundation could no longer afford the large-scale projects that scientists wanted to work on—the third-generation supercomputer, the long-delayed supercollider, fusion technology, and refinements in superconductivity to raise the ductility of the necessary ceramic materials and the temperature at which superconductivity could be sustained. Now Japan undertakes to support these scientific ventures and retains a monopoly on their technological and commercial applications.

American cities are more efficient than before and housing and commuting problems have been eased because Japanese trains drawn by magnetic levitation provide cheap and easy access to the central city even from remote suburbs four hundred miles away. To be sure, ethnic conflict has not been moderated or equality in living standards achieved. There is little Japanese money for the inner city: investment goes to majority groups who have the best education and the stablest family backgrounds. Welfare expenditures have been cut to reduce government expenditures and wage costs, and the homeless have multiplied by a factor of ten. Though wages remain low, housing costs are astronomical, fueled by Japanese purchases at multimillion-dollar rates. The American educational system has improved in science and technology and many Americans know Japanese, the language of business, industry, and government. The work week has increased to six and one-half days, and the average American gets a two-week vacation, which generally speaking he does not take, pressed to turn out more production for the Japanese business staff. Many Americans work more than 2,600 hours a year.

There is little time for foreign travel because of the demands of work, but even if there were, American wages would not support trips to Japan or Europe, where the dollar buys little. Mexico is the logical tourist haven for financially stressed Americans, but even its prices have risen, given high Japanese investment there. In fact, Mexico is now the major competitor of the United States, with Japan encouraging the latter to do better or Nippon might feel obliged to shift investment to Mexico City, Monterrey, and Guadalajara.

The other future is more hospitable to the United States. After years of running a trade deficit and borrowing to finance it, the United States girds itself for worldwide competition in the mid-1990s and begins to export high-quality products. It regains some of the market lost to Japan in electronics, cars, and financial services. During the period of great indebtedness to Japan, American business and government make a studied effort to apply Japanese technology and business practices to their own factories. As a result, they regain some market share in semiconductors and continue to maintain their lead in computers and software. As the U.S. labor shortage sets in, investment in robotics begins to automate electronics plants, giving the United States a new comparative advantage in foreign trade.

The American–Japanese relationship undergoes a major crisis in the early 1990s, as the American government demands and finally secures a more equal economic relationship with Japan. After that challenge, the U.S.–Japan tie strengthens and Japan continues to depend upon a progressive and expanding U.S. market for its goods. Increasingly, Japan invests directly in the American economy, building new plants to make all sorts of components as well as doing advanced research and development in the United States. This investment worsens the Japanese trade balance, which has already turned into a deficit, but like the United States in the postwar period, Tokyo is willing to finance ventures to stimulate the economy of a close ally. The new technology is transferred routinely to American business participants in joint ventures. The new commercial technology that America acquires as a result of Japanese investment allows American firms to emerge as new and tenacious competitors of their Japanese colleagues. Even more than is true now, Japanese business leaders come to realize that they cannot prosper without a vibrant and dynamic American economy at their side.

The dollar has slid to a value of 100 yen[1]; it stabilizes there, with considerable advantage to American exports. Japan begins to open its consumer economy to U.S. goods and for two reasons: first, they are reasonably priced and high in quality; second, it is in the Japanese interest to allow America to repay its debts through an export surplus in the Japanese market. In fact, Japan emerges as a benevolent creditor power, offering the United States and Latin America as well as East Asian nations the means of selling to the Japanese population. Meanwhile Japanese consumption has greatly increased, taxes have been reduced, and savings decreased as the Japanese population ages.

A new group of Japanese citizens, called *shinjinrui* (new breed), have stressed leisure and freedom from the demands of the work place. Vacations have lengthened and the work week has shortened. There has been a general recognition that the period of incessant Japanese export surpluses also hurt the Japanese population, who have a common interest with Japan's international competitors in increasing consumer access to a range of foreign goods. Japanese government has been broadened to include a range of democratic and socialist parties as well as the erstwhile ruling Liberal Democratic party. The Japanese agricultural market has finally been completely opened to outsiders. The Japanese rate of growth has declined from 4 percent to less than 3 percent per year.

Increasingly, there are American-Japanese consortiums to compete in other markets, but these are not simply dominated by Japanese managers. American science and technology remain the standard of the world as the quality of U.S. products greatly improves. American firms begin to invest for the long term and for competitiveness and market share, not just short-term profits. American growth rates rise to 3 percent and above. Though enmeshed in a worldwide network of interdependence, America retains its economic sovereignty.

United States investment in new industrial products is eased by a more benign climate in foreign policy, which permits lower spending on defense. In Western Europe, Eastern Europe, and the

1. In September 1989 the exchange rate hovered around 140 yen to the dollar.

Soviet Union, governments manage crises without wholesale resort to force. This is partly because tensions between East and West have greatly moderated and because Russian leaders are willing to experiment with mixed regimes in Eastern Europe. The United States does not try to take advantage of Soviet difficulties and instead a new foreign policy link develops between Moscow and Washington.

1

The Transformation of the American Dream

Which of these futures will the United States really come to experience? From the vantage point of the last decade of the twentieth century, the answer is not yet fully clear. From every standpoint the United States confronts a unique challenge. For many reasons a trend toward the pessimistic scenario sketched previously seems more realistic over the next few years than toward the optimistic one. Beginning with the 1990s and for the first time in their history, Americans face a gloomier economic prospect than did their parents. In industry after industry they have lost their lead. Americans as a nation now owe close to $1 trillion to Japan, Europe, and the rest of the world, a debt that will be paid back by their children in the form of lower living standards.

Though the pessimistic scenario has not yet become a full reality, modest houses today are frequently too expensive to buy. Middle-class families have difficulty educating their children at first-rate colleges and universities. Raising a family has become more complicated because two incomes are necessary to finance even a downsized version of the good life. Overall, it appears that the American Dream of unfolding opportunity is being transformed into one of shortening horizons.

The historical position of the United States is beginning to resemble that of sixteenth-century Spain, seventeenth-century Holland, and nineteenth-century Great Britain—each of which found that their great wealth led ultimately to national profligacy, overexpenditure, and finally decline.[2] America's great period of economic growth occurred before World War I. Since then, the United States has endured two world wars and a depression. The standard of living has dramatically risen, but the American economy has slowed down. Productivity no longer attains past levels (see Table 1). Though productivity rose rapidly in the aftermath of the 1981–82 recession, it then slumped to around 1 percent per year, much lower than historic levels of nearly 3 percent. Compared to neighbors and rivals (though not to the Soviet Union), the United States of America is a declining power.

Typically, history writes "finis" on the headstones of erstwhile great nations. Sweden, the Austrian Empire, the Ottoman Empire, Venice, and Burgundy all at one time were legendary powers in world politics. They had great economic as well as military potential. But they fell from the ranks of the major nations and today have been absorbed, subdivided by others, or exist in well-earned national retirement.

Is such a fate awaiting the United States? No one can be sure. The basic contention of this book, however, is that, unlike past powers, the United States can come back from decline. America's economic resurgence will occur. The nation does not have to face a continuing restriction of economic and political opportunities. This does not mean that over the next hill a rosy dawn awaits to bring "morn-

Table 1

Nonagricultural Productivity Growth in the U.S., 1945–1987
(Yearly Average)

1945–65	2.7
1965–73	1.8
1973–80	.4
1983	3.3
1985	1.2
1986	1.6
1987	.8

Source: Benjamin Friedman, *Day of Reckoning* (New York: Random House, 1988), pp. 188–89, 206–207.

2. Here and afterward the adjective "relative" should always be interpolated before the noun "decline." England "declined" compared to other nations even when its own wealth was absolutely increasing. "Relative" refers not only to the record of other nations but to one's own past performance.

ing in America." Americans face difficult days in the years ahead, and to brighten the long-term prospect their political leaders must take vigorous steps in the next few years to reshape the American future.

Among their tasks, they must oversee the remodeling of the U.S. economic plant. They must find a means of financing foreign policy and entitlement programs while reducing the government deficit. This almost certainly means tax increases as well as budget cuts. In the process Americans also have to stop contributing to the trade deficit by excessive federal spending, which typically incurs a short-fall of about $140 billion per year (irrespective of contributions to the Social Security Trust Fund).[3] In practical terms this suggests that Americans will have to produce more efficiently and work harder simply to earn their current (real) incomes. Instead of pur-suing the highest corporate earnings, businesses will have to aim at long-term growth. Working men and women face the need to forgo wage increases that are not justified by productivity gains, and corporation executives and white-collar professionals must trim their lifestyles to the incomes that their performance actually merits. To make the economy regain momentum, Americans will have to cooperate more in the country's interest, and not seek merely to advance their own.

Nor is it enough to bring the government budget into balance and to end the surplus of imports over exports. Many poor nations, like Bangladesh, have favorable balances of trade. The dollar can fall so far to achieve equilibrium that American assets become totally devalued. Already, metropolitan real estate in Tokyo (at the value of 130 yen to the dollar) is almost equal to the value of all

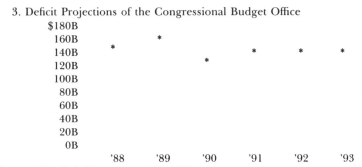

3. Deficit Projections of the Congressional Budget Office

Source: *New York Times*, August 18, 1989.

the land in the United States![4] What is important is to achieve a balance in which the United States continues to export highly valued products and the dollar retains enough purchasing power to buy the expensive goods of other countries. Thus Americans must invest to manufacture high-valued goods, not mere raw materials, food grains, or products produced at low labor cost. To do this, they need extra savings from government expenditure, which can be devoted to investment in production facilities for intricate and sophisticated new products. American production of high-value (but still much wanted) goods will enable them to reach a balance-of-payments equilibrium in which the terms of trade remain favorable (in which the prices of exported goods are higher than the prices of imported goods, on average).

In foreign policy the United States has to find a way of lessening the cost of the American military presence in Europe and the Far East and getting more defense per dollar. U.S. weapons systems now in the pipeline will require a 7 percent real increase in the defense budget each year for the next five years if we continue to fund them.[5] If government accounts cannot stand such a strain, Americans must find means of canceling or stretching out the procurement of such items. Congress and the Bush Administration are already grappling with this problem.

None of these tasks is impossible to perform. The world environment is now uniquely favorable to Americans' hopes and dreams, almost as their forefathers believed. The tide of world politics is going their way. With the temporary exception of postcrackdown Beijing, repressive regimes are becoming more democratic. Traditional foes who engaged in military conquest in the past are now emphasizing economic growth, foreign trade, and military retrenchment. Despite the check to political liberalization in China, the regime in power wishes to continue and intensify its economic links to the western world. Iran is moving to a more "economic,"

4. N. Amaya writes: "The total value of the land in the Tokyo metropolitan area has been estimated at Y400 trillion, which is reportedly close to the total value of all the land in the entire United States." N. Amaya, "The Japanese Economy in Transition," *Japan and the World Economy,* vol. 1, no. 1 (1988-89), p. 106.

5. See John Steinbruner, ed., *Restructuring American Foreign Policy* (Washington, D.C.: Brookings Institution, 1989).

as compared with its past "ideological," strategy. There are no new large states bent on expanding their territory against the United States and other countries. Indeed, most nation-states are small and content to remain within their borders. One hundred new (mostly small) states have joined the international system since World War II. Despite their size, these new nations have proved resistant to military pressures of all kinds: from their neighbors or from large states. Their nationalism and ethnic identity have not crumbled under assault. Their success has forged a kind of built-in deterrence against imperial or military expansion.

New states in the Pacific Rim and elsewhere have also shown that prosperity stems from rising exports and burgeoning foreign commerce. They chart a path that America might follow with profit. The United States can pursue this course because its traditional adversaries face problems keeping up and are also turning their attention to long-term economic growth. Allies have assisted America to begin retooling industries so that it can perform better economically. In fact, one of the tendencies of modern world capitalism is to develop regions where the returns are greatest. If investment funds pile up in Japan, they can usefully be diverted toward Latin America and the Third World. If certain industries are high-cost and overdeveloped in Europe, they can be exported to the United States and to other areas where local currencies and trained labor forces provide an incentive.

Despite the valid comparisons between America's present difficulties and the plight of nineteenth-century Britain, the United States retains unique strengths. It has a far larger manufacturing base than any of its predecessors. It has unmatched creative potential in pure science, an asset that can be transformed into superiority in industrial technology. Further, America's challengers—the Soviet Union in the military field and Japan in the economic one—are one-dimensional powers. They could threaten others only if they could combine. This seems highly unlikely. Historically and militarily the two nations have always been rivals in the Far East, clashing over China and Korea. Culturally and politically they have espoused dramatically contrasting systems of government and ways of life. The Soviet Union has little to offer Japan except mineral resources, and the Russian market will remain tiny for the foreseeable future. Certainly, it could not substitute for the huge attractions to Japan of American consumer buying power. And if, despite all obstacles, Russia and Japan did unite, they would force China and America into a military and economic embrace, an eventuality that neither power seeks.

Japan, moreover, the primary ally as well as competitor of the United States, rests its future on the further expansion of world trade, an expansion that cannot take place without higher economic growth rates in America. The United States still contains the greatest consumer market in the world, and as Table 2 shows, Japan cannot continue to prosper without selling in it. The fusion of European economies in 1992 will not greatly alter this situation because the new Europe may be surrounded by a restrictive tariff wall. Europe buys and sells mainly to itself, and in any event the European Economic Community has been much less hospitable to Japanese exports than the United States has been. As far as America is concerned, its ability to buy depends upon its capacity to sell—both at home and abroad. Japanese investment in the United States to modernize factories and outdated industrial practices is critical to America's new competitiveness, and it has so far been forthcoming.

But the Japanese will not solve America's problems. The American people will have to prod corporations, unions, and governments to abandon outdated economic practices and to reform themselves under the stimulus of foreign competition. Otherwise, as suggested in the Preface, the United States could become a kind of economic colony of Japan—a species of advanced developing country in which Japanese managers make the major deci-

Table 2

Japanese Exports to Selected Countries 1987
as % of Total Exports

U.S.	36.5
Rep. of Korea	5.8
Fed. Repub. of Germany	5.6
Taiwan	4.9
Hong Kong	3.9

Source: *Statistical Handbook of Japan 1988*, p. 85.

sions affecting America's industrial future and ultimately its way of life.[6]

To compete in the multifaceted world of tomorrow, the United States will need radically new policies—policies that increase savings and spur the transfer of savings into investment. It will need an educational system second to none, which must include a renaissance in state primary and secondary school systems, perhaps modeled on recent progress in South Carolina, where test scores, teacher salaries, and parent involvement in school programs have all increased dramatically. American managers need to reinvest in the future of their companies and industries. They cannot do this if they are harried by the prospect of hostile takeovers, or if they spend all their time arranging leveraged buyouts to feather their own nests. They cannot do it if investment capital is either too expensive or is available only on a short-term basis. They cannot finance new machines and technology through venture capital if lenders shrink in number or lose long-term perspective. They cannot issue bonds or stocks if markets do not sustain their value. They cannot appease stockholders if investors demand tangible, high, and rising profits in each quarter of the financial year.

The United States needs a tax system that rewards long-term capital investment and penalizes short-term returns, specifically a reduction in the tax on long-term capital gains. At the same time Americans need to curb indebtedness while they reward thrift, balancing the current advantages of borrowing against the socially necessary ones of saving. Ultimately, the United States, like most other developed democracies, must have an "integrated" tax system, which (instead of favoring debt) gives equal treatment to debt and equity. It will need government help akin to that rendered in Japan by the Ministry of International Trade and Industry in finding sources of finance for innovative new products. Many have advocated a new Reconstruction Finance Corporation to channel low-interest loans to industrial renovation. A National Technology Foundation (NTF), based on the National Bureau of Standards and Technology law introduced by Senator Fritz Hollings of South Carolina and passed by Congress, should be fully financed to create

6. See Clyde Prestowitz, *Trading Places* (New York: Basic Books, 1988).

a partnership with the National Science Foundation (NSF) and to facilitate the transfer of findings from pure research into civilian products and commercial uses.

Nor can Americans assume that the "market" will solve all their problems. Every society's economy is a reflection of its tax structure. In America, tax laws give an advantage to indebted individuals and corporations, so much so that the U.S. Government Treasury is raided periodically to create heavily mortgaged corporations, which, as a result, pay little or no tax. In Japan tax laws give an advantage to savers and investors (who are able to avoid tax on the dividends from savings accounts), but companies cannot escape tax by going into debt. Unless Americans change their laws, companies will not operate as effectively and freely as their Japanese competitors do. Indeed, it might even be advantageous for America and Japan temporarily to exchange tax codes.

Americans should also come to recognize that many of their organizations, public and private, military and economic, have too many chiefs and not enough Indians. Social organizations have embraced Max Weber's bureaucratic society with a vengeance, with overstaffed ministries and corporate headquarters, in which specialization has been narrowed to a pinpoint. In organization after organization committees proliferate, but the job does not get done. It is almost as if leading U.S. hotels and business establishments are run by a series of ganglia, but not by a single brain. In all too many of them, management specialties are the way to the top instead of production and meeting the needs of the consumer or customer.

But more than any single measure, the United States needs to recognize the challenge society faces, and openly acknowledge the impending crisis that lies before it. Otherwise efforts to solve long-term problems will be blocked by the short-term business-as-usual mentality. How can this occur? The crisis America faces will have to intensify and be made concrete—for only a sustained and powerful challenge can bring home the need for Americans to work together and to accept sacrifices: to help their country as well as themselves.

The coming crisis will manifest itself in a new fall of the stock market, followed by a sharp recession. It could arise from many sources—a sudden selloff in Tokyo; a collapse of the dollar, leading to a sudden flight of capital out of the United States (requiring much higher interest rates to prevent a further flight)[7]; the widespread failure of savings-and-loan institutions; or a general decline of consumption and investment. With consumer, government, and business debt over $7 trillion, even a small slump could trigger a default of highly leveraged corporations and thereby precipitate a crisis.

Where, normally, corporate debt shrinks in time of prosperity, in the past several years debt has risen as a result of takeovers financed by junk bonds. Corporate debt has risen to 33 percent of the GNP as compared with 26 percent five years ago. Under these circumstances, a Brookings Institution study has estimated that as many as 10 percent of public corporations would go bankrupt in a recession like that of 1973–75.[8] On the trade front, even good news has its darker lining: once Americans move their commercial account into the black, ending the flow of foreign capital into the United States, there could be a collapse in investment, triggering a slump.

Such a setback could be salutary. It could lead to new measures that would be politically difficult to embrace today—measures like those Franklin Roosevelt was able to adopt in the first months of the New Deal or that John Kennedy could put in place in the early years of the New Frontier. One may question the efficacy of many of FDR's measures and the wisdom of Kennedy's steel price rollback and his tax cut. Nonetheless, in both cases new presidential leadership was given greater scope to deal with national problems. In this way, the crisis could be restorative. America's trading partners would not let the United States plunge into a depression as

7. Robert Litan writes, for example: "The supply of foreign capital could suddenly dry up, throwing the U.S. economy into recession. Any number of events, real or perceived, could trigger a dollar strike: a failure by the United States to reduce its budget deficit, a perception by foreign investors that the United States will become less hospitable to their capital; or a drift by the United States toward protectionism, to name just a few. Fearing the inflationary consequences of a plummeting dollar, whatever the cause, the Federal Reserve could be expected to tighten monetary policy sharply." Robert Litan, "The Risks of Recession" in Robert E. Litan, Robert Z. Lawrence, and Charles L. Schultze, eds., *American Living Standards: Threats and Challenges* (Washington, D.C.: Brookings Institution, 1988), p. 74.

8. See Lindley Clark and Alfred Malabre, "Cooling Economy Puts Fed on Tightwire," *Wall Street Journal,* May 9, 1989, pp. A2, A14.

severe as that of 1929–38. In their own interest they would buy American goods and lend, perhaps even give, money to the United States. If it arose in the next few years, such a challenge would require George Bush to prove that he is more like Roosevelt (Franklin or Theodore) than Herbert Hoover.

In certain ways the challenge could not come at a better time. In the immediate future foreign problems will be more manageable than they have been at any period since the start of the Cold War. America's allies have strengthened greatly compared to her enemies. The people of the United States recognize the economic challenge that other countries pose and, given the stimulus of new leadership, are ready to work to meet that challenge. American business is ready to take on new responsibilities if the tax system and stock market pressures allow them. All Americans know that their educational system vitally needs repair and improvement. A new crisis would crystallize these ideas and sanction reforms that today still encounter political resistance. In the nineties a new administration will be ready and able to make difficult decisions.

The success of these reforms will depend upon a transformation of the American Dream and a new vision of the United States and its role in the world. Historically, the American Dream of national and individual achievement was based on U.S. "uniqueness" in social, geographical, economic, and philosophic terms. Gouverneur Morris, our informal emissary to France in 1789, believed that it was useless for the French to adopt new liberal institutions. "They want an American constitution," he thundered, "without realizing they have no Americans to uphold it." The American colonies were not riddled with European class divisions and pretensions. In fact, there was no "nobility" of the European sort, only a species of the upper middle class. In addition, a European lower class played no role in the settlement or the founding myths of the American social order. Despite the tincture of indentured servants, slaves, and poor farmers, most early settlers were essentially of middle-class stock. This was to change, of course, during the nineteenth century, but then the later immigrants had to adjust to a middle-class culture that was already in place.

America's social uniqueness—its essentially middle-class origins—colored the U.S. attitude toward Europe. American society had unique freedoms that the Europeans could not match, with their antagonistic three-class system. Social equality, at least at the level of theory and prescription, was endorsed by all Americans, though it was far from being achieved in practice. Hence, what worried Jefferson most was his fear of "contamination" by European influences: The United States should not be too entangled in the affairs of Europe or it would lose social innocence and the ability of Americans to cooperate with one another.

This social uniqueness was fostered and supported by geographic isolation. The United States was removed from European conflicts and in the nineteenth century could develop in freedom from war (with the exception of the Civil War) and the constant threat of external intervention. That isolation did not begin to break down until the First World War and it did not end until the Second. Until then, Americans were quite ready to expand their borders in the Western Hemisphere but did not want to be involved in European quarrels, at least until they seemed directly to affect the United States. For both social and geographic reasons, then, America could grow and prosper without reference to Europe.

Economically, it also could proceed largely under its own steam. British capital helped to develop the United States, financing canal building and railroads. But agricultural exports, including cotton and wheat, allowed the United States to pay back its debts in short order. America had a virtually unblemished record of export surpluses running from 1874 to 1970, nearly one hundred years! With new U.S. technology after the Civil War, Americans saw little need for European industrial exports: they could produce their own manufactures. And as far as minerals and food were concerned, there was an abundant supply at home. With its continental market, and plentiful raw materials, the United States needed practically nothing from the rest of the world.

Thus, after a brief period as a developing country, America became largely self-sufficient. Nor did it have to sell to Europe: the rising tide of immigrants provided a sufficient market at home, and the U.S. population grew by leaps and bounds. A huge continental market emerged as the western boundary was pushed to the Pacific. Again, there was little need to tailor American tastes or goods to Europe or the rest of the world. Indeed, in certain respects, the United States led the world. Its rate of growth in the late nineteenth

Table 3

Growth Rate of Manufacturing Production
of the Great Powers 1870–1913

Germany	1.9 %
France	1.5
Britain	1.3
Russia	2.0
U.S.	2.05

Source: Calculated from A. J. P. Taylor, *The Struggle for Mastery in Europe, 1848–1919*
(Oxford: Oxford at the Clarendon Press, 1954), p. xxxi.

century was equaled by that of no other country save Russia, and
Russian growth was episodic. (See Table 3.) By 1910 the United
States was the equal of Germany and Britain combined. Because of
the shortage of labor relative to the needs of a developing continent, America was among the first to invent and use labor-saving
devices in industry and mining. Mechanization went very quickly in
the United States, faster than in Europe. Machine-made interchangeable parts were pioneered by Colt, and the assembly line by
Henry Ford.

By the 1920s there was the belief, propounded by Horatio Alger
and modified by Scott Fitzgerald, that an American with pluck, luck,
and effort could proceed from "rags to riches" in one generation.
New immigrants shared that belief and many of them prospered
because of it. But Americans did not have to imitate the rest of the
world, only each other's success. Success was defined in terms of
the latest American invention, product, or social innovation. Many
believed that Americans "solved problems" while other countries
retained their traditional and habitual ways of doing things. There
was little reason for Americans to look beyond water's edge.[9]
Thomas Edison's work provided abundant evidence that new con-

9. This faith smacked of overconfidence, West Churchmen notes: "Given the
crushing advantages and overwhelming success the U.S. enjoyed, what possibly
could ever happen to derail the American dream machine? Or had there always
been a weakness lurking somewhere within it? The answer is not only 'yes,' but it
can be given a definite name: The Failure of Success. Ironically, it was not the initial
failure of the American experiment itself that led to the subsequent difficulties that
the U.S. is currently experiencing. Rather, it was America's huge unparalleled
successes. Or more precisely, it was our enormous failure as a culture to understand that it was only a very special, limited set of conditions that made for America's temporary success no matter how long they seemed to last." C. West Church-
man et al., *Business for Non-Business Majors* (mimeo, 1988), p. 16.

sumer inventions were likely to be American ones. In the 1930s Roosevelt's innovative Tennessee Valley Authority (TVA) offered an example of American ingenuity in spreading low-cost power to the southeastern states. In 1969 America put a man on the moon when no other society could accomplish such a feat.

The same strand of American uniqueness ran through American writing. The nation was philosophically unique because America gave rise to no class philosophies that might divide citizens. Its contributions, like pragmatism and instrumentalism, were philosophies of technique, which assumed fundamental agreement on underlying social and political values. The early settlers were seeking religious freedom from the established churches of Europe. They preached hard work and instilled guilt as a social incentive. Each person had to make a contribution to the community to justify his or her existence. Accepting such promptings, individuals by dint of effort and self-sacrifice could achieve the American Dream, success and happiness, in small communities or great cities. Effort, energy, and dedication were the keys to prosperity.

Nowhere in the American experience was attention to the outside world—its mores, practices, economic systems, and social usages—regarded as either useful or mandatory.[10] Thus, Americans, for the most part, did not learn European or Far Eastern languages, nor read the books of other cultures. Other nations, they thought, had little to teach them. The most American examples of the desire to create the rest of the world in their own image were Woodrow Wilson's Fourteen Points in 1917, the Hoover relief efforts in Europe after World War I, the Marshall Plan after World War II, and the Peace Corps of the Kennedy Administration.[11] Each assumed that the United States had something to teach or offer to others. With these assumptions, when were Americans ever going to learn from the outside world?

The time to do so has now arrived. The American Dream has been transformed. America's place in the world has fallen to "first

10. For an example of an American who refused to indulge in European social intrigue see Henry James, *The American.*

11. The primary value of the Peace Corps, as it turned out, was not in imparting American wisdom, educational practices, or technology to new nations: it was in informing a generation of young Americans about conditions in the rest of the world.

among equals" (*primus inter pares*). Within society, there is a growing gulf between rich and poor, the mainstream and the alienated.
Internationally, isolation has yielded to interdependence. Given
new technologies of transportation and communication, geographic remoteness has given way to military and economic proximity to others. The American economy no longer functions self-
sufficiently, but depends upon huge imports of oil, industrial
products, capital, and, maleficently, drugs from other nations.
Americans' dependence on others therefore obliges them to export
as they have never done before. Philosophically, American social
doctrines now have to adjust to a world of conflicting values, of
different ethnic and religious views. Technique alone cannot sustain America in the international competition of ideas, political
ideologies, and institutions. The United States needs a vision not
just of its own future but of where the rest of the world is going and
ought to go. America must broaden its understanding of the funda-
mentals of democracy so that they can be applied in a worldwide
context. This means it must begin to understand that past American emphasis upon social unity and uniformity at home (though
never in fact achieved) is not a prerequisite to democracy in other
countries. It is not necessary even in the United States. Many different social groups within one country can make an important contribution to economic transformation and growth.

At least in its early stages, economic development does not require democracy, as countries like imperial Germany and post-
Meiji Japan have demonstrated in the past, and China and Korea
have at present. It may be, however, that economic growth reaches
a plateau that cannot be transcended without social and political
reform—a sometimes barren region on which contemporary Russia
has been stranded for the past decade. Liberal-democratic societies
offer a free flow of information. They are open to the latest technological invention and quickly see the means by which it might be
further developed or put into practice. By monopolizing the exchange of information in order to retain control, authoritarian
regimes ultimately paralyze their own scientific advance. If this is
true, the United States does not need to try to "Americanize"
others, to impose its own peculiar liberal institutions on other
nations. Under the pressure of the need for economic reform, they
will seek political development in their own way.

For the past two generations, Americans have not always been aware of this lesson. They have striven to remake the world too much in the American image. They have succeeded in liberalizing and rehabilitating many parts of the world, not least in Europe and Japan. But much of Asia, Africa, and Latin America remains outside the liberal purview. Mired in poverty and inequality, these societies do not yet have enough social reform to sustain a lasting economic and political transformation. Further, while the United States can offer a beacon of hope to some oppressed nations through the force of its own example, it cannot impose a political or social metamorphosis upon them. They have to accomplish that themselves.

If that is true, the American role in world politics can be more modest in the generations to come. In the future the United States will have to articulate a philosophy of foreign policy in which the country achieves a balanced contribution, to Americans at home as well as to others abroad. Up to the 1930s, America put national goals ahead of world stability and neglected the foreign threat. In a 180-degree turn after 1945, the United States raised world stability above national progress. In the years ahead it will have to find a more equal balance between the two. In particular it will have to narrow the widening rift between rich and poor citizens. America will have to deepen and rechannel the wellsprings of national strength if it is to continue to have a useful mission abroad.

For both philosophic and economic reasons the American Dream no longer mandates either isolation or crusading interventionism, but rather partnership in a society of nations. As "first among equals" the United States will find that partnership demands a knowledge and understanding of other peoples that it does not currently possess. As the Third World develops in association with Europe and Japan, many Americans will spend half their lives working in other countries. The United States will have to learn more about them in order for its own society to function properly. In these circumstances, American long-term social strengths will be seen not in terms of "uniqueness" but rather in the way U.S. society shows how different ethnic, religious, and racial groups can work together. Ideally, the United States will serve as a microcosm of the way the world might function as a large commonwealth, an international melting pot. The fact that America has been able to design an economic and social system in which minorities and immigrants contribute greatly to the success of the whole community should give hope to heterogeneous nations like India, Brazil, Israel, and even the Soviet Union that they can do the same. In this way, then, America will be gradually transformed from a special, unique case to that of an exemplar—a kind of mirror of the world community. And in the future, U.S. international success, as George Kennan foresaw, will depend greatly on domestic achievement in solving pressing economic, social, and political problems.[12]

Will an America that focuses more on domestic problems lose out in foreign relations? Some may be tempted to think so. Yet, as even the Communists recognized, the ultimate influence of a society in world politics depends on whether it offers a model that others may seek to emulate. Nikita Khrushchev, the Russian leader in the late 1950s and early 1960s, believed that Communism would offer a more attractive economic and social system for the developing world to imitate than capitalism. The Third World would follow the Soviet pattern. With this same self-confidence, Khrushchev predicted that Communism would outlive Capitalism: "We will bury you," he pronounced. (He meant, literally, "We will be around to officiate at your burial rites.")

If Third World nations had generally embraced socialist models, the United States and the Western democratic nations would have suffered a great reverse. In fact, the less-developed countries did not adopt Russian-style socialist regimes. And those that did, like China, are now seeking to find a way back toward a more open economic, but not yet liberal political, system. The great success stories like Korea and Taiwan, Singapore and Hong Kong, have prospered from exporting to other nations under a Western capitalist pattern. There are no parallels in Eastern Europe, although Hungary has moved furthest in the direction of an open market, and East Germany, beginning to undergo political turmoil, has been an effective exporter. In this basic sense, the main issue of the Cold War has already been decided: the Western capitalist option has proved decisively superior to the Communist one.

This gives rise to a paradox: the United States has been doing

12. See George Kennan, *The Realities of American Foreign Policy* (Princeton: Princeton University Press, 1954).

less well economically than many of its capitalist colleagues. Its camp has won, but U.S. economic performance has proved decisively superior only to that of the Soviet Union. Still, international capitalist success gives the United States a breathing space to strengthen its foreign influence by improving its economic and social functioning at home. It must do this and not only for domestic reasons. Insofar as the American economy weakens and fails to perform, America's example becomes less attractive. A reconcentration upon domestic growth does not mean that the United States will not remain heavily involved in foreign relations: it does suggest that relatively greater attention to domestic economic matters will not impair its foreign standing and may even improve it. This will be no sectarian introversion; in fact America can only better its own record by being more aware of the practices of other nations. In other words, the United States will progress domestically only if it can apply resources, both intellectual and financial, derived from foreign relations.

To be a more successful economic power Americans will need to recapture their nineteenth-century heritage and social élan. Despite the huge wave of immigration that washed upon its shores then, nineteenth-century United States still faced a labor shortage.[13] And that labor shortage forced high investment in labor-saving devices and the mechanization of production. American economic growth raced ahead. In recent years the rather slumbrous U.S. rate of development has slowed new investment. (See Table 4.) After the Great Depression of 1929–38 high growth rates did not resume, or did so only temporarily. America avoided recessions too often through military spending to absorb excess industrial capacity. When military demand abated, the economy foundered and declined. After 1982 President Reagan was able to create many new jobs because low U.S. productivity (based upon deficient capital investment) guaranteed that labor would be employed before new machines would be built. America's relatively lower capital intensiveness increased the demand for labor. Workers found employment in low-skilled jobs and menial service tasks: in fast food emporia, as messengers and clerks. The lower American productiv-

13. Ronald Rogowski, "Political Cleavages and Changing Exposure to Trade," *American Political Science Review*, vol. 81, no. 4 (December 1987).

ity fell, the more jobs would be created when an economic upturn occurred. If this trend was carried to an extreme, America would become a labor- instead of a capital-intensive economy, and living standards would fall in proportion.

The United States now faces a situation, in short, which is fundamentally different from that of the nineteenth century. Low economic growth means low investment in new capacity; low investment in capacity means low productivity. When recessions occur, large numbers of people are thrown out of work, just as large numbers are suddenly reemployed when prosperity returns. If there were higher rates of economic growth, however, the United States could have higher productivity and the work force would be employed in "good jobs at good wages." High rates of growth could provide employment for a growing number of immigrants without fundamentally altering America as a country with a persistent need for labor.

How does the United States regain its nineteenth-century advantage? In the near-term future, the American work force will shrink as the children of today's baby-boom generation grow up. From now to the year 2000 there will be fewer eighteen-year-olds joining the work force and unemployment will decline demographically. The number of workers aged 16 to 24 will drop by almost 8 percent or two million people.[14] The existing working population will age.

Table 4

Growth Rates of GNP
United States 1870–1986

1871–1913	4.3%
1913–1929	3.1
1929–1950	2.9
1950–1960	3.2
1960–1969	4.5
1969–1980	2.8
1980–1986	2.6

Source: Data for 1871–1969 from U.S. Bureau of the Census, *Historical Statistics of the United States, Colonial Times to 1970, Part I* (Washington, D.C.: U.S. Bureau of the Census, 1975), p. 225; current data from U.S. Bureau of the Census, *Statistical Abstract of the U.S.: 1988,* 108th ed. (Washington, D.C.: U.S. Bureau of the Census, 1987), p. 407.

14. *Workforce 2000: Work and Workers for the 21st Century* HI-3796RR (Indianapolis, Indiana: Hudson Institute, June 1987), p. xix.

As the bulge in the American population moves beyond the 18–44 age group, spending will decline and savings rise. Fifty-year-olds have already made their major expenditures on housing, education, automobiles, equipment, and furniture. In the first half of the 1990s the fastest-growing age group will be 45–54-year-olds. As savings increase, the cost of capital will decline and investment will increase, much of it in the United States.

New capital investment in machines and technology will generate new jobs. As J. R. Hicks shows, new machines replace labor in the short run, but they require new employment to make the machines and to keep them running.[15] The nineteenth-century investment in the Industrial Revolution increased rather than diminished real wages and added to the demand for labor. Thus Americans need not fear that new capital expenditures will ultimately reduce employment. Since in the future fewer Americans will be entering the labor market in any event, immigration will supply some of the new workers that will be needed. Thus it may be possible to recapture some of America's nineteenth-century strengths. Fewer workers means a greater need for capital investment to sustain relatively high growth.[16] It also means that immigrants can be accommodated in progressively more technical jobs. For this, education will be required and the United States will need greater investment in human capital (the educational system) as well as investment in machines and information systems.

This does not mean that changing demographics will provide an automatic solution to America's problems. A persistent labor shortage will stimulate investment, but unless American saving also rises, the United States will be tempted to borrow the needed money abroad. This creates debt, which can only be financed by a trade surplus, and therefore accentuates the problem the United States currently faces.

A labor shortage, drawing in immigrants, thus does not solve the problem by itself. Still, immigration has traditionally eased U.S. economic problems. In the nineteenth century, the influx of new-

15. John R. Hicks, *A Theory of Economic History* (Oxford: Oxford University Press, 1969).

16. Dr. Edward Yardeni writes: ". . . business managers will opt to spend more on labor-saving, productivity-enhancing capital to substitute for scarce and expensive workers." Prudential-Bache Topical Study #16, *The Baby Boom Chart Book*, January 25, 1989, p. 8.

comers not only stimulated consumer demand but also provided the needed labor force. In the years to come, the challenge is to duplicate the achievement of the past, with a steady supply of eager and skilled workers.

Many Japanese observers, however, are pessimistic about this scenario. They believe that the United States is too diverse already in ethnic and racial terms to achieve rapid economic progress. It should not admit new immigrants. Only a socially homogeneous nation can attain the requisite cooperation to meet the economic competition of other states. A nation of blacks, whites, Hispanics, and Asians cannot do so. The lower educational attainment of minority groups, so it is said, will make it difficult for them to compete in the high-technology world of tomorrow.

This view cannot entirely be dismissed, but it neglects the question of incentive. As long as marginal groups looked forward to menial jobs with no future, they had little incentive to participate in the mainstream economy. For too many of the minority underclass, the crack and cocaine industry proved much more attractive than working for McDonald's. Alienated and less-educated workers participated without enthusiasm in the mainstream economy, or remained on the sidelines. There are many case histories in which low-wage employment turns out to be a less attractive choice than subsisting on welfare. If true economic growth returned to American industry, employment possibilities would open up and the minority stake in the society would greatly increase. The same would be true of the educational system. As long as jobs are menial, education makes little difference. But as high-tech jobs become more available and more highly paid, minorities will want the education that prepares for them.

And there is a further point. Societies define their objectives in different ways. Countries do not pull together unless there is some overriding reason for doing so. A long literature documents that, in the aftermath of an earthquake, disaster, or other social challenge, citizens can frequently cooperate at very high levels for short periods.[17] England's "finest hour" was during World War II, but

17. See Jack Hirshleifer, "Disaster Behavior: Altruism or Alliance?" in Hirshleifer, *Economic Behavior in Adversity* (Chicago: University of Chicago Press, 1987) and Howard Kunreuther and Douglas Dacy, "The Peculiar Economics of Disaster" in Dacy and Kunreuther, *The Economics of Natural Disasters: Implications for Federal Policy* (New York: Free Press, 1969).

thereafter social solidarity quickly dissipated. The challenge that confronts America is perhaps greater than that Britain faced. It is more than winning a war because the competition is continuous. Wars (or price and wage freezes) demand and justify sacrifices that can be quickly renounced once the war (or price freeze) is over. But the challenge of competing in an international economy endures. Outside competition could force the U.S. government to come to grips with what is—in the treatment of minorities—a great wastage of human capital. Investment in the American people and their children would not only be a great social blessing at home; it would also strengthen the United States internationally and in competitive terms. The immigrants who come to North America from Asia and Latin America also can lend knowledge and perspective to deal with their areas of the world. They can begin the reeducation of America.

America's past independence has given way to interdependence. Interdependence means not only that America admits and prospers from foreign workers, it suggests a world in which the United States prospers from foreign trade. Increasingly, in the future it will be foreign trade that buoys American growth, not military spending (which sufficed in periods of excess capacity or depression) or sales in the domestic market. Unless tariffs are put up that artificially recapture the domestic market for American industry (placing a crimp in the U.S. standard of living and range of consumer choice), America has to sell more abroad. Today the United States cannot be sure of winning its own market, so it must be ready to sell in other peoples'. This means not only new products. It means higher-quality products. American customers no longer tolerate shoddy goods; the Japanese tolerate them even less.

The tradition of American uniqueness has come to an end. Insofar as it continues it is disadvantageous: American wares and social usages are frequently seen as inferior to those of other nations. In social, philosophic, economic, and geographic terms, America has become more like other countries. The challenge of the future will be to build on similarity, not uniqueness: to fashion a society and a competitive economy that is interdependent and integrated with the rest of the world and yet excels. Americans have already had to learn how to reconcile conflicting ethnic and social values at home; increasingly they will have to apply those lessons abroad.

But others will attend to the United States only if it proves that it can perform economic feats as well as fashion a just society at home. Sweden offers the example of an egalitarian society, but it does not yet inspire imitators. A transformed American Dream will stress the economic and social contributions that the United States can make to others, not just the military contributions. But to be an exemplar for others Americans have to be an exemplar for themselves. People recognize that to succeed internationally they need to know more about other countries. But to succeed domestically Americans also must understand the methods and social solutions of other nations.

2

The Decline and Rise of Nations

THREE VIEWS OF THE PRESENT AND FUTURE

Contemporary America certainly faces major problems. How serious are they, measured in historic terms? To gain a more rounded view I will first consider the conclusions of current apostles of decline, then the arguments of their critics. Finally, I will attempt to draw a trial balance between them.

First, the decline thesis. In recent years there has been a spate of works claiming that the United States, following the example of nineteenth-century Britain, has lapsed into a terminal condition of economic lethargy and decline.[1]

A second view is that while the United States has experienced its ups and downs (during the Great Depression of 1929–38 as well as in the late 1970s and early 1980s), its position has not appreciably changed; few new measures are necessary to enable America to achieve its future economic and foreign policy goals.

1. David Calleo, *Beyond American Hegemony: The Future of the Western Alliance* (New York: Basic Books, 1987); Stephen S. Cohen and John Zysman, *Manufacturing Matters: The Myth of the Post-Industrial Society* (New York: Basic Books, 1987); Robert Gilpin, *War and Change in World Politics* (New York: Cambridge University Press, 1981) and *The Political Economy of International Relations* (Princeton: Princeton University Press, 1987); Paul Kennedy, *The Rise and Fall of the Great Powers from 1500 to the Present* (New York: Random House, 1987); Charles P. Kindleberger, "Dominance and Leadership in the International Economy," *International Studies Quarterly*, vol. 25, no. 2 (June 1981), pp. 242–54; Governor Richard D. Lamm, *Megatraumas: America at the Year 2000* (Boston: Houghton Mifflin, 1985).

The third view, shared by this author, is that the United States has demonstrably declined, but that it can and will come back. With important policy changes, it will regain the ability to meet its domestic economic and social problems and also to contribute to international stability in the years ahead.

The adherents of the first view point out that while at one time the United States had 45 to 50 percent of world gross national product, now it possesses only 21 percent. Some of these authors believe that the American share could fall to 15 or 16 percent. Part of this decline was to be expected as production resumed in Europe, Japan, and East Asia following the dislocations of the Second World War. But the exponents of the decline theory argue that the reverse in American fortunes is greater than the bare figures indicate. Since 1975, America has run a deficit every year in its balance of trade (exports versus imports), and that deficit continues at the high level of about $130 billion a year. At current rates of improvement and even with a further devaluation of the dollar, it will be more than five years before equilibrium is regained. Indeed, the current account deficit, after declining for a period, might even start increasing again as America faces deficits caused by transferring higher interest and dividend payments to foreign creditors. Any increase in the value of the dollar would also postpone or negate movement toward balance. From being the leading industrial exporting country, the United States has fallen to third, behind Germany and Japan.

Those who contend that America is in decline cite many features of the current situation. As American exports decreased, relative to those of other nations, the United States embarked on a love affair with foreign goods. To pay for Americans' preference for imports the country became the world's largest debtor. U.S. foreign debt exceeded $600 billion and at current rates will reach $1 trillion in the early 1990s. During the Reagan Administration government accounts swam into the red, more than doubling the national domestic debt accumulated in the past two hundred years of American history. Imitating their government, American companies and consumers also went in hock up to their ears. While America's total production of goods and services has shrunk as a proportion of the global sum, this staggering public and private debt has grown to more than one-third of world GNP: it represents nearly 200 percent of U.S. production.

The exponents of decline point out that in industry after industry American companies have lost their lead. U.S. companies used to set the standard of the world in autos, machine tools, and electronics. American farmers were more efficient and productive than any others. The United States once dominated the world market for computers, with IBM alone taking an 85 percent market share. Recent data indicate that the U.S. share of the world electronics market is falling rapidly, from 50.4 percent in 1984 to 39.7 percent in 1987.[2]

When America lost its lead in cars, consumer electronics, and advanced machine tools, people consoled themselves that the United States was tops in finance and services. But in each realm Japan and other nations have caught up. Now, of the world's ten leading banks, ten are Japanese. Nomura Securities dwarfs Merrill Lynch. Even in biotechnology, civilian aircraft, and advanced semiconductors and computers, Japan is beating at the U.S. door. Many analysts believe that the era of America's industrial leadership is over, never to return. In addition, challenged by Australia, Argentina, and Thailand, American farmers are no longer the world's most efficient producers of food. In comparable circumstances in the 1890s, British economists, industrialists, and exporters warned England of the German challenge, but nothing was done to meet it. Historically, there is little reason to believe that the United States will be more successful in reversing current trends.

The *Wall Street Journal* recently wrote:

> For two decades, the Made in America label has been vanishing as overseas manufacturers dominate entire industries. While U.S. manufacturers in 1969 produced 82% of the nation's television sets, 88% of its cars and 90% of its machine tools, last year they made hardly any TVs, and gave up half the domestic machine-tool market and 30% of the auto market. Even in a new industry like semiconductors, this country's world market share has shrunk to 15% from 85% in 1980.[3]

2. *New York Times,* January 5, 1989, p. C1.
3. *Wall Street Journal,* May 2, 1989, p. A2.

Under current conditions, those who foresee a significant American decline have begun to ask whether Paul Kennedy's apocalyptic book on *The Rise and Fall of the Great Powers* foretells the American future. If so, the United States may wake up to find itself sharing the fate of previous imperial powers. Historical critics point out that in the seventeenth century intelligent Dutchmen and in the nineteenth century prescient Britons were well aware of the plight of their nations, yet they could do nothing about it.[4] What role then awaits the United States in the twenty-first century? Is it that of an American Sweden, a benign social democracy with few abilities to assist other nations or to participate effectively in world economic and military politics? If so, Americans will simply have to accustom themselves to a less rapidly growing standard of living compared to other nations, and a greatly lessened influence in international politics. Paul Kennedy writes:

> The only answer to the question increasingly debated by the public of whether the United States can preserve its existing position is "no"—for it simply has not been given to any one society to remain *permanently* ahead of all the others, because that would imply a freezing of the differentiated pattern of growth rates, technological advance, and military developments which has existed since time immemorial.[5]

The second view rejoins that America has not declined, or that any temporary decline is explicable, harmless, or easily remedied. The Department of Defense sees the United States maintaining its position at least until 2010, when they believe China will have passed Japan and become America's leading rival.[6] Some conclude that America has suffered only minor reverses and that there is no project it cannot accomplish if citizens are willing to pay for it through new taxes.[7] The manufacturing sector, so it is said, is as

4. Charles Wilson, *Economic History and the Historian: Collected Essays* (London: Weidenfeld and Nicolson, 1969); Aaron Friedberg, *The Weary Titan: Britain and the Experience of Relative Decline, 1895–1905* (Princeton: Princeton University Press, 1988).
5. Kennedy, op. cit., p. 533.
6. Commission on Integrated Long-Term Strategy, *Discriminate Deterrence* (Washington, D.C., January 1988).
7. See, for example, the series of op-ed pieces by Herbert Stein in the *New York Times* during 1988–89.

vibrant as ever.[8] Or, if manufacturing has declined, then the United States can compete as effectively as ever in services. Others observe that there is nothing dramatically new in America's present situation. In the mid-1960s the United States produced about 24 percent of world GNP; today the figure is about 22 percent.[9] In fact, if we compare the U.S. share of world gross national product in the 1930s with today, there has not been a marked decrease. In 1938 the United States had only 28.7 percent of world manufacturing production.

If, however, America has measurably declined on some of the indices of national power, the approvers of its current position note that this is because of, not despite, American policy. In the late 1940s, "rather than seeking hegemony over its allies, the United States opted to stimulate their economic revival and create a strategic partnership balancing Soviet power."[10] In other words, America itself decided to help other nations and should not complain if these are now successful competitors.[11] The United States strove to undertake the historically thankless task of stabilizing world politics and supporting free and open economies throughout the globe. It largely shouldered the burden of containing the Soviet Union. As a result, the aggressive dictatorial states of the 1930s have either been defeated or transformed. The Axis countries and Japan were defeated in the Second World War. The Soviet Union was contained effectively after 1945 and appears now to be moving in a more liberal and democratic direction. Perhaps the United States lost economic power in the containment task, but it did so to benefit the rest of the world.

Also, if American influence is less now than it was then, it is not only because others have grown stronger in the interim, but rather

8. Robert A. Lawrence, *Can America Compete?* (Washington, D.C.: Brookings Institution, 1984); Susan Strange, "The Persistent Myth of Lost Hegemony," *International Organization,* autumn 1987, pp. 551–74. Note, however, the contrary view of Cohen and Zysman, op. cit.

9. Charles Wolf, Jr., in the *Wall Street Journal,* May 12, 1988. Joseph Nye's figures are similar. He depicts U.S. share of world gross national product as:

1938	1950	1974	1988
25%	36%	23%	23%

Source: "Interdependence and Grand Strategy," American Political Science Association paper, August 31, 1989.

10. Joseph Nye, "Understating U.S. Strength," *Foreign Policy,* fall 1988, p. 107.

11. Walt Rostow, "Beware of Historians Bearing False Analogies," *Foreign Affairs,* vol. 66, no. 4 (spring 1988).

because the United States now faces a more complicated and obdurate world in economic, political, and military terms. Even the strongest power cannot always expect to get its way in a context of complex interdependence. This is not just because of the growth of Japan, China, the new industrializing countries, and Pacific rim nations, it is because Third World countries now contain politically mobilized populations, which are ready to support their leaders and resist foreign pressure. The latent, unmobilized populations that yielded supinely to British imperialism in the nineteenth century now have been transformed into prickly and tough new nations, conscious of their ethnic identities and strength. Even if it wanted, a resurgent America could not tell them what to do.

In the present world, then, one actually needs less power. Small, formerly weak powers are now quite influential, as are private actors like multinational corporations. In a new world context, where power has become diffused, a great nation actually needs less physical power. It needs, rather, the power to persuade, a capacity that is not necessarily increased by possessing greater military force.

Economically, there has been a similar diffusion of power. No country now monopolizes raw materials and markets, but all need access to them. The United States now imports a greater proportion of its oil requirements than it has ever done before. Under these conditions, Americans cannot simply declare resource "independence" and make it stick. Finally, if the United States appears to have receded in influence in recent years, it is only because of policy mistakes made by the Carter and Reagan administrations. These can be and will be corrected, setting America on the course to greatness once again.[12]

Furthermore, the apostles of the status quo claim if the United States has declined, so has Japan. In the 1960s Japan grew, as we have already seen, at more than 10 percent per year. Since then she has been averaging around 4 percent annual growth. Samuel Huntington writes: "There is little reason why the Japanese economy as a whole should grow much faster than the U.S. economy and there is little reason why an individual U.S. worker should be significantly

12. Samuel Huntington writes: "The deficits stem from the weaknesses, not of the American economy, but of Reagan economics. Produced quickly by one set of policies, they can be reversed almost as quickly by another set of policies." Huntington, "The U.S.—Decline or Renewal?" *Foreign Affairs*, winter, 1988–89, p. 79.

more productive than a Japanese worker. On such indices of economic performance, one should expect long-term convergence among countries at similar levels of economic development and with economies of comparable complexity."[13] By 2010, as a consequence, the United States will still have twice the product of the second-strongest economic power. No one should have expected the United States to retain its 40–50 percent of world GNP; certainly nineteenth-century Great Britain never amassed half of world production. (See Table 5.) America, however, can continue to possess 20–25 percent of world product for a considerable period. Once again, these writers observe, little bad has happened, and little needs to be done.

The writers of the Defense Department's essay on *Discriminate Deterrence* plot American growth for the next two decades at 2.6 percent and Japanese growth at 2.8 percent per year. (Japanese estimates for their own growth, however, are at a rate of 4 percent.) According to U.S. analysts, the Soviet Union will limp along at 1.6 percent. Only China should greatly increase its relative position over the next generation, surpassing Japanese GNP by 2010. (These estimates, of course, may have to be deflated following the political and military crackdown in China.) According to them, the United States will reach a gross product of nearly $8 trillion (in

Table 5

GNP of the European Great Powers 1830–90
(At Market Prices in Billions of 1960 U.S. Dollars)

	1830	1860	1890
Russia	10.5	14.4	21.1
France	8.5	13.3	19.7
Britain	8.2	16.0	29.4
Germany	7.2	12.7	26.4
Hapsburg Empire (Austria-Hungary)	7.2	9.9	15.3
Italy	5.5	7.4	9.4

Source: Paul Kennedy, *The Rise and Fall of the Great Powers: Economic Change and Military Conflict from 1500–2000* (New York: Random House, 1987), p. 171.

13. Ibid., pp. 83–84. See also the argument in Martin Baily and Margaret Blair, "Productivity and American Management," in Robert E. Litan, Robert Z. Lawrence, and Charles L. Schultze, eds., *American Living Standards: Threats and Challenges* (Washington, D.C.: Brookings Institution, 1988), pp. 187–88.

1986 dollars) in 2010; China and Japan will be next at nearly $4 trillion each. The Soviet Union follows at $2.9 trillion. Then comes the Federal Republic of Germany at $1.5 trillion, France at $1.4 trillion, and India at $1.3 trillion.[14] (See Figure 1.) If the U.S. Defense Department is correct, the American lead (double that of the next power) will remain the same in 2010 as it is now. But Japan will no longer be the major economic challenger, and the Soviet Union will have failed to keep pace. The number of important players in world politics will have risen (including a more united Europe, plus Japan and China), but the bipolar relationship, with the United States twice as powerful as the second economy, will represent a continuing reality.

(It should be noted, however, that these Defense Department estimates are unduly favorable to the United States. The assumed Japanese growth rate of 2.8 percent between now and 2010 may understate the actual by as much as 1.5 percent per year. The Chinese growth rate starts from a current base of $1.2 trillion, instead of the $600 billion usually calculated. If more realistic estimates are used, the results twenty years from now, given in Figure 2, show Japan at $5.8 trillion, second to the United States at $7.4 trillion, with China [$3.2 trillion] and the Soviet Union [$3.0 trillion] in third and fourth place, respectively.)

Some of those who are content with American economic performance claim that "we may have declined, but who cares?" There is now "one world" economically speaking. American trade deficits with Japan and Korea don't matter any more than a Maine deficit with California. Political distinctions matter little in the big world market. Capital surges across national frontiers in this gigantic economy, and the fortunes of one entity don't mean much so long as the system as a whole works and stays intact. Some economists do not worry that Americans face huge government deficits and debt burdens to themselves and to foreigners. As a percentage of GNP the deficit has declined, not risen. The U.S. deficit burden is less than that sustained easily by Japan in the mid-1970s. Perhaps the United States does not even need to cut government spending.

14. For details see pages 1–5 of *Sources of Change in the Future Security Environment*, a paper by the Future Security Environment Working Group, submitted to the Commission on Long-Term Strategy, U.S. Department of Defense, October 1988.

Besides, America has a $5 trillion economy and can perform any task it wishes. U.S. aggregate wealth and power may have been shifted from one industrial category to another or increasingly from industry to services, but its total economic power and influence remain largely unaffected. In this view, America faces no crisis and needs to do little or nothing to improve its position.

Economically, a number of experts support the view that America's current course is the best one. Some think that the United States does not need to cut the government budget. The budget deficit has decreased from a maximum of 6 percent of GNP to only 3.45 percent today (a $150 billion deficit on a GNP of $4.5 trillion). Some believe that the deficit will continue to decline as a proportion of GNP for the next few years, before rising again.[15] Others claim that the deficit is positively beneficial. In Keynesian fashion it stimulates the economy, and the U.S. would have much slower growth without it.[16] When the deficit declines or is finally eliminated, the fiscal stimulus disappears, and the United States will move into a recession. This could be alleviated by an easier monetary policy, but that would lead to a sharp fall in the dollar, higher import prices, and greater inflation.

Thus those who deny America has declined believe it can continue to afford its foreign commitments and troop dispositions as easily as (and perhaps even more easily than) in the past. All Americans need do is be ready to pay for them with taxes. If it proves necessary, the funds needed to reduce the government deficit by one-third might be provided by a higher tax on gasoline. And as one foreign leader commented recently to the *Wall Street Journal:* "It's hard to take seriously that a nation has deep problems if they can be fixed with a 50-cent-a-gallon gasoline tax."[17] Since the United States could afford to devote 10 percent of its GNP to national security in the 1950s and 9 percent under the Kennedy Administration, it can certainly spend 6.5 percent on it now. Equally, those who support this argument contend that the American economy will continue to grow and prosper, at least commensurately with other major nations.

15. Robert E. Hall, *New York Times,* December 21, 1988.
16. See the series of pieces by Robert Eisner in the *New York Times* during 1988.
17. *Wall Street Journal,* January 23, 1989, p. 48.

Figure 1

Future GNP Growth—Future Security Environment Working Group

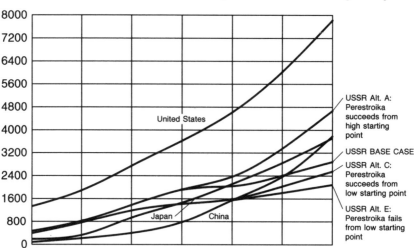

Source: Future Security Environment Working Group, *Sources of Change in the Future Security Environment,* a paper submitted to the Commission on Integrated Long-Term Strategy, October 1988.

Others argue that the very diversity of American society ensures its strength over the long term. The *Wall Street Journal*'s correspondent Karen Elliott House wrote recently:

> Economic strength, of course, ultimately rests on human resources. Here too, America has the advantage. While Japan, despite a rapidly aging population, works hard to maintain its racial purity by closing its doors to outsiders, America's human resources continually are replenished by waves of immigrants. Some 600,000 legal immigrants arrive each year, far more than go anywhere else in the world. And many more arrive illegally.

Ms. House observes:

> These people restore national energy and enthusiasm and bring new talents. They live and thus keep alive the American dream. In this sense, America isn't doing immigrants a favor by letting them in; it is the immigrants who strengthen and thus favor America by coming. Moreover, while Japan largely excludes women from its work force,

Figure 2

Future GNP Growth, Revised Projections

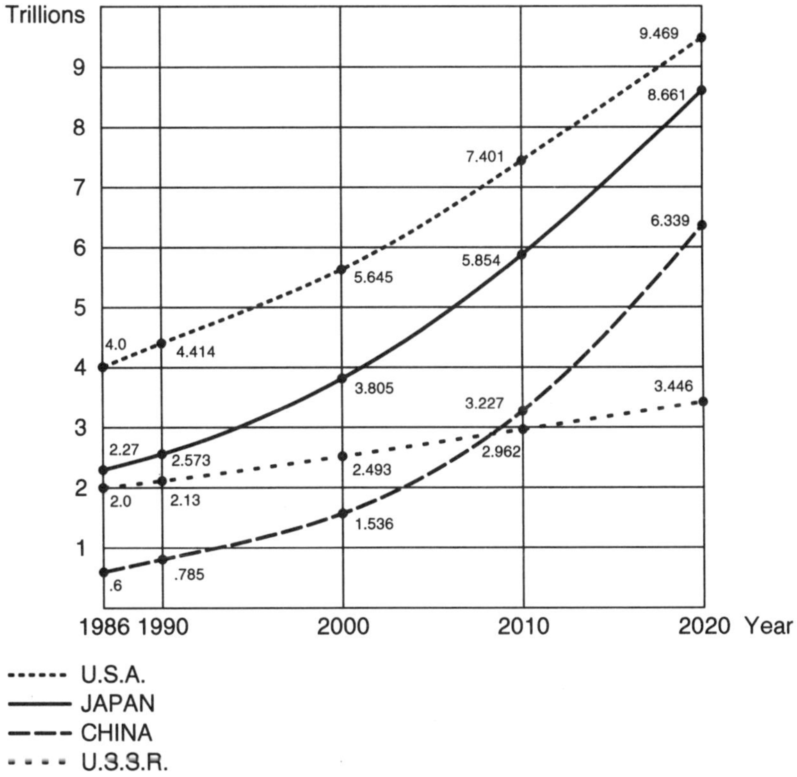

Trillions

9 — 9.469
8 — 8.661
7 — 7.401
6 — 6.339
5 — 5.854, 5.645
4 — 4.0, 4.414
3 — 3.805, 3.227, 3.446, 2.962
2 — 2.27, 2.573, 2.493, 2.0, 2.13
1 — 1.536, .785, .6

1986 1990   2000   2010   2020 Year

······ U.S.A.
——— JAPAN
— — CHINA
· · · · U.S.S.R.

America has led the industrial world in recognizing and using the talents of its women.[18]

Finally, there are those who accept part of the "decline" thesis, but believe that the argument has been carried too far. Aaron Friedberg contends that defense spending was not the *cause* of decline in any of the historic cases; at best defense burdens accentuated the problems of a country already facing economic weakness. In some cases, the difficulties were caused by a rise in consumption or in welfare programs. If higher taxes had been levied, defense spending could have been sustained without limiting eco-

18. *Wall Street Journal,* January 23, 1989, p. 48.

nomic growth. Alternatively, a cut in welfare budgets would have made space in national accounts for continuing foreign policy burdens. In the United States today, defense has not grown appreciably as a proportion of GNP; indeed, it has declined from the 10 percent reached in the 1950s. (See Figure 3.) Rather, it is the entitlement (social security and welfare) programs that have necessitated a cut in government spending. Thus Friedberg recommends either social welfare cuts or higher taxes. There is no necessity to cut defense. This argument is supported by Herbert Stein, former chairman of the Council of Economic Advisers. All that is needed to rehabilitate America is *will*—not a change in foreign policy.

The third possible view, and that held by this author, is that the United States has demonstrably declined, but that it can and will come back. One can hardly contend that America's share of world gross national product has not fallen markedly. In 1929 America had more than 43 percent of world manufacturing production. As late as 1937, its share had only been reduced to 35 percent, and this low note was reached because the Depression had hit the United States harder than its European rivals. Assuming no change in current trends, one foresees a less comfortable situation than that outlined by the Department of Defense. Japan estimates that her growth rate will average 1.5 percent per year higher than that of the United States (4.0 for Japan; 2.5 for the U.S.A.). If this is true, twenty years from now Japan will be a close second to America, with the momentum to pass the United States in the decade of the 2020s.[19] China will have ousted the U.S.S.R. from third place. (See Figures 2 and 4.)

The resulting quadripolar world will be more uncertain than our present system. If economic conflict breaks out among the four major states, Americans could witness a rivalry with consequences similar to those of the 1930s. This prospect would not necessarily entail a new round of major war, but it could invoke momentous conflicts over trade and the creation of new and feuding tariff blocs.

19. The statistics used by the *Wall Street Journal* in preparing its GNP comparisons are questionable, based as they are on "US purchasing power equivalents" and not real exchange rates. Using such figures, it is possible to conclude that Japanese GNP is 40 percent lower than it is in terms of international buying power.

Figure 3a

Government Outlays as a Percentage of Total Outlays

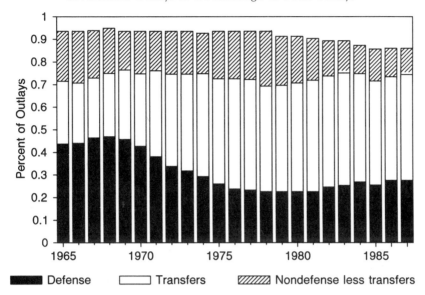

Figure 3b

Government Outlays as a Percentage of GNP

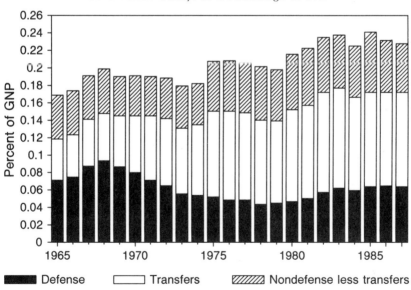

Source: Aaron Friedberg, "The Political Economy of American Strategy," *World Politics*, vol. 41, no. 3 (April 1989), p. 386.

One cannot rest content with the assertion that in a world economy it does not matter what happens to the constituent national units so long as the whole system prospers and remains open. The American interest is not identical with that of every other nation, certainly not if Americans want to continue to live well. They should be concerned about the relative decline of U.S. growth and purchasing power. Those who plan to continue to sell in the American market should also be worried that that market is not expanding rapidly enough.

There is a whole literature on what happens when a previously dominant economic power declines. Many social scientists and economists conclude that without the steady hand of a single leader on the world's economic tiller, the international ship of state may founder. Rising challengers will not pay the costs of keeping the international economic system open by providing markets for countries in balance-of-payments difficulty and loans to needy debtor nations. The result is that when the leader declines, the three or four successor nations will tend to implement high-tariff policies, and world trade will fall significantly, as it did in the Great Depression. In this view, it is far better to maintain one large power steadily at the helm of the international economy.

The United States, however, may not be able to continue its leadership role. It may lose further ground and find itself unable to exercise hegemonic power in the international system. It is significant that on many important measures of economic and trade policy even close allies such as the United States and Europe cannot today agree, with the European Commission refusing American requests.[20] At the moment America is far stronger in relative terms than it will be in twenty years' time. In the future, will a triumphant Japan and a resurgent China be more tempted to reach an accommodation with the United States than Europe is now? The answer is not clear. It will take higher U.S. growth rates and a dynamic American marketplace to convince others that they need to respond to U.S. policies, and that their own economies ought to open their doors. Without rapid U.S. growth, Japan and China will surely

20. One example is the prospect of continuing friction over American meat, television, and motion picture exports to Europe.

Figure 4

How Fast the Superpowers Are Growing

	United States	Soviet Union	Japan	European Community	China
Population (in millions)	243.8	284.0	122.0	323.6	1,074.0
Gross National Product (in billions of 1987 U.S. dollars)	$4,436.1	$2,375.0	$1,607.7	$3,782.0	$293.5
Per capita GNP (1987 U.S. dollars)	$18,200	$8,360	$13,180	$11,690	$270
GNP Growth Rate					
1966–70 (annual average)	2.8%	5.1%	11.0%	4.6%	N.A.
1971–75 (annual average)	2.3%	3.1%	4.3%	3.0%	5.5%
1976–80 (annual average)	3.3%	2.2%	5.0%	3.0%	6.1%
1981–85 (annual average)	3.0%	1.8%	3.9%	1.5%	9.2%
1987	2.9%	0.5%	4.2%	2.9%	9.4%

The data presented here—with a few exceptions—are for 1987, the latest year for which comparable data are available for all countries.

Source: Karen Elliott House, "The '90s and Beyond," *Wall Street Journal,* January 23, 1989, p. A8. House cites as her source *CIA Handbook of Economic Statistics.*

face temptations to remain largely closed to the rest of the world, China even more so in light of the present grip of the party and the military on Chinese politics. If America could regain stable economic growth rates of 3 percent or more per year, however, it could maintain its present approximate position for a long time to come, and its influence would endure (for previous growth rates, refer back to Table 4).

Higher growth rates, however, require a massive change in American priorities. If the United States is to regain productive strength, it needs a new "grand strategy" that takes into account economic as well as military factors, and the efforts of allies. National security has to be redefined to include the strength and productivity of the economy, which is after all the mobilization base on which military capability rests. This means that the United States must reconsider past policies, which involved mobilizing too large a proportion of American economic strength. Paul Kennedy is right to say that the recessional of a major power is both economic and military in nature.

An American resurgence thus awaits change in American foreign policy as well as in domestic priorities. Two stages are involved here. In the first, some cuts in foreign policy programs will be required to finance domestic resurgence. In the second stage, greater American economic growth will allow the United States to offer enhanced support to countries in trouble. In the first phase of this agenda, higher taxes and perhaps some cuts in social programs will be necessary. Congress has found it impossible to balance the federal budget without including cuts in entitlement programs as well as new taxes, and thus the budget remains in the red. But, politically speaking, it is impossible to achieve a consensus to impose new taxes on the American people and cut social programs without trimming defense at the same time. Any administration that sought to do one without the other would be risking political suicide. Thus, some degree of foreign policy realignment will be an inevitable result of the budget crisis. Defense economies are also justified by emergent Soviet policy.

But will the world permit an American retrenchment, a partial shifting of alliance and military burdens from the American Atlas to two or three new Herculeses? That depends on the future of world politics, and on the willingness of others to assume novel responsibilities. It also depends upon a hoped-for liberalization of U.S. adversaries. If these transitions occur, a future world environment could be much more hospitable to America. If they do not, it could be much more hostile.

This is one of the points sometimes neglected by those who believe that domestic reform will suffice. The commission appointed by Governor Mario Cuomo of New York to survey means of regaining U.S. economic growth and competitiveness discussed a wide range of domestic initiatives that America might take to recharge the batteries of economic growth. But it did not take account of the fact that the problem has to be attacked on both foreign and domestic fronts. If the United States cannot solve the international aspect of the problem, it will not be able to solve the domestic part. Unless America gets some savings in the foreign policy budget, it will not have enough new investment.

Future American prosperity is thus predicated on a better atmosphere in world politics, and not just on a more favorable distribution of the burdens with allies. It depends on finding cheaper ways of dealing with the Soviet Union and even on less hostility in world politics generally, reducing the total foreign policy burden that America and its allies would have to shoulder. A new grand strategy must address these questions so the United States can achieve economic progress at home.

This being said, U.S. resurgence also depends upon Americans. Since the era of John F. Kennedy, American leaders have issued no call to personal sacrifice and given no reason to renounce the ethic of "borrow and spend." Rampant inflation in the 1970s schooled a generation of Americans to buy, rather than save, to borrow, rather than invest. The "me" generation propelled a consumer spending spree. But history suggests that great civilizations have sometimes been fatally weakened through indulgence. David Landes, the great historian of the Industrial Revolution, observes that the third generation of industrial entrepreneurs tends to lose its edge:

> Thus the Britain of the late nineteenth century basked complacently in the sunset of economic hegemony. In many firms, the grandfather who started the business and built it by unremitting application and by thrift bordering on miserliness had long died; the father who took over a solid enterprise and, starting with larger ambitions, raised it to undreamed-of heights, had passed on the reins; now it was the turn of the third generation, the children of affluence. . . . Many of them retired and forced the conversion of their firms into joint-stock companies. Others stayed on and went through the motions of entrepreneurship between the long weekends; they worked at play and played at work.[21]

21. David Landes, "Technological Change and Development in Western Europe, 1750–1914," in H. J. Habakkuk and M. Postan, eds., *The Cambridge Economic History of Europe, Vol. VI, The Industrial Revolutions and After: Incomes, Population and Technological Change* (Cambridge: Cambridge at the University Press, 1965), p. 563.

Others note that first-generation pioneers innovate and save; they create new products and industries. The second generation manages the successful enterprise without greatly modifying the product, while extending its corporate reach. The third generation lags in its ability to innovate and excel. Savings are no longer accumulated at the old rate; new products languish on the drawing board. Financial strategies maximizing short-term profits replace the long-term goals of industrial competitiveness and market share. The industrial pioneers' ethic of hard work and team effort degenerates into the pursuit of individual goals and conspicuous consumption in the grandsons and granddaughters.

Perhaps more important, the new generation sometimes forgets that social cooperation to assure the survival and prosperity of the national community against the challenge of other nations is a prerequisite to continuing future success. Business, labor, and government go their separate ways and consumers take their cue to maximize consumption in the now-unraveling social contract. Great Britain reached this phase during the Edwardian period before World War I. The United States too appears to have reached the "enrich yourselves" stage. Narrow interest groups proliferate, and the national interest is lost in the unruly scuffle for sectarian advantage. Phrases from the history of the Roman Empire apply surprisingly well to the United States after Vietnam. "The prevalence of the idea of the Welfare State little by little imposed upon the State great charges and tasks, that were out of proportion to the possibilities of its income especially when, after the end of wars of conquest, the contribution of extra treasures failed." (In other words, foreign receipts were no longer available, and domestic taxes could not be increased to pay for welfare expenditures.[22])

THE POSSIBILITY OF RESURGENCE

In sum, if critics of the contemporary American situation are correct, the United States has now entered a well-nigh irrevocable decline. But pessimists, even historically trained ones, are not al-

---

22. Aurelio Bernardi, "The Economic Problems of the Roman Empire at the Time of Its Decline," in Carlo Cipolla, ed., *The Economic Decline of Empires* (London: Methuen, 1970), p. 79.

ways right.[23] The typical pattern of rise and decline has important exceptions. Nations can decline and still rise again. Both Germany and Japan appeared to have reached their economic summits in the 1930s, yet both underwent a remarkable renaissance after the Second World War. Tsarist Russia reached a major economic peak in 1913, but Stalinist Russia grew rapidly through the late twenties and thirties (see Table 6). Some will contend that Russia had to undergo a revolution and Japan and Germany to be defeated in war for the economic transformation to take place. The United States surely does not want to engender such trauma in order to shake up and reinvigorate its economy. Also, it seems to be true that no declining power of hegemonic rank made a real comeback. Spain, Holland, and England underwent no renaissance in power relative to other states, and they still remain pale replicas of past majesty and power.

Their historic challengers fared no better. France and Germany were the challengers of England, as in contemporary terms Russia has been the challenger of the United States. France and Germany rebounded to some degree after 1945, exceeding their absolute position of the first half of the twentieth century, but they did not achieve premier status. Russia has lost the relative gains that it made in the 1930s (economically) and in World War II (militarily). But with the possible exception of Russia, none of these nations was a continent-sized power endowed with enormous resources and a great and trained population. None, including Russia, possessed, as the United States does today, a vast and sophisticated industry and the ability to create technology of the highest order.

America, in short, remains in a distinctive position. Despite certain parallels with Holland and Britain, the United States retains unmatched historic strengths. No hegemonic state in other periods of history remained far ahead of its competitors in the total production of goods and services. None of the imperial predecessors had almost unlimited investment funds available to it through the contributions of other nations. No other state was preponderant in research in pure science, an unexampled asset, which could generate a profusion of new technologies and products.

Furthermore, the United States, unlike its hegemonic counter-

---

23. Henry Ford once remarked dismissively: "History is bunk!"

Table 6

Annual Growth Rates 1913–50

	Germany	Japan	Russia
1913–29	0.4	3.9	0.19
1929–50	1.9	0.6	6.04
1950–69	6.8	9.7	5.22*

*Figure is for 1950–73.

Source: U.S. Bureau of the Census, *Historical Statistics of the United States, Colonial Times to 1970, Part 1* (Washington, D.C.: U.S. Bureau of the Census, 1975), except Russian figures, from Paul Bairoch, "Europe's Gross National Product: 1800–1975," *Journal of Economic History,* vol. 5, no. 2 (fall 1976), pp. 273–340.

parts of yesteryear, is bargaining to maintain its position. Britain did not negotiate an opening of the German or American market at the end of the nineteenth century when economic decay had begun to undermine British industry. Holland did not manage to persuade Britain to revise its high tariffs in the mid-seventeenth century. America, however, is not willing to offer an unlimited market to others when theirs are closed to American goods. The next few years will witness one challenge after another to the mercantilist and closed economies of Japan and the developing nations, which strive to prevent the importation of industrial goods. Japan, in particular, will be forced to open up its agricultural sector to exports from other countries. Given these attributes and new policies, today's America possesses unequaled strengths if their potential can only be harnessed.

THEORY OF THE DECLINE AND RISE OF NATIONS

In history, it is traditional to chart rise and then decline. Historians have assumed that nations, like biological organisms, rise to power and then age and wither. Likened to death or suspended animation, that decline signifies a relative final stanching of national energies or a permanent relegation to lower national status and power. It is important to remember, however, that decline can be the prelude to rebirth, and that for important countries (though not yet for the greatest powers) decline and loss have frequently preceded economic revival. Indeed, countries which have not declined enough, which have not been subjected to the national shock of defeat and despair, have had more difficulty maintaining their growth rates than those who have. Japan, Germany, France, the small countries of East Asia, the small democracies of Western and Central Europe—these gained a powerful economic impetus from defeat and occupation in war. In contrast, Britain, Canada, Australia, New Zealand, and the United States—victors all—did not strive toward economic resurgence and revival because they suffered no defeat.

Rather, the victors chugged along on a curve of moderate military and tepid economic success, spending (at least in the British and American cases) large amounts on arms and ultimately enfeebling their productive processes. The worst outcome of a challenge, therefore, is expensive but narrow triumph. Victory in World Wars I and II sanctioned a history of indolent economic efforts and impaired social progress in Britain. The loss in Vietnam was not a sufficient social shock to change traditional habits of investment and work in the United States. In fact, Vietnam was a reverse shock. It caused Americans to become alienated from their government and its foreign policies, to challenge leadership, and to distrust authority. After Vietnam, Americans were not shocked out of their lethargy; they were not convinced they had to become more productive or to work together as a people; instead, they did nothing. Many young Americans believed that a United States that did nothing was better than an America that did wrong.

If Vietnam did little to awaken Americans, the earlier onset and pathology of the Cold War also produced no desirable reevaluation of economic strategies. Instead the arms race inhibited needed reinvestment in the civilian economy of both adversaries. In Paul Kennedy's words, military "overstretch" and high defense spending captured the very investment capital that was needed to regenerate economic growth.

Yet the matter is not so simple, for military spending may not disable an economy if domestic consumption is held in check. This was undoubtedly the case in Britain's costly wars with Napoleonic France, which did not short-circuit the high voltage of the Industrial Revolution in Great Britain. Military spending may even spur industrial growth if, in conditions of depression or recession, there is large unused industrial capacity. That can be true when a country does not have to export in large amounts and when consumption lags.

In this way, President Franklin D. Roosevelt got America out of the Depression, not primarily by social spending, but by rearmament. Through high military spending, he largely put the country back to work by 1940. Defense expenditure at the time of the Korean War did not create inflation or divert civilian investment, it reversed the recession of 1949 and stimulated a boom. During the 1930s, Japan's initial imperialist gains in Manchuria (prior to 1937) did not slow down Japanese growth. The conquest proved incredibly cheap, and the Chinese province (joining the previous acquisitions of Taiwan and Korea) was quickly integrated into the Japanese metropolitan economy.[24] Japanese economic growth spurted upward. In the case of Nazi Germany, the rearmament program of 1934 stimulated heavy industry, which had been depressed, and German growth quickly exceeded that of the rest of Europe. Likewise, there appears to be little question that military spending under the Reagan Administration helped get America out of the recession of 1981–82.

Excess capacity and civilian consumption, then, have to be included in any account of the effect of military spending upon economic growth. In Britain in the first half of the nineteenth century, investment and savings remained very significant, while consumption did not yet attain high levels. After mid-century, however, when the rate of investment began to decline, an increase in consumption could continue to prop up British national income, though growth proceeded more slowly. Military spending did not intrude upon this benign but placid condition because from the Crimean War (1854–56) until the very end of the nineteenth century (with the Boer War and the beginning of the naval race with Germany) England did not need to rearm. Her antiquated navy was still much larger than that of any possible foe, and her overseas empire was quiet, needing little policing. Even after 1897 there was no initial disadvantage because England had excess capacity remaining from the depression of 1873–96. It was not really until the First World War that military spending displaced civilian investment. And it was not until the 1920s, and particularly the 1930s,

24. Miles Kahler, "External Ambition and Economic Performance," *World Politics,* vol. 40, no. 4 (July 1988), pp. 419–51.

that British governments began to worry about the tradeoff between military preparedness and industrial rejuvenation.

All imperial powers have had to balance consumption, investment, and the military. Early seventeenth-century Spain engaged in an orgy of consumption; this spending raised prices and wages. Military demands pushed inflation further, but the remaining price increases stemmed from the inflationary effects of the vast inflow of bullion from Peru and Mexico. As a result, Madrid lagged behind in productive investment in new products. Her traditional wares—silk, textiles, leather, wood, wool, and iron—were now priced out of their customary markets on the continent.

A century later Holland had to tax at confiscatory rates (much higher than those of her competitors) because of the cost of wars against Louis XIV of France. These wars increased prices and reduced the competitiveness of Dutch goods. In the later stage of the Dutch Empire lavish display and unbridled consumption reigned: gilt was everywhere.[25] Dutch merchants failed to reinvest sufficiently in the now less profitable foreign trade, preferring to send their money to London, where the return was higher. Meanwhile, Holland's streets were filled with the destitute. In this phase, short-term economic profits for the upper and middle classes took precedence over building a strong national (commercial and industrial) economy at home.

Thus economic growth appears to require: (1) high savings and investment, with consumption remaining at a relatively fixed share of GNP, and (2) low military and foreign policy expenditure, except where there is excess capacity owing to recession. Three combinations of these factors can be identified in the rising, declining, and resurgent state.

The nation on the rise has large reserves of savings, which it ploughs into investment in new products and the new machines to make them. Some of these savings occur in agriculture, where new methods of production produce a surplus which can be invested in industry. Consumer demand, of course, must increase if there is to

25. Simon Schama, *The Embarrassment of Riches: An Interpretation of Dutch Culture in the Golden Age* (New York: Knopf, 1987).

be a justification for buying new machines. Typically, at the outset a rising nation faces a labor shortage conjoined with increased demand, at home or abroad. If labor is costly, there will be an incentive to turn to machines. Then enhanced and cheaper production comes to depend on labor-saving devices. At the same time, relatively highly paid labor will also help with the demand side.

For example, in England in the late eighteenth century food costs were relatively low compared to British wages. Workers could therefore afford to spend money on better clothes than were available on the continent. They wore full leather shoes, rather than clogs, and dressed in wool, not the drafty and inferior linen of their European brothers. Their needs could stimulate a new textile industry. This increase in consumption, however, did not diminish investment; it stimulated the creation of new industrial capacity.

There was also an even greater market abroad: in America, Africa, and India. Foreign trade thus became an even greater impetus to production than was home consumption. And Britain developed economically during the Industrial Revolution, first on the basis of her exports and then later on her surplus of "invisibles" (shipping, insurance, financial services, and income on foreign investment). These sustained a continuing surplus in the balance of payments. Of course, new advances in technology were critical to supply the British industrial machine. Spinning and weaving devices and the steam engine stoked by coal were necessary, and Britain required a new iron industry to build machines and factories that would serve the new market.

Ample sources of capital were needed to finance investment. Britain had begun to establish a new capital market as early as the 1690s. But the important point was that as capital was drawn to London, the interest rate fell, making investment cheaper for British entrepreneurs. The capital market was so powerful that it would finance (through government borrowing) the Napoleonic Wars without encroaching much on investment in the Industrial Revolution. Britain did not try to pay for her struggle with the French Emperor through new taxes, and when, after 1815, government expenditures were radically cut, there was no long-term disadvantage. Rising economic growth easily covered the tax burden. Equally, while consumption had provided an initial spark to the introduction of machine production, it did not absorb all the products of British industry. Savings remained high, and much of textile production was sent abroad to clothe foreign peoples. Thus Britain continued to invest at high rates, and she was not (initially at least) primarily reliant on the demand of the home market.

Nor did her military endeavors upset her growth rate. When Britain took her North American and Indian colonies in the seventeenth and eighteenth centuries she did not have to spend a great deal on them. She did not station large garrisons of British troops abroad. Her continental strategy was equally economical: it generally relied on others to do the land fighting. The peripheral and naval strategy that she adopted (and largely carried through, even during the Napoleonic Wars) was far less expensive than the exactions that enormous continental land armies placed on France and Russia.

This pattern, of course, does not fully apply to the growth of the United States, Germany, and Japan. In the United States' case much more industrial momentum was speeded by the demand of a continentally expanding home market, and less by exports. But America's ability to stay out of European quarrels for a century certainly averted military diversions that might have cut into her rate of investment. At the same time, while the Civil War (1861–65) certainly reduced the proceeds from exports of raw cotton, it increased American self-sufficiency and assisted the growth of an autonomous American industrial capacity, centered largely in the North and Northeast. The Civil War introduced the process of tariff protection and insulation that continued down to World War I.

Germany also relied on tariffs after 1879 to capture her own grain and steel markets. Her growth depended on protection, but it also relied on exports, which bounded upward in the last quarter of the nineteenth century at a rate higher than Britain's. Until the mid-1860s, however, Prussia-Germany was a net importer of capital and still depended on Britain for some of her imports. Her pace of investment in the domestic economy was two or three times as fast as that of Britain. Germany's military adventures and military spending did not disable her industry. The Austro-Prussian and Franco-Prussian wars did not require a wholesale mobilization of the domestic economy, and the military phases of the wars were short and decisive. German domestic consumption buoyed the German economy, but it could not sustain the capacities that had

been built up to serve export markets as well. Soon German industry would be needing even wider outlets for its goods.

Under the spur of military necessity (lest she be subjected to the
same extraterritorial demands Europe levied on a weak China),
Japan also achieved remarkable rates of industrial growth in the
nineteenth century, while avoiding too much dependence on Britain and Europe. But since her home market was inadequate to
sustain a modern industrial technology in textiles and machinery,
she needed new markets, which initially could be found in China,
Korea, and Taiwan. She celebrated her rapid-fire industrialization
by defeating China in 1894–95, thereby laying claim to equal treatment with the European powers in the division of Far Eastern
spoils. Her military exploits, like Britain's imperial ones, were carried out against less organized and less developed states, and did
not issue in life-and-death struggles that would have consumed her
industrial plant. In fact, Japan, like Germany, pioneered in winning
lightning victories, quickly followed by peace. Her wars involved no
large or permanent diversion of industrial capacity.

Latecoming industrial developers have frequently capitalized on
what Alexander Gerschenkron called the "advantages of backwardness," importing technologies developed by others for their own
use.[26] They could then leapfrog the industrial pioneers and move
quickly to the forefront, with new machines and larger plant. Japan
and Germany certainly did so, as did America for a time. But the
newcomers, particularly nineteenth-century United States and imperial Germany, also developed new technology on their own in a
series of new industries: chemicals, automobiles, and electric
power. Some latecomers found new and more efficient ways of
meeting their capital requirements through investment banks in
Germany, and in the Russian case (a late, late developer) the state
raised capital for industry. Late development has tended to be
larger-scale in character than that of industrial pioneers. Thus,
England, Germany, Japan, and the United States all stimulated
their industry with rapidly increasing demand; in the British, German, and Japanese cases, exports played a major role. In America,
domestic demand was paramount in the nineteenth century, but it

26. Alexander Gerschenkron, *Economic Backwardness in Historical Perspective, A Book
of Essays* (Cambridge: Belknap Press of Harvard University Press, 1962).

was a domestic demand that doubled and redoubled as America expanded to the Pacific. Large industrial capacity developed in all four instances.

Often there was a kind of protective relationship between early and late developers. The first industrial nation and hegemonic power opened the international system and helped to sustain the balance of power, so that other new developers could stretch their wings and strengthen their industrial muscles in peace. When the latter emerged from the nest, they tested their new-found strength in short, quick wars, contests that did not interfere with their industrial growth. Only later did they challenge their industrial mentors. Rising developers saved their capital for investment and did not allow consumption to encroach upon its share of income. They frequently based their development on exports. Even in the United States increasing consumption did not preempt investment funds; rather, the size of the total economic pie increased.

The rising power, however, ultimately confronts two challenges: (1) it may encounter rival military nations; and (2) it eventually has to provide consumers with rewards for their past abstinence and restraint, in other words, consumption rises and savings and investment decline. As political development proceeds, it creates a larger and more powerful electorate, which in turn demands a greater share of national product and a greater range of consumer choice in imports as well as domestic goods. If military rivalry and high consumption occur at the same time, the nation is forced to deplete its productive assets and the underlying productivity of the economy decreases markedly.

When Great Britain was a rising power, her people invested and saved and aimed for long-term growth. As the British achieved preeminence, however, they began to yield to the temptation to relax and enjoy their position. Short-term returns became important to appease stockholders and investors and to minimize risk. Factory owners kept overage equipment because buying new machines involved a high fixed cost. Frequently they neglected to make new investments unless they were justified by immediate profits. Thus, after 1870 the British spent less to innovate in new products than did Germany and America. They did less to improve worker productivity, and they acquiesced in a less educated and less technically proficient labor force than that of their rivals. When they confronted less profitable short-term opportunities at home, they increasingly chose to send their money overseas. Little by little, they moved toward a financial strategy focused on investment abroad and away from an economic and manufacturing strategy centered at home. This worked so long as foreign investments and the British money market provided for a balance-of-payments surplus. When those investments had to be sold off to finance two world wars and America emerged as the leading creditor nation, however, Britain had to fall back on merchandise exports at just the time when her past comparative advantages were running out.

The first indications of decline showed up in productivity. At the apogee of her economic power in the third quarter of the century, Britain's factor productivity (labor and capital) grew at the solid rate of 1.2 percent per year. For the next forty years, however, it fell to only 0.4 percent. In the same period German productivity rose at 0.9 percent and American at 1.2 percent per year. Subsequently, some economic historians have explained the decline by claiming that the "advantages of backwardness" accrue to rising economies, which can simply apply the industrial lessons and technologies already created by others. This is no doubt true. But Britain slowed down relative both to other nations and also to her own past performance. In a later period, the supposed limits on continuing industrial growth of industrial pioneers (confronting the competition of new latecomers) did not prevent Japan and Germany (whose industry reached an initial peak in the 1930s and the early stages of the war boom) from regaining speed for a second "takeoff" after 1950. Unlike contemporary Japan and Germany, however, the British after 1880 failed to reinvest in their own industries on the scale of their competitors.

The failure to invest was complicated by failings of labor and management. Increasing unionization led to demands for higher wages and shorter hours. If these had been offset by higher productivity, there would have been no disadvantage, but they were not. Unlike some of her rivals, Britain did not offer enough incentives to improve the performance of labor. Under pressure to reduce costs, British managers were likely to lower wages rather than install labor-saving machinery, which, given low labor productivity, would not have increased profits. But wage reductions alienated the labor movement and further reduced productivity.

The net result was that the British worker was less motivated and technically trained than competitors in Germany and the United States. In steel and engineering Britain tended to rely on the talented "tinkerer" while Germany stressed technical skills and spent 2.5 percent of its GNP on education by 1914. British entrepreneurs generally confined their research activities to those areas that would return an immediate profit, while German managers engaged in painstaking attempts to discover and create new products in chemicals and other lines.[27] Britain did not even introduce compulsory primary education until 1880. Nor did managers recruit and pay scientists and engineers at the scale of their competitors. At the Woolwich Arsenal, for example, chemists were paid £100 a year, the same as workers.

Perhaps Britain could have compensated for deficient labor productivity by higher investment. But after 1900 she sent an even greater proportion of her funds abroad, particularly to the empire. In the two decades after 1860 British capital formation was just under 10 percent of GNP, and only 3 percent was invested overseas. By the last decade before the First World War, however, domestic investment had declined to 8.7 percent and over 5 percent was invested in foreign countries. At a time when the United States was devoting more than 21 percent and Germany 23 percent of its gross national product to investment at home, the British failure to reinvest took its toll in overall productivity. How could this occur? Arthur Lewis contends that the productivity of the British working man was already so much less than his American counterpart that even labor-saving machinery would not pay, at least in the short term.[28] The benefit would not outweigh the costs. While British businessmen were explaining their failure to buy new machinery, the United States was introducing automatic looms and mechanical coal cutters. The ultimate effect was that Britain did not

27. D. H. Aldcroft, "Investment in and Utilisation of Manpower: Great Britain and Her Rivals, 1890–1914," in Barrie Ratcliffe, ed., *Great Britain and Her World, 1750–1914* (Essays in Honor of W. O. Henderson) (Manchester: Manchester University Press, 1975).

28. Arthur Lewis, *Growth and Fluctuations, 1870–1913* (London: George Allen and Unwin, 1978).

invest to expand production; rather, she surrendered part of the growing market to others.

Instead of aggressively increasing her ability to compete in Western Europe and the United States, Britain sought to sell existing production in third areas. New continental tariffs encouraged this practice. As late as 1870 Europe took 42 percent of British exports, but by 1910 the figure had declined to 35 percent. Meanwhile, the total sent to Africa, Asia, and Australasia went from 29 percent to 43 percent. And if we consider agricultural countries as a whole (including the Empire), the shift is even more dramatic. In the 1850s exports to these countries were less than 60 percent of the British total; by 1910 they consumed more than three-quarters of Britain's export trade. Britain's inability to make headway in the markets of her principal rivals—Germany and the United States— led her to an easier strategy. Still, confronting her competition, Britain could have moved to higher-quality products (enhancing profits); she could have tried to reduce costs (through labor-saving devices); or she could have directed traditional products to new markets. Largely, she adopted the third alternative, a palliative which would last only until her competitors turned their sights on the developing world and her own free-trading empire.

A fourth tack might have led Britain to innovate and introduce new industrial products. America and Germany were rapidly turning their attention to electrical appliances, automobiles, and chemicals. Like the United States today, Britain had initial advantages in all these areas. The British made the essential discoveries in steel-making, but like latter-day America, they often found that their designs were put into service by others. Britain had the world's first functioning electric power station, but America and Germany spread urban electrification more quickly and then applied electric motors to industry. In such new fields American and German worker productivity coupled with new machines entirely outpaced their British rival.

Ultimately military problems in two world wars defeated British economic pretensions. In the first great encounter, Britain could pay for only 36 percent of war costs, borrowing the rest from her citizens and from the United States. This might have been no disadvantage if British exports had retained their power and competitiveness, but they did not. During World War I, Britain lost her primacy in shipping and textiles and had to sell off half her foreign investments. John Maynard Keynes managed the Treasury portfolio during the war. With remarkable dexterity he balanced foreign borrowing (mainly from the United States), tax revenues, Treasury bonds, and judicious disposal of foreign assets to finance the war. Despite overall success, Keynes calculated on February 22, 1917, that Britain's gold stock would not last "for more than four weeks from today."[29] Only America's entry into the war averted fulfillment of the prediction and saved Britain. It was true, as Paul Kennedy wrote: "The harder the British fought, the more they had bankrupted themselves."[30]

What does the British example tell us about the process of economic ossification and decline? From 1860 to 1913, Britain invested too little in her home industry and consumed too much. The record does not demonstrate that military spending was the cause of British decline. Britain was already failing to invest at German and American rates long before military pressures forced her to divert funds from the civilian economy to rearmament. Consumption as a percentage of gross national product increased and savings declined in the second half of the nineteenth century. The funds available for investment thus decreased. Furthermore, Britain did not distribute and use her investments well. Too much went overseas, too little to Britain's home economy. British entrepreneurship became listless and flaccid. The drive to excel and to innovate diminished.

Britain had supported her worldwide commitments with a tiny defense budget, so tiny that it had only limited deterrent effect on her major adversaries. It is possible that Britain could have defended her commitments more adequately if she had been willing to tighten her belt to pay for them.[31] But by the turn of the century, Edwardian luxury came to compete with defense obligations. And the First World War completed the process. By 1917 the combina-

29. Robert Skidelsky, *John Maynard Keynes* (New York: Viking Press, 1986), p. 336.
30. Paul Kennedy, "Strategy versus Finance in Twentieth Century Britain," in Kennedy, *Strategy and Diplomacy, 1870–1945* (London: Fontana Paperbacks, 1984), p. 106.
31. Friedberg, *Weary Titan.*

tion of military spending and relatively high consumption had damaged the underlying productivity of the economy.

Not surprisingly, the Dutch Empire, Britain, and the United States all confronted the twin problems of high consumption and high military exactions, though the sequence differed in the three cases. Holland had to fight Louis XIV on land and, for a time, Britain at sea. In World War I, England had the burden of maintaining her dominance at sea at precisely the same time that she had to raise an expeditionary force to resist the German challenge on land. She did this carefully and in a calculated manner, always husbanding her forces and hoping to keep France at the forefront of the continental military effort.[32] But the role left for Britain was still too much for her.

In comparison, the United States today not only seeks to maintain superiority at sea but also to offset the land armies of Russia in Europe. With the continuing but reduced priority given to the Strategic Defense Initiative, America continues to aim at military dominance in space. But with all the high postwar defense budgets, U.S. decline did not reach exaggerated proportions until the military spending of the Reagan Administration. That was because, even more than in the Vietnam War buildup, defense expenditure was not allowed to lessen civilian consumption, but was financed by domestic and international borrowing. That strategy perhaps created no difficulty for post-Napoleonic Great Britain, because England maintained a solid surplus in her balance of payments. But in the 1980s American exports were allowed to fall well beneath imports, and there was no immediate means with which to repay the debts.

In short, all three military leaders tried to combine high domestic consumption with their substantial defense exertions overseas. Holland and Britain failed to do this successfully. This combination of too-high defense spending with unlimited consumption was devastating not only because of its amount; its timing was also important. In the Napoleonic Wars, England restrained domestic consumption through taxes while borrowing and spending heavily to finance her military effort. By World War I, however, consumption

32. David French, *British Strategy and War Aims, 1914–1916* (London and Boston: Allen and Unwin, 1986).

was already too high. Civilian investment could not continue in face of the need for guns and soldiers. By the time the war was over, Britain had already lost her markets in crucial industries; it was nearly too late to redeem her industrial future.

The yet-unanswered question for the United States is whether it can increase savings and investment in time to achieve high productivity in new realms of technology. Can America surmount the limitations that history traditionally seeks to impose upon once Great Powers?

Some will say that the mere conception of a world hegemonic power renewing its energies is a historical anomaly, perhaps even a contradiction in terms. In this view, world leaders bear burdens and ultimately sacrifice their positions to benefit the welfare of others. They switch from economic strategies to military ones in order to buttress the international balance of power. Inside their protective cocoons, others' economic development undergoes peaceful metamorphosis. Ultimately, the new butterflies take wing, and the protection of the world leader is no longer necessary. But meanwhile, the leading power's energies are spent; markets are lost and new products have been slighted.

We have already seen that no truly hegemonic power has ever come back. The powers that have regenerated themselves (like Japan and Germany) have done so under the beneficent protection of others. It would seem to follow that America cannot come back without similar protection, with a greater freedom from military responsibilities, and new capital and markets given to it. It cannot at once develop economically and still carry the bulk of world military burdens.

But history does not lend us enough perspective to determine the result of America's present condition. In certain respects that situation is unparalleled. The military load never lightened in past international systems. Every hegemonic power kept looking over its shoulder to see who might be gaining on it. Spain had to worry about France and the Netherlands; Holland had to contend with both France and England; and Great Britain could not neglect the German challenge. In every case new and growing powers presented a looming military menace. There was never a respite, a period in which the drive to military expansion was more than briefly abandoned.

In the 1990s, however, the world will confront an entirely new situation. There is and will be no hegemonic successor to the United States. Though there will be military threats to guard against, no single military challenger will be capable of wresting leadership from the United States. As America looks over its shoulder, the country gaining on it is not a great military power, the Soviet Union, but rather a "trading state," Japan. There is no great and sustained territorial threat to the existing order. Thus the choices that world leaders faced in the past were different from those to be confronted in the future. In past history, the choice was to continue to struggle with disastrous economic consequences, or to drop out of the Great Power race. Facing such decisions, Spain, Sweden, Holland, and England renounced their leadership. Sweden and Holland withdrew from the system and embraced neutrality. The United States faces no such alternative. It can continue, albeit as a lessened military and strategic power, because there is no combined military and economic challenger. In other words, the costs of international leadership have greatly declined.

We have previously stressed that shocks are sometimes necessary to bestir a complacent social and economic system. Some, however, contend that only defeat in war administers the necessary cathartic. If they are right, the United States will never regain its economic momentum. Despite imperial reverses it has not been defeated militarily or occupied by some hostile power. Its territories have not been stripped away. Americans have not been conscious of the degree to which their nation has slipped. They will thus do little about it.

But four factors suggest that a shock to the system, short of war, will suffice. First, there will be a major economic challenge to the United States even if there is no military challenge. That challenge will be posed in the form of a decisive economic crisis. Second, there is the challenge of foreign trade. Of course, other world leaders, particularly Holland and Britain, were major trading powers, but the dangers of military expansion did not allow them to pursue their trading vocation unhampered by military distractions. For too long, they limped along, attempting to combine their Great Power role with a flourishing export sector. By the time they realized that they could not do both, they had lost their trading advantage. In the Dutch case, Holland even missed the first installment of the Industrial Revolution, thereby postponing industrialization until after the third quarter of the nineteenth century. When it came Britain's turn, she labored so hard in World War I that she lost markets and market share that she still has not regained.

The third factor reverses this situation for the contemporary United States. America, unlike her predecessors, will increasingly be able to face the challenge of foreign trade free from onerous military distractions. Other countries have proved that they can respond to a trading vocation if foreign policy burdens are not too heavy. Since the Second World War, the small trading states of Western and Central Europe have reestablished growth rates and social cooperation under the stimulus of foreign trade. Holland, Austria, Switzerland, and Sweden have done so with notable success. Since growth in their gross national product depends heavily on exports, these countries have had to embrace social compromise and sacrifice to keep wages and prices in line with those of competitors. The small democracies of Western Europe have employed liberal and social corporatism to regain their trading advantage.[33]

Fourth, the international economic and financial system is now uniquely favorable in that support for foreign trade has risen in domestic politics. Since World War II major domestic groups and producers have had a significant stake in low tariffs and increasing foreign trade. Always before, there were major conflicts between countries in which capital was scarce and those in which capital was abundant. Broadly speaking, capital-abundant countries wanted low tariffs and benefited from expanding trade.[34] In contrast, capital-scarce and land-scarce economies relied on high tariffs. As nation after nation (most recently South Korea) has entered the phase of capital abundance, dominant economic interests within these countries have also acquired an interest in low tariffs. This may well be the reason why there has been no general move to higher tariffs in the United States, despite the unfavorable trade balance. Specific

33. See particularly Peter Katzenstein, *Corporatism and Change* (Ithaca, N.Y.: Cornell University Press, 1985).
34. See Ronald Rogowski, "Political Cleavages and the Changing Exposure to Trade," *American Political Science Review,* vol. 81, no. 4 (December 1987), and *Commerce and Coalitions* (Princeton: Princeton University Press, 1989).

sectors have asked for and received relief, but Japan continues to sell 36 percent of its exports in the American marketplace. Thus the stimulus of foreign trade as a prod to revivify and modernize industry is likely to be a continuing one.

In summary, given a major shock or stimulus and a favorable economic and military environment, nations can alter a trajectory of decline. Resurgence becomes possible when the fact of failure can no longer be denied and when new resources become available to finance an alternative strategy. Then the resultant challenge to the national psyche shatters past assumptions and breaks conventional models of behavior. Afterward, the newly chastened state can retrench and regroup, cut military spending and consumption, and rededicate itself to a new strategy combining industrial modernization and expanding exports. Timing here is very important. Too great a delay in returning to an export and trading strategy can do irreparable harm to domestic economic institutions and make it impossible for them to catch up. In the United States' case, scientific and technical research is still the standard of the world. Many industry groups like civil aviation, chemicals, computers, and software retain their cutting edge. The United States still leads in research on the possibilities of digital television. But if America is to revive, progress must be made soon, *before* further inroads take place in its overall competitiveness. Assuming this, Americans will find that a strategy of economic resurgence depends upon beginning to see themselves as growing progressively poorer under ruling economic practices, while recognizing that conventional navigation has failed to steer the ship of state in the correct direction.
   Foreign policy ultimately permits national economic development. A benign international environment and a cheap and efficient foreign policy, of course, do not guarantee that the savings that accrue will be used appropriately, and not simply be absorbed by increased consumption. Yet, if foreign policy burdens are too heavy, growth will not take place or it will be quickly stunted.

To achieve economic growth through foreign trade, domestic electorates as well as nations must increasingly tailor their coats to the cloth meted out by the international system. While it is very difficult to gain new territory, states can more easily improve their economic performance. The conflict among countries lessens when they take aim at economic growth, for the development of one nation does not impede the growth of another and it may even assist it. In addition, as international politics becomes a less threatening environment, nations can make great savings on their military budgets. This does not mean that international politics presents no competitive challenge, but it is typically, among developed countries at least, the challenge of economics and foreign trade, not warfare. This challenge is even a desirable one, for societies do not concentrate upon efficient production of economic goods if they face no competitive rival. Under these circumstances, decline is no longer final; nations can go down, and still up the economic scale. They can recover and ascend.

ADDENDUM ON THE PUBLIC GOODS PROBLEM

Public goods are benefits that, once provided, can be enjoyed by everyone. Consumption by one individual does not diminish consumption by another. No one can be excluded from benefiting from them. Clean air, clean water, sidewalks, roads, public health, an electoral system, police protection, economic growth, and a generally cooperative international environment are examples of public goods.

The economic account of such goods, however, does not explain how they could be created, except by government fiat. Each potential consumer of public goods should adopt the maxim: "Let George do it." Once national public radio, a welfare system, or clean water have already been provided, then the consumer can be a "free rider"—contributing nothing, but benefiting from the public good provided by the efforts of others. From a sheerly self-interested viewpoint, a person has an overwhelming reason *not* to contribute to such goods. If their benefits are greater than his costs, he would offer funds to create them *only* if his share made the difference between provision and non-provision of the good in question. The chance, however, that a single individual's contribution could itself make the difference between creating and not providing the public good is negligible. Tens of millions of people are involved in the public act of voting: one individual's vote does not spell the difference between victory and defeat of a national candidate. Economic growth depends upon an overwhelming number of people making particular choices on consumption and saving. The likelihood that one individual decision would affect the outcome can be dismissed. If others save, a particular individual can afford to consume and still expect to benefit from rising growth rates in the society as a whole. Yet, if all members of society reasoned in this way, consumption would rise and investment decline. The public good would be lost.

It thus appears that if public goods are to be created, government must mandate them and, if necessary, impose taxes to ensure that they are paid for. This is how police protection is guaranteed. Welfare and social security systems come into being in this way; penalties are thus applied to polluters and in Australia to those who don't vote. Alternatively, government may offer rewards to those who contribute (as the U.S. Federal Government did a few years ago in striving to persuade home owners to insulate their houses, thereby conserving energy for all). In many cases, however, government is powerless to achieve mandatory results. One can penalize those who transfer capital overseas, but if financial conditions are desperate, such measures may only stimulate illegal flight. A democratic government can try to establish the political conditions in which economic growth will occur, but it cannot actually guarantee development. That will depend on individual decisions made by entrepreneurs, consumers, savers, and investors aiming their actions toward compatible goals. If, despite government regulations and tax policies, individuals consume virtually all of their disposable income, there will be no saving and little investment. Growth will be restricted, and inflation will rise. Worker productivity, thrift, and social cooperation cannot be legislated, though all three are necessary for continuing economic growth. If this is true, public goods which cannot be brought into being by the government's tax and enforcement powers will not be created.

Yet this model of economic man's rational decision making cannot be correct. People and organizations have broader social objectives than those suggested in the study of public goods.[35] Except

35. See particularly Howard Margolis, *Selfishness, Altruism, and Rationality: A Theory of Social Choice* (Chicago: University of Chicago Press, 1982), and Robert Frank, *Passions Within Reason: The Strategic Role of the Emotions* (New York: W. W. Norton, 1988).

in a definitional sense, individuals are not self-interested beings, seeking only to advance personal welfare at the expense of the group. If people really acted the way economists assume, they would be "rational fools."[36] Nor is there any evidence that economists, in their daily lives, act in the way they prescribe.[37]

Evidence of behavior that is not purely self-interested in character is legion. At least 50 percent of those eligible do vote in U.S. presidential elections, though no one can believe that his individual vote will make a difference in the outcome. In Europe, the figure is much higher. A very large proportion of Americans are vaccinated against smallpox, even though the "rational" incentive is not to be, so long as others are. University faculty meetings regularly achieve quorums even though each professor can convince herself that as long as many of her colleagues attend, she need not be present. Individuals continue to support public radio and television with their donations even though one other person's pledge of the same amount should "rationally" obviate one's own contribution. In Los Angeles in 1976 the water shortage should have produced a community of free riders (free floaters?), each member of which used water to his heart's and his lawn's content. Yet conservation was the rule, rather than the exception. For a long time Japanese citizens paid high prices for food, housing, and consumer goods because they agreed with their government's rationale that they must save and not consume in order to leave a vast supply of goods for export. Political action on behalf of women's rights, a nuclear freeze, or against abortion has generated more than local support even though partisans might rationally have expected to achieve as much by staying at home.

Nor does the pattern of philanthropy support the strict public-goods argument. As Brian O'Connell shows, the poor, who can least afford to be generous, give a greater proportion of their incomes to charity than the rich. Nor, despite public-goods arguments, are people now less willing to give up their time to work for volunteer organizations. O'Connell points out: "A far larger pro-

36. See Amartya K. Sen, "Rational Fools: A Critique of the Behavioral Foundations of Economic Theory," *Philosophy and Public Affairs*, vol. 6, no. 4 (summer 1977), pp. 317–44.
37. Though it does appear that economics graduate students are more disposed to think in terms of material payoffs for their actions than others. See Frank, op. cit.

portion and many more parts of the population are now involved in giving and volunteering than at any time."[38] Nor are corporations and foundations largely responsible for public giving. The combined total for the two is only 10 percent of the total; individuals give the other 90 percent. Studies show that more than 85 percent of Americans donate to charities. In 1981 orchestras received $150 million in gifts, religious groups $10 billion, and hospitals over $7 billion.[39]

These examples certainly make clear that private individuals contribute to public goods. But it remains uncertain why public giving goes up and down, why societies elicit more cooperation from their members at some times than at others. There can be no doubt, however, that up to some point, societies under stress or pressure from outsiders will cooperate more intensely among themselves. This suggests, as we have seen above, that some institutional or social stimulus to the giving of one's time, effort, and money may be necessary to bring forth a response. Mancur Olson puts this in extreme terms, arguing that defeat in war, occupation, revolution, and change in frontiers may be necessary to shock the national psyche into a regenerative response.[40]

But too much shock may be positively harmful to the system. Many defeated nations have in the past simply declined and dropped out of international politics. Some victors did far better than many would have us believe: the northern states of the U.S.A. after 1865; Germany after defeating France in 1871; and Great Britain after dispatching Napoleon in 1815. In fact, it appears that social cooperation to overcome special-interest division of the social spoils is greatest in the case of *medium* levels of challenge to domestic institutions. Victory and its aftermath can still pose a challenge. Defeat may be too sweeping to engender a revival. Too great a challenge, like that suffered by Spain after 1640, Sweden after 1709, Turkey after 1900, and Austria after 1916, brings a social dissolution.

The outcome is like that in a lifeboat. If there are plenty of provisions, water, and nearby assistance, survivors need not coop-

38. *New York Times,* January 25, 1989, p. A19.
39. Frank, op. cit., p. 222.
40. Mancur Olson, *The Rise and Decline of Nations: Economic Growth, Stagflation, and Social Rigidities* (New Haven: Yale University Press, 1982).

erate to any great extent. If, on the other hand, there are no provisions, little water, and no help forthcoming, each passenger adopts the attitude of *sauve qui peut* and perhaps even connives to throw another person overboard. In the intermediate or medium case, social cooperation, both to ration the supply of water and to bail out the boat, may make the difference between survival and death for those on board. Cooperation leading to economic growth and internal consensus would then seem to depend on a challenge to the social fiber that does not cut its threads. This can occur in a number of different ways, not only by military defeat. In fact, the opening up of a nation to foreign trade and imports forces an important change in economic strategies. More than this, general awareness of the fact that the nation is declining and the presence of leadership to fashion a new approach could also lay the groundwork for a transformation in performance. In this context, an economic crisis would also have a profound effect in changing economic strategies.

3

The Preconditions
of Resurgence

As the historical legatee of Spain, Holland, and Great Britain, the United States is the fourth world power to try to understand and to reverse the seemingly inexorable processes of decline and decay. None of the first three succeeded in this task. Yet, with the possible exception of Spain, the others were well aware of what was happening and were resolved to alter their course. Neither Holland nor England found the social will to cope with societies that were fragmenting, dissolving in a welter of individual consumption and excess.

The difference between the Victorian and Edwardian ethos symbolizes this change in Britain: Queen Victoria was a model of nineteenth-century propriety, her son, Edward VII, a well-known rake. The general population was unlikely to heed calls for greater self-discipline from dissolute ruling classes. In the late nineteenth century the British worker had already been forced to accept a gradual but constant fall in his real wages under the impact of the European depression from 1873 to 1896. With growing prosperity in the first decade of the twentieth century, he was understandably unready for a new round of austerity. His middle-class colleagues—the merchants, manufacturers, and clerks—were also eager to enjoy their suddenly bettered fortunes, rather than save for the future.

England's manufacturers of textiles and machinery were aware of

71

the German and American challenge. They watched with appre-
hension the march of German goods into traditionally British markets on the continent. They knew that American mining and textile
mechanization was ahead of theirs. But they could not bring themselves to invest in new labor-saving machinery to increase productivity. As economists have since recognized, the efficiency of the
British work force was so far below that of the American that marry-
ing it to new labor-saving machines would not have yielded a
greater short-term profit. British managers had tried to force
economies by cutting wages, and their workers had responded by
slowdowns. If labor-saving machines had been installed, costs
would have risen, and production would not have grown enough
to compensate for them. Long-term British competitiveness, however, obviously required new mechanization.

Another course Britain might have tried was to bargain down the
tariffs of major competitors. Germany could perhaps justify some
slight protection of infant industries as late as 1879. She could
scarcely do so at the beginning of the twentieth century when her
steel, machinery, and chemicals industries had come of age and
were stronger than their counterparts in Britain. Then Germany
should have reduced tariffs proportionately. Despite some minimal
reductions in the 1890s, however, German tariff protection came
back with a vengeance in the early years of the new century. In
response, Britain's Joseph Chamberlain campaigned for "tariff reform," hoping to negotiate lower continental tariffs or to surround
the empire with a higher tariff wall. But he could not win support
from workers who savored their cheap food or from businessmen
who counted on cheap raw materials and believed, erroneously,
that the market for British goods would continually expand.

If Britain had seriously sought to impose higher duties, rivals
would have rushed to dismantle their own tariff barriers. The British had great bargaining leverage because their home market, like
the U.S. market today, was the most open and prosperous in the
world. Their most notable high-tariff competitor, of course, was the
United States, which did not seek real tariff cuts until Woodrow
Wilson carried the day in their favor in 1913.

All the while, British capital was developing other nations. Interest returns were higher abroad, and railway bonds for Australia or
Argentina (to say nothing of the United States) represented a prof-

itable investment. But what of the British manufacturer in the Midlands and the North? His access to capital was circumscribed by regional banks, and the London money managers did not always deem him the most attractive risk. So their funds went preponderantly to rising countries overseas.

In the third quarter of the century particularly, Britons loaned and invested large sums in European and Latin American nations, the United States, and the Empire. Having done so, they had to allow them to pay back their debts. The borrowers could do this only by exporting to England. In fact, they had to run an export surplus in the British market, while restricting British imports at home. In both cases Britain was disadvantaged: Britons lent capital to their competitors, not to their own country, and then they had to keep their market open and not threaten others that it might be shut. In effect, in the nineteenth and early twentieth centuries, Britain helped to create and then sustain her own competitors!

The American historical situation is all too similar. In relative economic terms the American advantage peaked in the late 1920s and 1930s. But many believed that her edge continued into the 1940s and early 1950s. In one sense, it did. World War II destroyed European and Japanese production, and thus measurements of shares of world gross national product taken in 1945 and 1950 artificially inflated the American proportion. When the continentals and Japan regained their productive feet, however, America promptly fell in relative share.

Also, because of the Communist threat, America saw economic growth by key East Asian and West European allies as building "situations of strength," an essential foreign policy task. The United States not only opened its markets to Western and Japanese goods, it allowed the presumably weaker, war-damaged economies to discriminate against American products. Further, it provided in the Marshall Plan and subsequent military aid the resources needed to restart and sustain economic development in Europe. In the late 1940s and early 1950s, the dollar was regarded as a "scarce currency" and continental states in the European Payments Union were allowed to discriminate against it and to clear payments among themselves through barter and other exclusive arrangements.

Not until 1958 did such financial barriers fall. When they did,

Europe had already proposed to substitute for them a far-reaching plan of integration, which, while moving toward internal free trade, would raise a common external tariff against the United States and the rest of the world. And the United States not only acquiesced in this movement, but encouraged it. Why America did not foresee the consequences of her aid to Europe is still a historical puzzle. Perhaps the United States could not understand that Europeans might come to have a contrasting and sometimes conflicting point of view on major world problems.[1] In justification, however, one should remember that this was precisely what Britain had done in the nineteenth century, and that the United States was not the only beneficiary of England's bounty.

In many respects, the United States between the late 1950s and early 1990s came to resemble its imperial predecessors. It provided loans and grants to its competitors. It retained markets for their produce. It committed itself to defend them against external attack. It shared its technology with them. In the process, America neglected to renew its own sources of industrial strength. Though helpful to American consumption in the short term, America's trade deficits provided needed resources to others. The United States devoted very large amounts to the military protection of its postwar allies and clients. In short, it continued to act as a Great Power so that others would have the ability to act as free-riding economic developers. In so doing it planted the seeds of its own decay.

Aside from growing economic weakness, the United States experienced draining foreign policy challenges, which further poisoned the attitudes of Americans toward their leadership and each other. Vietnam, of course, was the classic cause of disaffection. Normally, countries and individuals learn the proper lessons from foreign policy failure: they conduct an inquisition within, find out what is wrong, and strive to eradicate the faulty trait.

Countries which lost World War II surmounted that crisis and emerged in sounder economic and political condition. Under the stimulus of the Allied occupation, they rapidly concluded that undemocratic leaders and military policies were at fault, and replaced

1. Max Beloff, *The United States and the Unity of Europe* (Washington, D.C.: Brookings Institution, 1963).

them. Social learning in Germany and Japan dealt appropriately with the causes of the war and helped to ensure that they would not be repeated. To reverse the failures of the past, Germans worked hard, and Japanese even harder, to redeem themselves. In both countries, social cohesion rose. To be sure, they had help in rehabilitating themselves. Others carried most of the military burden so they could lay it down; economic assistance was forthcoming, and the outside world's unanimous condemnation of fascism assisted the two defeated nations' intellectual and social reorientation.

The Second World War offered useful lessons and a purgative experience for the vanquished nations. But America's defeat and withdrawal from Vietnam had a much less salutary effect. The moral to be drawn was unclear, and in some cases the Vietnam episode taught the wrong lessons. Positively, it suggested that in certain "imperial" conflicts (involvements well beyond concrete spheres of interest as interpreted by Western Europe and Japan) the United States would have to go it alone. Quickly, Europeans detached themselves from American policy in Southeast Asia, the Middle East, and to some degree as well in the Persian Gulf. There were thus some Americans who became convinced that the United States would have to carry on in these peripheral areas without the blessing and support of allies, and others who believed that the United States should not be there in the first place.

After Vietnam, Americans came to disagree about foreign policy in ways they had not done since the "loss of China" in 1949. But Vietnam was a much more divisive case than the Communist victory in China. Then, few people except Senator Joseph McCarthy believed that America's China policy was immoral or based upon duplicity. Most Americans concluded that the United States did not have the military, political, or economic strength to prevent a Communist takeover there. Few recommended a wholesale commitment of American forces to the mainland of Asia in those years. Indeed, there were few enough who supported the defense of Japan, and many who were willing to place Korea outside the U.S. defense perimeter. Not morality but the physical limitations on U.S. strength were at issue here.

Vietnam created much deeper divisions. In China there was no need to create an independent national government. Even the Kuomintang were "nationalists," ruggedly independent of foreigners. Many Americans were convinced that, in Vietnam, the cause of the rise of the Viet Minh and Ho Chi Minh was not the attractions of Communist ideology, but rather nationalism: the desire to be free from French or American dictation. American intervention was seen as preventing the logical completion of a national revolution.[2] The United States was, in short, on the wrong side, morally speaking, and the issue was not simply one of deficient American strength.

Great Britain also had questionable motives in the war against the Boers in South Africa, 1899–1902. The British tried to convince themselves that they were on the side of humanity in striving to prevent Afrikaaner discrimination against the British South Africans and the blacks (whom the Boers wanted to use as slaves), but mostly they were aware that the Boers were fiercely defending their own territory against a British attempt to amalgamate them with the Cape Province. Nevertheless, using extremely punishing counterinsurgency tactics—burning the homes of the Boers and putting their wives and children into newly invented "concentration camps"—the British prevailed. Britons scrutinized their purposes in South Africa more carefully than they had done at the time of the Crimean War in 1854–56. The Boer War also led, as did Vietnam in the American case, to a recognition of how "isolated" Britain had become from European nations (all of whom, not just Germany, supported the Boers). In victory, the British later conceded defeat by allowing the unification of South Africa under Boer leadership. Still, the Boer War did not continue to reverberate as an issue in English politics, inhibiting further foreign policy commitments. It did not, obviously, prevent the British from joining the French side in the First World War.

For the United States, the impact of Vietnam was more severe. It not only made other commitments more difficult, it also questioned the morality of American leadership. Leaders were not only misguided, but perhaps dishonest. Americans were not only hesitant to follow them in foreign policy, they were also doubtful of obeying them in other, domestic disputes. Watergate, coming on

2. George McT. Kahin and John W. Lewis, *The United States in Vietnam*, rev. ed. (New York: Dial Press, 1969).

the heels of Vietnam, taught the lesson that American leaders frequently lie and deceive, and that the people might do better disregarding them.[3] Two of the next presidents, Carter and Reagan, essentially agreed on this issue. Carter tried to return American leadership to the people as a moral and incorruptible force and source of inspiration for policy, but his presidency did not accomplish the needed reform. Reagan's election campaigns ran against Washington and the Washington élite, and he won them even when he was running the bureaucracy himself. Nor did he become markedly less popular when it was clear his own presidency was tainted by duplicity, misleading both Congress and the public about his administration's intentions and actions in regard to Iran, the hostages, and the Nicaraguan Contras. Perhaps this was because, as the testimony of Oliver North suggested, his actions could be defended by an appeal to principle, both in freeing the hostages and in supporting the Contras, despite congressional restrictions.

In any event, the Vietnam episode led some Americans not only to distrust leaders but also to distrust each other. For a time many young Americans believed that a truly moral life could be lived only in self-sufficient communities or communes, free from the restrictions of middle-class morality and from the international constraints of the energy crisis. Their elders had been responsible for the war; they were also the polluters of the 1970s. Those over the age of thirty had already been corrupted by "the system." Basic foundational myths of American society already overemphasized the need to be isolated to be pure. Society corrupts and international society corrupts absolutely, suggested the founding fathers from Jefferson to Thoreau. For an individual, too much social involvement was a sin, detracting from the purity of isolated effort and family life. For a nation, too many international entanglements would weaken the country and corrupt its moral calling. Vietnam

3. In December 1970 college students were asked in a Gallup Poll how they thought change would come about in America during the next twenty-five years. Forty-two percent said by "revolution" (as compared to 50 percent by "peaceful means"). In 1972, 43 percent of college students said "yes" to the question: "Do you think violence is sometimes justified to bring about change in American society?" (54 percent said "no.") In late 1973 the *Congressional Quarterly* asked Americans to list the biggest problems facing the country. In 1972 in a similar survey only 5 percent had listed "integrity in government" as a major unsolved problem. In late 1973, 43 percent did so.

offered proof of both: it had the effect of taking Americans out of public life and America out of the world.

Thus the Vietnam calamity did not convey useful social lessons. Instead of rededicating and reuniting a social community confronted with the fact of failure, it raised the question of whether there should be unity at all. Individualism could then be carried to excess: in the 1970s in radical communities that hoped the immoral nation would fail; in the 1980s in untrammeled money making, which put the interest of the individual over and against that of the group and country. America as a country was not worthy to succeed, only individuals were.

The recommitment to social values that should have begun in the mid-1970s thus never occurred. And there is another reason for that failure. None of the protest groups against the Vietnam War seriously questioned the strength and power of the American economy. Some saw that economy as a strong instrument of capitalist oppression. No one initially said, "Stop Vietnams. They will sap our economic strength." The Berkeley radicals expected to get good jobs in the expanding economy of the late 1960s and early 1970s. The problem was not that the corporation was feeble or impotent, it was that it was malign and evil. There was nothing in the Vietnam crisis that fundamentally pointed to weaknesses in American economic or military power; it suggested only their misuse and misdirection. Social disunity could thus be tolerated without any effect on the standard of living.

Largely symbolically, the Reagan presidency changed this ethos. Now it is popular to be patriotic, but patriotism involves no concrete restriction on the individualistic pursuit of Mammon. Reagan offered "costless" patriotism, symbol rather than substance.[4] The problem for the future, however, is that Americans will have to work together in support of community goals and will pay a cost in doing so. It does not seem that they will do so without undergoing another and more dramatic economic crisis, one that overcomes the remaining antisocial lessons of Vietnam.

The historic position of America thus has been eroded in two ways: by the concrete damage that too great an international role

4. In the words of the liberal weekly *The Economist,* "Mr. Reagan promised a revolution and delivered a dinner party." January 21, 1989, p. 13.

and too many formidable competitors have created, and by a decline in domestic cooperation.

TRAITS OF THE AMERICAN ECONOMIC SYSTEM

America's imperial role and the loss of Vietnam did not simply dictate internal economic policies. These policies also played their role in fashioning the current U.S. predicament. A few well-known but still extremely important traits of the American economic system need to be underscored: American corporations have aimed at short-term profits; their short-term strategy often decrees buying other companies, rather than investing in new plant and equipment. American companies have too frequently developed an antagonistic attitude toward labor. They have focused too much on marketing older products on a product-life-cycle basis, rather than on developing new products. American society saves too little and consumes too much, and the American work force is undertrained and underprepared for the competitive task it faces in the years ahead.

•

U.S. corporations have tended to aim at short-term profits rather than long-term market share. Their goal has not primarily or even particularly been the survival of the individual firm as an economic unit, but rather profits for each financial quarter, even if these are realized by selling off the assets of the corporation. Some of these practices have stemmed from the dominance of financial criteria in making investment decisions. Financial texts often stress maximizing the value of the firm's stock as the major goal.[5] To do this, the return on investment must improve the earnings of the corporation and thereby sustain or increase the stock price. "If the greater expectation of profits outweighs the increase in risk [from making the investment] we expect the price of the stock to rise if the project is undertaken."[6]

Typically firms compute what they could achieve with capital funds in the money market if they did not make the proposed

5. See Haim Levy and Marshall Sarnat, *Principles of Financial Management* (Englewood Cliffs, N.J.: Prentice Hall, 1988), p. 5, as one among many examples.
6. Ibid., p. 5.

investment. The Net Present Value criterion compares the cash-flow returns from the investment over a period of years with the interest rate (or market capitalization rate) of today. If the cash flow of the proposed investment (discounted by time) is inferior to the amount that would be provided by a similar investment in the money market, the proposed investment should not be made. In many firms, the rate of return on a new investment had to exceed 20 percent for that investment to take place.

But as Robert Hayes, Steven Wheelwright, and Kim B. Clark of Harvard and Stanford business schools point out, one has to compare the investment's return not only with returns in the financial markets, but also with what happens if the firm does *not* make the contemplated investment.[7] One cannot assume that the firm will remain equally profitable and that the status quo will remain fixed. "Companies today are locked in fierce battles with competitors who are continually jockeying for position, introducing new products, attacking new markets, and adopting new process technologies. Therefore the choice of a base case must reflect a company's best assessment of what it, its competitors, and its customers are likely to do if the proposal is not adopted."[8]

For example, as Hayes and his collaborators note, a prime competitor who does decide to invest in new equipment may reduce prices and go for market share. Can the other firm compensate? Its overage machinery may make it difficult, particularly if the competitor is lowering prices. A revised calculation of the desirability of investment in new equipment will now yield an even more unfavorable outcome, because the project returns, given lower prices, will be even lower. In this way, the authors point out: "companies . . . often become trapped in [a] disinvestment spiral."[9] Also, "to regain its position, [the firm] may actually have to expend far more in the way of resources than would have been necessary if the investment had been made when first proposed."[10]

In this way, American electronics and then semiconductor firms lost ground to Japan. First, they did not make initial investments

7. Robert Hayes, Steven Wheelwright, and Kim B. Clark, *Dynamic Manufacturing* (New York: Free Press, 1988), p. 74ff.

8. Ibid., p. 74.

9. Ibid., p. 75.

10. Ibid., p. 76.

to capitalize on American inventions in videotape recorders and players. Then when Japan and Korea did make such investments, companies found investment even less remunerative and left the field entirely. U.S. semiconductor manufacturers fought the battle of the 64K memory chip, but then did not invest fast enough to get any of the market for the 256K successor chip. Now, though American firms are contending, they may still lose out in the race for the market for chips of 1, 4, and 10 megabytes.

In neglecting to invest, American business leaders have confirmed SONY chairman Akio Morita's warning that they are endangering the long-term competitiveness of U.S. industry. Deploring American business practices, Morita wrote: "The annual bonus some American executives receive depends on annual profit, and the executive who knows his firm's production facilities should be modernized is not likely to make a decision to invest in new equipment if his own income and managerial ability are judged based only on annual profit."[11]

Chief executive officers of many U.S. firms serve only for a short five-to-seven-year period. Their objective, like that of American presidents during the Vietnam struggle, is all too often to make profits and not to "lose the store" on their watch, rather than to devise strategies that will ensure the long-term survival of the company, in short, to prevail against the competition.

•

This short-term strategy that dominates American business often dictates manipulating assets rather than investing in new plant and equipment. Companies on the prowl for new capacity will buy assets, rather than add to their own production capacity. Companies that have been subject to takeover bids will frequently sell assets to pay the stockholders, to increase profits, or decrease debt. In one phase, the cash-flow surplus of the firm is spent in the temporarily more lucrative practice of mergers and acquisitions, where immediate profits may be made. Indeed, from the short-term point of view, market share may be gained more rapidly through purchase than via production and sales. In a later phase, the newly acquired companies are frequently split up and units sold off at

11. Quoted in Chalmers Johnson, *MITI and the Japanese Miracle: The Growth of Industrial Policy, 1925–1975* (Stanford: Stanford University Press), p. 313.

higher prices, showing a profit on the balance sheets of the con-
solidated firm, but leaving the company with little new production
capacity. In recent years, there has even been a tendency for firms
to reduce assets because profit rates then attain higher levels. This
in turn pushes their stock upward and guards against hostile takeovers. It also, however, diminishes the capacity of the company to
produce.

The conventional wisdom in the marketplace is that companies
which are targets of a takeover bid are badly run by managements
that do not get full value from their assets. Takeovers force management to obtain the profits that stockholders demand, and produce a "lean and mean" management style, which has to increase
revenues and cash flow to pay off debt accumulated in the takeover
process. It is very difficult to get data to learn whether companies
that were taken over did better or worse in the aftermath. Only for
a short period did the government ask companies to keep records
on how the previous target company performed when broken into
subsidiaries after the takeover.

Using this information, D. J. Ravenscraft and F. M. Scherer provide nine years of performance data on sixty-two companies taken
over or merged in the early 1970s. They found that these companies, prior to takeover, did slightly worse than their peers in the
industry (by 1.57 percent). After takeover or merger, however, they
performed even less well (by 3.10 percent). If a change in accounting procedures that occurred with the merger is taken into account,
however, the deterioration in profit rates was as much as 5.91
percent. In other words, they received an overall return on assets
of 7.43 percent compared to the industry average of 13.34 percent.
This, however, did not mean that the companies failed to make
money: it meant that the adding up of their assets (which occurred
during the takeover battle) reduced profit rates on those now too
highly valued assets. Still, as Ravenscraft and Scherer point out:
"Those premiums were supposedly paid in anticipation of enhanced profitability," a profitability which, they note, did not
emerge.[12]

The problem with takeovers is that they induce companies to

12. D. J. Ravenscraft and F. M. Scherer, "Life after Takeover," *Journal of Industrial Economics,* December 1987, p. 154.

take on more debt to pay returns to the stockholders, raising the stock price. While the debt might have been useful to finance new investment, the increased payout in dividends does nothing to increase the long-term survivability of the firm. In addition, the pyramiding debt and cash-flow requirements leave companies vulnerable to bankruptcy in a recession.

•

Third, in the past American business developed too much of an adversary relationship with labor. Until very recently workers have not been able to participate in decisions made on the assembly line or "quality circle." Employees have had too small a financial stake in the success of their companies. American business executives have sometimes taken bonuses when the underlying success of the firm does not justify them, while denying such rewards to labor. Not too long ago, Elmer Peterson, an heir apparent to the presidency of General Motors, resigned because he could not persuade management to forgo its bonuses in unfavorable years, years in which workers would not get extra compensation.

•

Fourth, as two keen students of industrial practice at the Harvard Business School, Robert Hayes and William Abernathy, observed in their prescient article "Managing Our Way to Economic Decline," marketing functions appear to be more important than production functions in many U.S. corporations. Rather than designing new products, executives spend their time finding ways to market old ones. Alternatively, they design utterly useless products. The reductio ad absurdum of this practice was the designing of a "pet rock," which each consumer could keep near the desk, offering reassurance and solidity in times of stress. Hayes and Abernathy's initial survey of business methods was made in 1980. But later reviews did not suggest significant change in the dominance of marketing over production strategies.[13]

The product-life-cycle concept, developed at Harvard, also contributed to prevailing beliefs that products have a long life and can

13. Robert Hayes and William Abernathy, "Managing Our Way to Economic Decline," *Harvard Business Review,* July-August 1980; Robert Hayes, "Strategic Planning—Forward in Reverse?," *Harvard Business Review,* November-December 1985; Steven Wheelwright and Robert Hayes, "Competing through Manufacturing," *Harvard Business Review,* January-February 1985.

be sold in a variety of markets. According to that concept, the "pioneers" of any new product, say a television set, would first capture their own domestic market. In the next phase, they would export it abroad. When competitors developed there, the pioneers would directly invest in production facilities in the foreign market. As European and particularly Japanese competitors not only began to recapture their own markets, but also to export successfully to the United States, American multinational firms would move their production facilities to less-developed countries—to "export platforms," where they could produce televisions at low labor cost, importing the finished product into the U.S. market. In fact, with the exception of Zenith, no electronics companies are still manufacturing television sets in the United States. With higher labor costs, even the Japanese have been forced increasingly to manufacture (that is, assemble) their electronic products in Korea, Taiwan, and Singapore.

The product-life-cycle concept has had two major impacts upon the production of new American products. First, it has let firms believe, in many cases unrealistically, that each new product would have a relatively long life cycle—twenty years or more. Now compact disks are rapidly replacing LP records, but they are themselves vulnerable to copying by cheaper digital audiotape machines, which achieve the same fidelity. The life cycle of new products in the highly competitive consumer electronics field is becoming ever shorter, with laser disks (which provide video as well as audio reproduction), high-definition television (HDTV) (the next hopefully long-lived product), camcorders, and other new products rapidly outmoding their predecessors.

Some, of course, contend that HDTV may not turn out to be as big as its backers think: it is apparently difficult to notice the difference in resolution unless you have a TV set bigger than twenty inches. Also, HDTV is still based on analog (not digital) reproduction techniques. Fidelity will increase much further when digital audio and video, processed by personal computers, can be meshed with fiber-optic cable transmission. As George Gilder writes:

> The video computers of the future will have virtually no current
> television technology in them—no high voltage vacuum tube with an
> electron gun spraying serial streams of charge millions of times a

second, no high powered, high frequency antennas, transponders and gigahertz converters, no processing of analog waves, interference and weather spikes. The telecomputer of the future will be a solid state computer cheaper, more energy efficient and far more powerful than any television-based technology.[14]

This is an extremely important point because while Japan has focused on processing and interpreting analog signals, the United States leads in computers with their digital format (the U.S. has 70 percent of the worldwide computer market). Unlike analog TV receivers, besides, the computer promises interactive transmission. With digital video interactive (DVI), as Gilder points out,

A feature length movie will soon be held on just two compact disks, and any frame can be randomly accessed and interactively manipulated. For example, in a real estate presentation, the viewer sitting at a screen can enter the picture and "walk through" a room, he or she can repaint the walls of or move and reupholster the furniture or even open shades and look out the window—all on the screen. Or a medical student could perform a simulated surgery, or a student pilot could fly a plane. The viewer of a televised football game could record and watch it from different vantage points.[15]

It is therefore just possible that when the analog HDTV age arrives in several years, it will already be out of date. In any event, technical revolutions seem to occur about every half decade: American companies can no longer count on a long-lasting product.

Second, the product-life-cycle theory had the disadvantage of convincing American businessmen and women that the ultimate stage in production is to be found in a cheap labor market located overseas. Venture capitalists seek to enforce this orientation by persuading developers of new products to demonstrate their seriousness and commitment by producing them in Malaysia, Taiwan, or Singapore. This argument may have had some merit before the 50 percent fall in the value of the dollar since 1985. It has no longer. As the Korean won and the Taiwanese dollar rise in value it will lose further force. In many new industries labor is in any event an increasingly smaller fraction of the cost of the finished

14. *Forbes Magazine,* February 20, 1989, p. 72.
15. Ibid., p. 74.

product. Japan has certainly made a profit and is now exporting from its production facilities in the United States.

Why can't American manufacturers do so? The labor-cost argument becomes increasingly weak as robotics and automation replace workers. The latest VCR production facility in Japan employs only three workers. Thus, the argument to produce in the United States should now be greatly reinforced, canceling the old suggestions of the product-life-cycle hypothesis. Nonetheless, in 1986 the United States had as much as 20 percent of its industrial production concentrated overseas. Akio Morita comments:

> Unless U.S. industry shores up its manufacturing base, it could lose everything. American companies have either shifted output to low wage countries or come to buy parts and assembled products from countries like Japan that can make quality products at low prices. The result is a hollowing of American industry. The United States is abandoning its status as an industrial power.[16]

·

In America since the 1970s there has been great emphasis on individual consumption but a low rate of savings, as young professionals and others have amply demonstrated. What is surprising is that this new fetish for consumption takes place against a background of the highest real interest rates in the industrial world. Savers should abound in such a context, but the savings of American households rarely exceeds 3–5 percent of GNP. In contrast to Americans, foreign savers are delighted to hold their money in short-term U.S. accounts. Even if inflation starts to rise, they still benefit because rising prices will cause the Fed to raise interest rates, increasing their return. This will also have the desirable effect (from the foreign investor's point of view) of increasing the value of the dollar. Americans, strangely, seem to be uninfluenced by these incentives. And unlike foreigners, since they maintain their savings in dollar accounts, they do not run any foreign exchange risk.

In Japan, on the other hand, saving amounts to 18 percent of GNP even though interest rates are very low. Japanese have a high disincentive to save and yet they save in prodigious amounts; Amer-

16. Quoted in Stephen S. Cohen and John Zysman, *Manufacturing Matters: The Myth of the Post-Industrial Society* (New York: Basic Books, 1987), p. 60.

icans have a high incentive to save, and yet they spend almost all their money. Different tax systems help to account for this result along with historical factors. Americans spend because they remember the inflation of the late 1970s when they first got used to the credit-card economy. Now that inflation has greatly declined, they behave as if it has not. Japanese thrift is based on the penury of the past and the uncertainty of the future. Japanese save for their old age. But now the Japanese population is becoming much older and should be beginning to spend its hoard of savings. To date it has hardly started to do so.

•

The American work force is relatively undertrained and undereducated as compared to its developed-country competitors. Former Governor Richard Lamm of Colorado points to the sad record of American students on standardized mathematics tests given around the world. A Japanese eighth grader typically knows more mathematics than an American holder of the Master of Business Administration degree. It is no wonder there are limits on U.S. worker productivity.

•

Each of these aspects of the current economic scene indicates that serious problems face the renewal of American productivity. Together they suggest a corporate and public leadership that lacks a long-term strategy to equal U.S. competitors in the decade ahead.

Can the United States save money in foreign policy costs to devote more resources to economic growth? It appears, fortunately, that the international situation does not require that America gain superiority over both its allies and the Soviet Union in deployed forces. American allies are much stronger now than they were before and well capable of bearing some of the burdens that the United States has carried. The Soviet "threat" is getting smaller. Soviet capabilities have not measurably decreased, though the reduction of tanks and associated forces from the Eastern European theater will be welcome when it occurs. But Soviet intentions are now much more tolerable: the likelihood of a direct Soviet attack upon Japan or Western Europe is now low and getting smaller. In some measure the better international atmosphere is due to the failure of Soviet expansionism in the past, in Afghanistan and elsewhere. But it is

also explained by the relative growth of other states as real or
potential members of the club of great powers: Japan, China, Brazil, and Mexico. India will one day join their number. As the two
erstwhile "superpowers" see others gaining on them (and in the
Soviet case, passing them), they have a greater common interest in
agreeing to reduce the tension between themselves.

This is particularly so if, as is now being suggested, the Soviet
economy (previously estimated at 50–60 percent of U.S. gross national product) is only about one-quarter to one-third the size of
the American economy. If it were true, for instance, that the USSR
had only a $1 trillion GNP, and a growth rate of 2 percent or less,
the Soviet Union could actually be pushed from the ranks of the
great powers in twenty years' time. Japan, a united Europe, and
China would all rank much higher in 2010. At that time, Japan
would attain a gross national product of $5–6 trillion and, if it
wished to reach such heights, a military budget of $200 billion a
year (2.5 percent to 3.0 percent of GNP).

It is the prospect of such relative decline that impels Mikhail
Gorbachev and his Russian colleagues to strive to achieve *uskorenie*
(acceleration) in economic and scientific fields. "Acceleration,"
however, will not be achieved in the short run. For the next five
years or so the disorganization caused by *perestroika* (restructuring)
will more than compensate for any growth either in the consumer
or manufacturing sectors. In fact, the Soviets have provided few
incentives for their people to work harder or improve the quality
of their products. The money that Soviet citizens earn cannot be
spent on superior products because they don't exist in that country.
Only if the leaders adopt the risky but still plausible course of
importing some high-quality Western and Japanese goods will the
Soviet population be rewarded for its sacrifices and its past saving.
With a greater range of consumer choice, Soviet men and women
would work harder and spend more, taking up the slack in the
economy produced by the coming slowdown in military production. Thus, it is possible that Soviet imports of Japanese, American,
and Western goods could increase in the short term. They would
particularly do so if the most favored nation restrictions of the
Jackson-Vanik Amendment were modified. The probability is that
Soviet preoccupations with economic growth will free America to
devote more of its own resources to the same task.

The world environment may also be ready to support greater American growth in another respect. American exports to the Third World and particularly to indebted Latin America have suffered since the late 1970s as a result of the international debt crisis. Countries like Mexico, Brazil, Argentina, Peru, and others have bought far less than their share of U.S. goods because of the economic stringency forced on them by creditors. Unless they control domestic demand for imports, they cannot run the export surpluses needed to repay the banks and international lending agencies. Despite rescheduling and refinancing, however, the debtors will not be able to repay the full amount. This means that at least some of the debt must be written down, that is, sold off at a portion of its par value or canceled outright. The banks have resisted taking such losses, but the ultimate impact of pressing for full repayment will only be the threat of default. When this is hinted, even the banks will be ready to sell their paper on a secondary market, accepting perhaps 60 percent of its face value. When the banks respond, they will relieve many of the pressures on debtors, who will then be able to accommodate some growth in domestic demand. This will in turn help to buoy American exports. Not surprisingly, America and the debtor countries have many important common interests; both would wish to see world growth at a much higher level in order to increase their ability to export.

America's present situation cannot be taken lightly. Judged from a historical perspective, the United States is now facing the prospect of continued economic decline. The Vietnam episode taught Americans not only to distrust their leaders, but also to contribute less to general social cooperation. The "free rider" phenomenon has become a characteristic of American social life. The corporate power structure has also not shown flexibility in face of new challenges. Short-term thinking continues to animate the chief executive officers of many corporations. Here and there, however, longterm thinking dominates: at Boeing, IBM, Hewlett Packard, Merck, and other forward-looking corporations. While the domestic prospect is scarcely rosy, international relations hold the key to greater flexibility, a flexibility that would allow the United States to concentrate new funds and energies on reviving its productive apparatus.

THE PRECONDITIONS OF RESURGENCE

Despite the favorable international circumstances of the moment, few theorists believe that nations can indefinitely cooperate. They have generally believed that independent nation-states seek power and come into conflict doing so. Even if there is a balance of power to restrain an aggressive state, there will still be war. Sooner or later a leader bent on expansion will fail to heed the warnings of his brother statesmen. Then war against the aggressor is the only means of maintaining the balance.

From this point of view, one can explain the origins of the First and Second World Wars as conflicts brought on by the balance of power. In 1914 Germany would not moderate its arms race with Britain and Russia or its support of Austrian expansion against Serbia in the Balkans. A quarter of a century later, Hitler disregarded Britain's and France's guarantee to Poland and Rumania and marched on Warsaw. Thus the restraints on power—or deterrence—have not universally operated to prevent war. And some believe that nuclear weapons will not always deter. In 1973 Egypt and Syria attacked Israel—a state they knew to be equipped with nuclear weapons. In 1950 North Korea and China were not hesitant to engage the forces of the world's leading nuclear power, the United States. Nor did North Vietnam cancel its campaign in the South in face of the mounting presence of American troops.

Beyond these conflicts, in the past kings and queens recognized that, if cooperation was beneficial, there was still more to be won by capitalizing aggressively upon an opponent's concession. In technical parlance, a state can usefully "defect" when its rival "cooperates." If power is defined strictly in relative terms, what one state gains the other loses, and there can be no cooperation between them.

Many theorists have believed that the existence and increase of interdependence among states would make for cooperation.[17] But

17. Norman Angell, *The Great Illusion: A Study of the Relation of Military Power in Nations to Their Economic and Social Advantage,* 3rd ed., rev. and enl. (New York: Putnam, 1911); Henry Thomas Buckle, *History of Civilization in England* (New York: D. Appleton, 1863); Richard Cobden, *Speeches on Free Trade* (London: Macmillan, 1903); Richard Cooper, *The Economics of Interdependence: Economic Policy in the Atlantic Community* (New York: McGraw-Hill, 1968); Edward Morse, *Modernization and the Transformation of International Relations* (New York: Free Press, 1976); Oran Young,

we now know this is not necessarily true: the mere division of labor among units does not engender a harmony of interest among them. Although business and labor are mutually interdependent, they have frequent conflicts. Allies in war have fates that are joined, but they do not always work in harmony. Sometimes international leaders seek to manipulate the interdependence to produce greater advantages for themselves at the expense of others.[18]

Enhanced trade among nations, which is beneficial to all, may help some more than others. Trade may not be balanced; instead, one side may run an export surplus and get most of the revenue, while the other suffers a deficit. Since this situation cannot go on indefinitely unless the debtor has an unlimited gold supply, the debtor country must take action to correct its imbalance. At this point conflict arises, for the debtor country's measures may involve tariffs, quotas, the attempt to get foreign suppliers to impose voluntary export restraints (VERs), and other restrictions. These acts may all be in the interest of the state running a trade deficit, but they will conflict with the interest of the state with an export advantage. Then, if the surplus country imposes a countervailing tariff, trade is cut and the problem remains unresolved. If the surplus nation allows the deficit country to restrict its exports, it loses foreign sales and concedes part of the international market. Neither solution is satisfactory to both sides, and the conflict simmers.

In the historic past a series of "trade wars" occurred with tariffs ratcheting up like old-fashioned barber chairs. In the 1920s and 1930s, France, Britain, and the United States, one after another, devalued their currencies. Each nation sought to get the edge in international trade, only to find that its competitor's devaluation

"Regime Dynamics: The Rise and Fall of International Regimes," *International Organization*, vol. 36 (1982), pp. 277–97; Robert Keohane and Joseph Nye, Jr., *Power and Interdependence: World Politics in Transition* (Boston: Little, Brown, 1977); Robert Keohane, *After Hegemony: Cooperation and Discord in the World Political Economy* (Princeton: Princeton University Press, 1984); Richard Rosecrance, *The Rise of the Trading State: Commerce and Conquest in the Modern World* (New York: Basic Books, 1986); Richard Rosecrance and Arthur Stein, "Interdependence: Myth or Reality?" *World Politics*, vol. 26 (1973), pp. 1–27; Peter Katzenstein, *Small States in World Politics: Industrial Policy in Europe* (Ithaca: Cornell University Press, 1985).

18. See Arthur Stein, *Why Nations Cooperate: Circumstance and Choice in International Relations* (Ithaca, N.Y.: Cornell University Press, 1990) and A. Stein, "Governments, Economic Interdependence, and International Cooperation" (UCLA, October 1988).

had countered its initial gain. The only result was that foreign trade collapsed, leaving everyone worse off.

But the fact that nations learned some lessons from the world-wide Depression of the 1930s by no means guarantees cooperation today. Japan would like to keep its foreign trade surplus, which allows that nation to buy up the assets and products of other countries. The more others devalue without achieving balance, the more Japan can acquire the assets of the world at low prices. Other things being equal, then, Japanese interests lead to a partial conflict over trade with the United States. Meanwhile, the United States, faced with trade deficits of the order of about $120 billion a year, has to bring them to a halt. Already, Americans are building up a debt that ultimately will have to be paid back by cuts in consumption.

Both the United States and Japan are democratic countries. Japanese leaders do not relish telling their people to sell less abroad or to buy more, and in any event such advice has not often been heeded. It is even harder for U.S. leaders to try to curb American consumer appetites through taxes or tariffs. But some agreement must eventually be reached between these governments, or the U.S. trade balance will get completely out of control, and the dollar will lose its value.

In certain respects the achievement of a reasonable balance in trade today requires weak governments to say "no" to the most powerful domestic constituencies in their society. They cannot easily do this, and this means that conflict between countries is an ever-present possibility. In a sense, governments form a kind of international pressure group, a corporate body directed, at least in part, against their own populations. Each government is aware of the risks their counterparts face in domestic politics. Each is eager to solve problems in ways that do not rile internal opinion. Yet each is also conscious that if the problem is not solved in the short run, even more drastic measures ultimately will have to be taken.

Of course, governments hope that the "market" will bring a solution if they do nothing. But often the market exacerbates the problem, with a flood of capital leaving a country whose policies have not brought equilibrium to the balance of payments. Ideally, monetary policy alone will suffice. Monetary decisions are generally made by arcane bodies such as the American Federal Reserve System or Germany's Bundesbank, relatively far from public scrutiny.[19] If interest rates go up and down with fluctuations in the money supply, experts notice but people only feel the effects later on. But if governments have to cut social programs or raise taxes to achieve a balance in their international payments, the whole world knows. And reacts. Governments understand that it is hard for one of their number to cut spending or institute taxes and so they are tolerant of their colleagues' delays.

At some point, however, either other governments or the market itself demand action, with the threat of sanctions. In their trade dispute, Japan and the United States have generally been quite tolerant of one another, at least in public. But Japan has not been able radically to increase its imports or to reduce its exports, and the United States has not been able to reduce the fiscal stimulus of its government deficit. The failure of both countries to adjust only makes the problem bigger, and ultimately harder to solve. Eventually, governments may have to risk unpopularity by imposing restraints on their own people. That is the test of international cooperation in the present era—whether governments can take that risk and recalibrate the benchmarks of social performance and economic welfare in their own countries. If they cannot, then international cooperation cannot generally be relied upon.

Still, the old notions of repetitive and inevitable international conflict are losing their validity. The theories of conflict specified that national "separateness" and "autonomy" (expressed in the doctrine of "sovereignty") would require one state to avoid becoming dependent on another. A nation would fight to avoid compromising its territorial integrity, but it would also fight to remain capable of defending itself and providing access to needed resources. Historically, this meant that each state should have a relatively independent economy and should be able to defend itself without foreign help. The very term "Great Power" meant a state that could not surely be defeated even if all other states ganged up against it. But that notion of "power" as "independence" has surely withered (though, like the Marxian state, it has not yet "withered away").

A more contemporary view is that "power" can be achieved not

19. William Greider, *Secrets of the Temple: How the Federal Reserve Runs the Country* (New York: Simon and Schuster, 1987).

against but within a certain degree of dependence on others. Japan has brought this conception to the fore, and it is an efficient one. According to this idea, one does not need to provide for all aspects of one's defense by oneself, nor must one contain all needed economic resources within one's own territory. Access to assistance, markets, and resources offered by others suffices and satisfies the now restricted demands of sovereignty. In other words, the new conception is that a nation does not have to do everything itself. It can focus on the functions it does best and, through alliance or purchase, obtain assistance from others. Collective alliances can reduce the security expenditures of each state member. International markets can make available at lesser cost items which a country would have difficulty producing on its own (such as oil, iron ore, bauxite, or coal). If we add to this the difficulty of a country's getting *physical* access to such resources through military conquest, one can see why at least a limited degree of mutual dependence is economically efficient.

This analysis, however, does not easily apply to the leading contenders for power in the international system. They may seek support by allying with other like-minded states and they may develop interdependent economic ties with the same group of nations. But vis-à-vis each other, they seek *independence*. Potential enemies do not like to rely on each other. During most of modern history, the two greatest powers in a system have typically been rivals. The primary question for the future is whether dependable cooperation can exist between the United States and the Soviet Union (and if the USSR fades, between the U.S. and Japan and/or China). The world has no experience, thus far, of a long period of continuous peace among the greatest powers. The forty-five years since the Second World War is longer than the generally peaceful period between the end of the Napoleonic Wars (1815) and the beginning of the Crimean War (1854). Trends in power help to account for this record. Frequently war occurs when the leading military power starts to decline and another rises to challenge it. If the challenger seeks to take territory or colonies from the leader, war is certain. In the American and Russian case, however, the Soviet Union is certainly not rising even if America has declined from its previous estate. The United States was so far ahead of the Soviet Union in 1950, however, that it could tolerate a considerable loss in relative strength without jeopardizing its territorial position. In this sense the two major military powers in the system are both declining. They have reason to cooperate to prevent further mutual decline.

If so, cooperation among the two leading powers in the system can continue. This may be less true if Japan or ultimately China supplants the Soviet Union. If Japan emerges as the challenger, she might be less tempted to agree with the United States than Russia would, because Japan would be a rising state. But there is a real question whether Japanese military power and political influence would be sufficient to take international leadership from the United States. Even more than the Soviet Union (which sought to rule restive and rebellious peoples in Eastern Europe, and hoped to colonize Western Europe), Japan lacks a coterie of friendly and powerful allies on which to base its power overseas. Its nearest neighbors—Korea, Taiwan, Malaysia, Hong Kong, the Philippines, Singapore, and Thailand—are economic but not political or cultural allies. Japan proved in the Pacific War that it could mobilize the labor forces and direct the economies of such nations, but (with the exception of Thailand) not that it could work with them. Traditional Japanese culture seems ideally suited to understand and cope with the stations of social superior and inferior, but it is less comfortable with relationships of equality. Nor, for similar reasons, could Japan hope to base its power on a durable friendship with China.

One of the strange outcomes of postwar world politics was that the United States benefited in both hemispheres: in the West because of the similarity in culture and institutions; in the East because of the very difference in both. The distinct civilizations of Asia have created natural cultural and ethnic rivalries, which seek friendship and support from nations outside the region. The notion of particularly sympathetic economic and political relations within the Pacific Rim is acceptable to East Asians only because of American, Canadian, and Latin American participation. In this very sense, Japan has no ethnic or cultural power base from which to launch a program of leadership of the world at large. If that is true, even a stronger Japan would likely remain associated with the United States.

The same need not necessarily be true of China. Overseas Japanese, other things being equal, are loyal to their adopted country.

In the United States, Hawaii, Brazil, and other places this is a fact of social life. Overseas Chinese, on the other hand, retain important loyalties to and cultural contacts with their motherland. These will endure despite the present climate of repression in Beijing. Though Chinese minorities are frequently discriminated against in local contexts, mainland China can use its connections with its overseas people to improve its political relations with a series of countries along the rim of the Pacific. The growing Asian migration to the United States will benefit China far more than it does Japan. On a similar basis, China, more than Japan, would be able to develop friendly relations with the emerging nations of East and Southeast Asia. Some of this latent solidarity would rest on a cultural desire to prevent further Japanese penetration. Perhaps this is because China's traditional policy toward foreigners, when it has been faced with outside threats, has been to assimilate the intruders. Japan's traditional policy has been to exclude them. The most numerous and one of the most resilient races in the world, Chinese have never had to fear cultural extinction. Japanese traditionally had to insist on their distinct cultural identity in order to be sure of preserving it.

Unlike Japan, China also has the ingredients of traditional power: population, resources, and a large geographic base. Once mobilized, they would make China much more independent of other nations than Japan could ever be. At some time in the first quarter of the twenty-first century, China might even be tempted to try to cut the remaining ties with supporters who now provide markets and technology for Chinese products. Yet one should not try to look too far ahead. In the intervening years, and particularly given the military suppression of dissidents, China will need all the help it can get, and that help may be declining. Ultimately, China will emerge as an independent national economy in ways very different from those of countries that rose in the nineteenth century like Japan, Germany, and the United States. After the shock administered by Commodore Perry, Japan fashioned its own distinctive industrialization, much less capital-intensive than that of European developers. The United States became capable of creating its own new technology in the 1870s. It still needed British capital, but was able to innovate on its own. Germany pioneered in the chemical and motorcar industries with limited help from the "first industrial nation." In terms of real wages, Germany, America, and even Japan were relatively well off even on a pre-industrial basis.

China, on the other hand, seeks to quadruple its income in twenty years, starting from a much lower industrial and much higher population base. China may thus be the first country to complete its modern industrialization in intimate association with and even dependence upon technological suppliers and markets. Existing industrial powers will be the midwife to China's technological rebirth. Any major withdrawal of Western and Japanese capital assistance will reduce China's growth rates. The re-establishment of rapid modernization in China would depend upon a reintegration of China into the world economy. The ultimate emergence of modern China thus could increase rather than diminish the economic links among the most important powers of the world. Under these circumstances, the association between China and the United States could continue relatively undisturbed.

Assuming that the overarching military bipolarity (of the United States and the Soviet Union) declines in intensity, the world will need new guidance in fashioning economic cooperation among nations. In the post–World War II period, intense economic interdependence was largely confined within one pole. Ostensibly it was the very hostility to the Communist bloc that strengthened the economic relations of the industrial democracies. Military and security mandates spurred common economic interests. When the Soviet Union and China begin to join fully the community of Western economies, this reason for special democratic cooperation will fade. Some theorists predict a possible breakdown in relations among Western and industrial nations. With markets available in China and Russia, why should Japan and the United States remain the closest of allies? The answer is that America and Japan will have to cooperate because theirs will be the largest economies. Japan will not find a substitute for the American market in either China or Russia. The United States will not find needed capital in either Moscow or Beijing, only in Tokyo.

Great powers today, in short, have to consider their economic interests, not merely the past pattern of military rivalries. If the two or three leading economies do not cooperate to manage imbalances, the world system will head for a crash, perhaps even greater than that of 1929. This could definitively shatter the prospects not only for Third World growth, but also for the export-led growth of China's and ultimately Russia's economy. In the final analysis, therefore, it is economic imperatives more than military ones that govern what will happen. The fate of the future hangs, essentially, on the ability of the United States and Japan to agree on how to manage the system. Thus far, the evidence for such continuing agreement is conflicting. On some matters, the two economic giants have been able to reach accord—on exchange rates, interest rates, and access to Japanese capital. On others they have not, particularly on the opening of the Japanese market to U.S. agricultural and industrial produce, and on a reduction in the Japanese savings rate through further fiscal stimulus. It remains unclear what will happen in the future.

It remains true, nonetheless, that the ultimate outcome will be contingent: there is no reason to believe in the inevitable occurrence of military conflict, as decreed by previous theory. The mere fact that the essential "good" which is now being pursued by most nations is economic rather than territorial in character gives room for hope. The amount of territory in the world is fixed and disputes about it constitute a game of constant sum. If one nation gets more, another must have less. But economic goods do not total a fixed amount. They can be increased. Countries negotiating over growth rates and trade balances can, over time, both improve their positions. Expanding trade is a rising tide which floats all ships, even if the wave of trade, growth, and markets temporarily lifts one more than the other. Nations with a long-term perspective can adjust to the ebb and flow, and short-term losses can often be the prelude to greater gains.

Whatever may be said about cooperation in international politics, however, economic growth requires cooperation at home. Citizens can usually cooperate when faced with a foreign threat. If there is no external challenge, however, domestic agreement may be much more difficult to achieve. This is partly because it is sometimes harder to demonstrate the need for cooperation domestically than it is internationally.

Unless internal difficulties spring from identifiable foreign causes, people do not always cooperate or know what to do. As President Carter found, a vague malaise does not inspire coherent action. If things are going wrong, should citizens blame the government? Perhaps business or labor is at fault. Perhaps it is the polluters. The temptation is to locate a culprit and take revenge. It is harder to say with Pogo: "We have met the enemy and he is us!"

Even if there is a clear social crisis, like depression or war, leadership still has to identify the problems and possible solutions. In 1933 Franklin Roosevelt recognized that consumer demand for products of the U.S. economy had collapsed. Business was not investing. Government spending programs thus were needed to augment private purchases and business investment.

But in the 1990s the government's problem will not be to get people to spend. The problem will not be employing unused industrial capacity, but creating new capacity to export American goods. If the Republican administration merely stimulates the domestic economy, it will preempt that capacity, bid up prices, and reduce the attractiveness of U.S. wares in world markets. The problem instead will be to create capacity that Americans do *not* use. U.S. citizens in fact will be pressed to save more, while foreigners are induced to buy more from the United States. In short, American citizens will be asked to change consumption and spending habits that are more than a decade old. To be sure, the government and private banks will have to offer interest rates that attract savings, but as many economists observe, they already do so. America has the highest real interest rates in the industrial world, but the lowest rates of actual saving. Japan in contrast has the lowest interest rates, but the highest percentage of savings as a portion of GNP. Of course, Japan allows savers to exempt their dividend income from income tax, while the U.S. taxes these proceeds at regular rates. But this alone does not explain the difference. (See Table 7.)

Yet interest rates should not be too high. If they are, business cannot finance its capital expansion, and investment slumps. Thus the leaders of America's economic rejuvenation campaign will have to persuade consumers to do something that they might prefer not to do on the basis of strictly individual calculations. Since many now believe that spending is the best prescription for the country's economic health, they will need to learn that saving, under current circumstances, is one way of solving our trade deficit and increasing productivity.

There will need to be tax incentives to achieve this outcome.

Table 7

Japanese and U.S. Savings and Consumption
(As a Percentage of GNP)

	U.S.		Japan	
	Savings %	Consumption %	Savings %	Consumption %
1982	12.82	87.18	31.18	68.82
1983	13.80	86.20	30.49	69.51
1984	15.50	84.50	31.51	68.44
1985	13.25	86.75	32.14	67.86
1986	12.60	87.40	32.33	67.67
1987	12.60	87.40	32.76	67.24

Source: Percentages calculated from data in Organization for Economic Cooperation and Development, *Economic Surveys: Japan 1984/1985* and *1987/1988;* and *Economic Surveys: United States 1986/1987* and *1987/1988* (Paris: OECD).

Interest on small savings accounts should be exempt from tax. Long-term capital gains taxes need to be reduced and perhaps abolished. But government expenditure will also have to be cut, and ultimately higher taxes will be necessary. Social security benefits will have to be taxed at higher rates. Government retirement programs may have to be trimmed. Real sacrifices will be involved in the programs of economic revitalization. On the other hand, the country will gain and individuals will benefit in the longer term.

Can such sacrifices be made? Social science theory and leading economists say "No." According to them, individuals will act as "free riders," capitalizing on the cooperation of others. They will not lift a finger to help their country. In the mid-1970s, President Jimmy Carter tried to persuade Americans to see the challenge of the energy crisis as "the Moral Equivalent Of War" until he found out that the acronym for his recommended response was "MEOW." But despite impressive displays of technical brilliance, the arguments of social scientists and economists cannot be entirely correct. If they were, no Americans would vote, because no individual could believe that his or her vote would itself decide who gets elected. From a single individual's point of view, efforts on behalf of political and social causes are unproductive. They detract energy and time from personal money making, and one individual's contribution will not make the difference between failure and success for such enterprises. Yet people still subscribe to them. In the

United States a truly important moral, political, or economic issue can tap deep wellsprings of cooperative effort and support. The task of national regeneration can also attract constructive social effort.

A nation's capacity for social compromise and cooperation is partly related to its demonstrated abilities to overcome past challenges and threats. Thus it is not only the experience of war, occupation, or change in frontiers that may forge a national consensus. The severity of the original struggle in which a colony became a nation may be equally important. That contest stamps the national identity and marks the boundaries in the first place.

Notably, Australia, New Zealand, and Canada, which had no colonial conflict with the mother country, experienced proportionately greater difficulty becoming fully unified national states. Instead of having to fight for it, independence was thrust upon them. Australia and New Zealand did not achieve fully defined national identities until they fought in World War I. India's Congress party did not engage in military combat to win independence from Great Britain. The Congress party had already been given administration of local areas in the late 1930s. Partly because the Gandhian independence movement was nonviolent, it also did not fully integrate all of British India as a new country. And Pakistan hived off when independence loomed.

The United States, however, won its defining characteristics through war with the British. That it was victorious is beside the point: in a struggle for independence, even if the colony loses it gains a disciplined and dedicated population. That is why in the Boer War the Boers (the Afrikaaners), and not the English South Africans, bore the stamp of national identity in South Africa. One fought the British, the other did not, or fought on the wrong side. This tends to suggest that new nations in Africa will face difficulties in carrying out a united and coherent economic plan, for they rarely have had to fight for their independence. But the United States possesses the underlying historical unity to weld a new national consensus on behalf of sacrifice and competition.

Americans have proved in war that they can sacrifice for a greater common interest. What remains uncertain is whether that martial spirit can be evoked again in the service of an economic cause.

Whether the United States can come back in the next few years depends on whether American decline proceeds imperceptibly down a gradually sloping path or plunges over a steep gradient. No one can say for sure what will happen, but the odds are better than even that a new crisis is not far away. The executive-congressional negotiations in 1987 and 1989 did not eliminate the budget deficit. This was either because the existing crisis was too mild or because its true severity was not perceived.

The budget deficit is even more significant because it is directly linked to the trade deficit. As we have seen, the trade deficit is a product not just of too much private consumption, but of too much government spending. In economic terms, the government deficit plus the excess of investment over savings equals the trade deficit.[20] The investment goods that Americans buy over what can be financed domestically plus the government purchases that are bought in excess of taxes together equal the amount by which imports exceed exports.

The government deficit is thus a major structural element in increasing the debt we owe to foreigners. Unless it is reduced and eliminated, devaluation of the dollar will not produce a long-term solution. By itself, devaluation will stimulate price increases, requiring a further devaluation unless and until the government deficit is cut. Since those cuts almost certainly await new taxes, which will not be risked in the first year of the Bush administration, the trade balance is not likely to improve in the short run. Ultimately this will signal the markets that the United States is not in control of its own house.

Along with higher inflation and higher oil prices, this will lead to higher interest rates, which in turn could trigger a sudden selloff in the market, not unlike that of October 19, 1987. Foreign monies

20. Avinash Dixit, *New York Times*, July 15, 1985, p. A18, as quoted in Gilpin, *The Political Economy of International Relations* (Princeton: Princeton University Press, 1987), p. 371. The formal relationship is as follows:

$$(G - T) \quad + \quad (I - S) \quad = \quad (M - X)$$

| Budget deficit | Investment minus savings | Trade deficit (Imports minus exports) |

(G = Government Spending; T = Taxes; I = Gross Private Domestic Investment; S = Private Savings; M = Imports; X = Exports)

would then leave the market and interest rates would have to be raised further, pushing the American economy into recession. A swing in the business cycle, which will occur ultimately in any event, could then magnify the cash-flow problem of many overindebted corporations and thrifts, which might then be forced to default, laying the foundation for a recession.

If this happened some would be tempted to turn on the government spending valve and pump-prime the economy with new deficit financing. Then the Federal Reserve and the Treasury (plus Congress) would be forced into a clash, with the threat of well-nigh permanent stagflation. The markets would not be likely to tolerate any such policies: attempts to pull a financial rabbit out of an inflationary hat could push the Dow-Jones average into a free fall.

The beginnings of recession following upon another drop in the stock market would do several things. First, it would automatically increase the savings rate as consumers began to save for a now more uncertain future. Second, if prices fell, American goods could become more attractive on world markets. Third, the lessons drawn from the slump would question government nostrums which achieved prosperity only through borrowing from foreigners. Americans (business, labor, and consumers) might then pay close attention to a reform government which told them what had happened and what needed to be done. A new crisis leadership, either in Congress or the executive, could produce a sea change in attitudes and create an entirely new climate of opinion—one that would welcome change and instill greater social cooperation to find a solution to the American predicament.

The preconditions of U.S. resurgence are threefold in character. First there must be reliable international cooperation. Historic practice would militate against this condition, but the increasing preponderance of economic goals over military ones lends new hope that it may be achieved. Second, domestic cooperation must rise. It can do so if there is a domestic or international challenge and if there is enough underlying unity among the people in support of national goals. Third, there must be a spark to ignite new social energies. Friction to produce it is being generated in the form of a new economic crisis.

4

Meeting the Domestic Requirements

THE PRODUCTION SYSTEM

Historically, one of the great strengths of the American system of production was specialization—breaking down the elements of a process into components and then engineering solutions for each element, one by one. From the Tayloristic school of management to Henry Ford's assembly line, time-study experts approved the division of complex manufacturing into defined operations, to be repeated in sequence. The assumption was that, with practice, a harmony of man and machine could be attained to produce a uniform product. How would this product of manufacturing compare with others? Nineteenth-century British workmanship, and indeed craftsmanship, might be superior to American, but the result was not as practical. Individual products from the British workbench would perform well, but parts were not initially interchangeable.[1] Repairs and replacements were difficult and expensive. Thus

1. T. K. Derry and Trevor Williams write: "The spread of the so-called 'American system'—that is, the improvement of the economy of manufacture by producing fully interchangeable parts—is one of the most striking technological developments of the second half of the nineteenth century. At the Great Exhibition in 1851, British engineering reigned supreme; the space allocated to the Americans was not even filled. Nevertheless, the American exhibits included half a dozen army rifles manufactured on the system of interchangeable parts, and within two years the system was being studied by a British committee." Derry and Williams, *A Short History of Technology: From the Earliest Times to A.D. 1900* (Oxford: Oxford University Press, 1960), p. 355.

America took the lead on cost, if not always on quality, and the Ford Model T earned its manufacturers millions more dollars than the builders of Rolls Royce made. By the 1920s, American mass production outstripped all competitors.

Others have noted that this bias toward mass production on an assembly line led to inflexibility.[2] The line could not easily accommodate a change in standardized products. Workers were tied to one repetitive operation; perhaps they could not perform another equally well (although this was certainly questionable). Yet it was General Motors' introduction of a limited number of variations (or options) on a standard model that won the initial victories over Ford. As William Abernathy has noted, however, the American automobile industry as a whole still emphasized productivity (in the sense of reducing costs in the production of a standard car) over innovation.[3] Even in recent years, General Motors has suffered because its Chevrolet, Buick, and Oldsmobile cars frequently represented minor modifications on a single chassis and body design. Engines from one division were used in others. When Chrysler emerged from the doldrums of the 1970s, it was with the K-car, still the basic box for many Chrysler automobiles. In the United States it was too long assumed that profit depended on long production runs of a standard unit. Only recently has American industry begun to learn how to do flexible manufacturing, as practiced by Japanese competitors. Flexible manufacturing, of course, requires a more expert labor force and speedier shifts from one product line to another. It therefore depends on flexible or soft automation, rather than hard automation, on robots which can do more than one thing. It also uses state-of-the-art machine tools, numerically controlled by computer. New flexible manufacturing techniques in turn need technological generalists who move easily from one problem to another, not the typical products of a vocational or trade school.

The assembly-line approach to specialization affects white- as well as blue-collar work. Administrative bureaucracies, perhaps reflecting generations of managers trained on the doctrines of Max

2. Charles Sabel, *Work and Politics: The Division of Labor in Industry* (New York: Cambridge University Press, 1982).

3. See William Abernathy, *The Productivity Dilemma* (Baltimore: Johns Hopkins University Press, 1978).

Weber, have pressed toward specialization. Inevitably, the more a task is broken down into separate components, the more specialists one must recruit to perform it. The greater the number involved, the smaller the purview of each. Ultimately this leads to one aspect of the "age of the smart machine," where the computer largely substitutes for human creativity and initiative, where it literally tells each worker what to do.[4] Self-esteem and the value of one's work (though not the rate of pay) decline commensurately. One of the workers that Shoshana Zuboff of the Harvard Business School studied complained:

> It robs me of my dignity of what I know how to do. They are removing my job, the job that lets me use my judgement. Now if you work on any one piece of the process, you have access to information about the entire bleach plant; you have access at your finger-tips. That means that my knowledge—which used to be special knowledge—becomes open and available to a lot of people.[5]

With the coming of the Industrial Revolution, machines came to regulate and lessen labor's contribution to total output; smart machines could render it a nullity. In this way, the computer did not eliminate specialization, it reinforced it by reducing further the individual worker's scope and initiative.

Nor at least initially did the computer increase the purview of middle managers. A giant corporation has many divisions, each with its own cadre of managers and engineers. The financial controllers at the top have to have a general view of all the operations of the corporation. But division and plant managers focus on the balance sheets of their own unit. As the corporation becomes larger, more operating divisions are set up, each given a smaller slice of the overall action. In these circumstances, it is not surprising that the major problem in large organizations, both public and private, is *coordination*. Unless divisions consult with one another, the components they produce separately are not likely to interface smoothly. Nor is it sufficient to leave all coordination to top management. By the time the problem reaches the highest level, its

4. See Shoshana Zuboff, *In the Age of the Smart Machine: The Future of Work and Power* (New York: Basic Books, 1988).
5. Ibid., p. 303.

solution will already be more difficult and costly. Thus the structure of the modern organization, with specialists at the bottom and generalists at the top (and no coordination in between), is not likely to cope with the challenges of tomorrow.

The old way of designing, producing, and marketing a product reflects this outdated orientation. Someone in a lab comes up with a new idea. It is sent on to engineering to produce a design. Next it goes to production, which has to figure out how to manufacture it. Finally, the product is dumped on the experts in marketing to sell it. At each stage one division "throws it over the wall" to another. But the process does not have to be performed this way. A company can bring together a team from all divisions that works with the product from inception to sales, smoothing obstacles and untying knots in the process. The result, as the Japanese have proved in the auto industry, is a car that moves from drawing board to driveway in three years, as opposed to the Detroit norm of five.[6]

A bassoonist cannot substitute for a violist in a symphony orchestra. But players of different instruments have to listen and respond to the playing of other sections, much as they would in a string quartet. The natural coordination among symphony players abets the coordination imposed by the conductor.

It is by no means clear that this coordination naturally or automatically occurs in large organizations. In fact the dramatic increase in the number of managers in recent years makes final control and coordination even more difficult. Production workers must specialize to some degree to carry out their tasks. But if middle management is also very specialized, coordination becomes episodic and difficult.

Not only this. The performance of the organization actually deteriorates. Endless meetings must be held to solve (coordinate the response to) simple problems.[7] U.S. automotive manufacturers are not as fast and agile as their Japanese counterparts. American hotels cannot respond as quickly as Japanese hotels to their guests' complaints: there are too many largely autonomous divisions be-

6. The Ford Motor Company, however, produced the 1990 Lincoln Town Car in just 41 months.
7. See Ross Perot's criticism of GM's operations in *Fortune*, January 1988.

tween the client and the management. American government cannot decide (or decide quickly enough) on a response to the Japanese commercial challenge, because every move by the Department of Commerce and the U.S. Trade Representative must be coordinated with the State Department and the White House national security staff. The State Department itself is a maze of bureaucracy. There are not only country specialists, but specialists on every conceivable topic within a foreign country. In U.S. embassies overseas, there is so much specialization that few political and economic officers have a full understanding of what is going on in the country as a whole.

Outside of the federal government, there are similar problems in public schools. Rarely do schoolteachers have leeway to teach classes the way they want and are trained to do because state educational bureaucracies and the personnel experts from the office of the superintendent frequently stand in their way. Teachers are so burdened with administrative duties that they have little time to prepare and to teach. Is it any wonder that private schools (where teachers may receive even less pay) do a better job than U.S. public systems of education?

To solve the problem, the United States needs less specialized middle managers and fewer layers of management between the enterprise and the public it serves. This almost certainly means fewer executives and a greater authority and responsibility for each. Correspondingly it means more teachers. In the past, managers proliferated because each one could not exercise more than a limited "span of control." Information technology, however, permits each executive to increase her range of supervision. As a result, over time corporate, government, and educational bureaucracies can and should be ruthlessly pruned.

Today, however, their proliferation has increased dramatically. Among the top ten of the Fortune 500 companies, a surprising percentage of employees are supervisory white-collar personnel (see Table 8). Even if we admit that the growth of service specialties within the corporation should increase the number of white-collar employees, that *more than half the modern corporation* should consist of individuals uninvolved in operations or production work is little short of astounding. The ratio in typical corporations in Japan is approximately one-sixth of the American figure.[8]

Americans have frequently wondered why U.S. military performance in recent years does not compare to that in World War II. One critic contends that the answer is that there are unified commands (where no service actually is in control), rather than specified commands (where a particular service governs), *and* that the officer corps are chronically overstaffed.[9] In unified commands, all the services are on an equal footing, and in Vietnam, as Edward Luttwak comments, "Corporate harmony was judged more important than the needs of war."[10] Another disadvantage was the overstaffing of headquarters and support personnel. It is the typical but highly relevant complaint of too many Chiefs and not enough Indi-

Table 8

Employment Structure of Top Ten
Fortune 500 U.S. Corporations, 1988
(Percentage of Work Force)

	White collar/salaried	Blue collar/hourly
General Motors	77.5	22.5
Exxon	43.0	57.0
Ford	37.0	63.0
IBM*	91.5	8.5
Mobil	61.5	38.5
General Electric	60.0	40.0
Texaco	n.a.	n.a.
AT&T	42.0	58.0
Du Pont	57.1	42.9
Chrysler	44.4	55.6

*It is not surprising that IBM manufacturing staff in the United States is relatively small compared to managerial staff—IBM does much of its manufacturing overseas.

Sources: Corporate annual reports for 1988 and personal communications to the author, June 1989. Data may not be completely comparable owing to differing measuring systems at each corporation.

8. See James Abegglen and George Stalk, Jr., *Kaisha: The Japanese Corporation* (New York: Basic Books, 1985), p. 105. Abegglen and Stalk compare the number of American and Japanese supervisory personnel needed to produce a given output.

9. See Edward Luttwak, *The Pentagon and the Art of War* (New York: Simon and Schuster, 1985).

10. Ibid., p. 27.

ans. In Vietnam only about 60,000 troops formed the maneuver battalions doing the actual fighting on the ground, but nearly 500,000 more military personnel supported this fighting. Table 9 (compiled from Luttwak's figures) demonstrates the increase in command positions since World War II.

Although there were slight reductions in the ratio of flag-rank officers to enlisted men during the Korean and Vietnam wars (when large numbers of men were mobilized), afterward the numbers resumed rising. Congress halted the increase in 1981–83 by fixing the number of generals and admirals. The rate of growth in numbers of flag-rank officers is even greater if one looks at the senior general officers, three-star ranks and above. As Edward Luttwak points out,

> In 1945 the 12 million at war were managed and commanded by a total of 101 three-star officers . . . and 38 full generals and admirals. . . . In 1983, a total of just over 2 million in uniform enjoyed the attentions of 118 three-star officers and 34 full generals and admirals. In other words, the number of these most senior officers *is now actually greater than in 1945,* even though command positions in the combat forces have diminished to roughly one-sixth of the 1945 levels.[11]

For most of these individuals there was no command position. The United States Army has 17 divisions, and thus needs 17 major generals, but has in fact 140. The Navy has 3,738 captains, but lists only 100 positions for captains aboard ships.[12] Luttwak comments:

Table 9

Ratio of Flag-Rank Officers to Enlisted Men
(Per 10,000 Enlisted)

1945	1.9
1952	3.5
1965	5.2
1980	6.4

Source: Edward Luttwak, *The Pentagon and the Art of War* (New York: Simon and Schuster, 1985), pp. 191–92.

11. Ibid., p. 192. Emphasis in the original.
12. Ibid., pp. 195–96.

Unable to command, because only a fraction can be accommodated in bona fide command slots, all these senior officers must manage instead; but there is not enough management to keep them occupied, so they must overmanage and micro-manage, or else "coordinate" the massive complications that overstaffing has caused in the first place.[13]

This tendency toward bureaucratization in modern American life is not confined to business and the military. In school districts the number of service and supervisory personnel has risen relative to the number of teachers. Current ratios in selected urban school districts are as shown in Table 10.

In universities, the number of administrative personnel has increased relative to the number of professors. And in state universities where there is more than one campus, there is a statewide administration to "coordinate" them all. In every area, there is a great surplus of captains over sergeants and lieutenants. As a result, each realm of activity is less productive.

For these very reasons, economists and business analysts have long recognized that white-collar productivity is the lagging element in the overall productivity of the American economy. While manufacturing productivity rose after 1985 to about 3 percent per year, overall U.S. (including white-collar) productivity has lagged at 1 percent or less. Stephen Roach (Morgan Stanley) hypothesizes that this is because business bought large numbers

Table 10

Percentage of Teachers as Compared to Total
Employees, Selected School Districts

Chicago Public Schools	56.4
Denver Public Schools	24.0
Houston Public Schools	53.1
Los Angeles Public Schools	50.6
New York Public Schools	46.3
Philadelphia Public Schools	47.6

Source: Personal communication with school boards by the author, June 1989.

13. Ibid., p. 192.

of computers and word processors, but then did not diminish the number of clerical employees.[14] The modern computer processor was supposed to give the individual manager the wherewithal to be his own secretary and research assistant, but those who hold those positions were retained. Two systems were engaged to perform the work of one. In time, Roach believes, the modern data-processing machine will be fully utilized, and when it is, white-collar productivity will rise. There are good reasons to doubt, however, that this will happen under current circumstances, because the net tendency toward fatter layers of white-collar bureaucracy appears to be continuing. Richard Darman's accusation of "corpocracy" continues to reverberate in the corridors of economic and military power.

Shoshana Zuboff shows how reform can nonetheless be accomplished. In the age of the "smart machine" information that was previously the privileged resource of managers can be shared with workers. When this happens, as Zuboff testifies, there is a flattening of the bureaucratic pyramid, and some managers can be dispensed with. For this reason, managers may hesitate to share information. But the performance of the firm nevertheless improves at all levels of the corporate hierarchy if changes are made. In time, therefore, the current division of labor between workers and management will alter, and the information revolution and the modern computer can help bring it about.

In these circumstances, as Zuboff writes: "The rigid separation of mental and material work characteristic of the industrial division of labor and vital to the preservation of a distinct managerial group (in the office as well as the factory) becomes not merely outmoded, but perilously dysfunctional. Earlier distinctions between white and blue collars collapse."[15] When these conditions are achieved, as they partly were in the paper mill Zuboff studied, workers feel differently about their task. One commented: "It is a different kind of decision making now. The computer is already making the smaller process decisions that I used to make. So that means I have

14. Stephen Roach, *White-Collar Productivity: A Glimmer of Hope?* (Morgan Stanley, September 16, 1988).
15. Zuboff, op. cit., p. 393.

to make the larger decisions and I have to have the information to make those decisions."[16]

In the industry of the future, there will be fewer executives because operators with appropriate training will be able to solve problems on their own; work will begin to include a managerial and self-controlling function. Employee-involvement (EI) programs will carry this process further. Now many companies are setting up self-managing work teams, the most advanced stage of EI programs. Under this concept, five to twelve multiskilled workers rotate jobs and take responsibility for an entire product or service with only limited supervision. As *Business Week* points out: "Adopting the team approach is no small matter; it means wiping out tiers of managers and tearing down bureaucratic barriers between departments. Yet companies are willing to undertake such radical changes to gain workers knowledge and commitment—along with productivity gains that exceed 30 percent in some cases."[17]

What will this reduction of administrative layers mean for the number of workers and executives? For particular industries, automated plants where the flow is entirely monitored by computers will be set up, dispensing with workers altogether. The newest Japanese VCR production unit employs only three operators. However, erstwhile workers may have become managers. In other cases, given greater information, a much leaner and flatter management corps will respond more effectively to the challenges of competition than the overstaffed bureaucracy of today. Two countervailing trends will obtain: on the one hand, cutting back on management, U.S. business will increase the ratio of operators to managerial staff; on the other, workers will increasingly be endowed with a management function, raising the white-collar total. In the far-distant future, perhaps, as Zuboff suggests, the difference between white and blue collars may disappear.

16. Quoted in Zuboff, op. cit., p. 302. Note the difference in response to information sharing in this instance and the one cited on page 107. In the previous case a worker objected to sharing his specialized knowledge with others. In this case the worker gains from *acquiring* new information.
17. *Business Week,* July 10, 1989, p. 57.

THE CONTINUING ROLE OF THE STATE

If bloated bureaucracy impedes the U.S. response to challenge, it does not follow that the state is itself the culprit. Some believe that the government is of limited utility in the solution of modern problems: business, volunteer organizations,[18] and transnational links are supposed to be the creative instrumentalities, molding the future. For others, the relevant unit is the globe and the appropriate instrumentalities of action are multinational in character: corporations, private and public international organizations. For these people, to seek to solve American problems is as parochial as thinking of the problems of Maine or California, divorced from a national context.

Yet, as we know, while the globe may have progressed, many countries perished or became impoverished in the process. Holland and Britain lost their economic edge and their ability to lead the world into new pathways of trade. Instead, continental monarchies and the United States came to the fore. If Britain had been as strong as the United States in the 1930s, the German challenge could have been dispatched much more easily. If Holland had remained powerful in the nineteenth century, the career of Napoleon's aggression would have been checked early on. Today the question is whether American strength serves a purpose beyond that of a narrow definition of U.S. interest. If American economic and political momentum is necessary to stoke the fires of political reform in China and the Soviet Union, and to help the Third World solve its economic problems, then a vital and resurgent America is a requisite for future world politics.

Why does America need to buttress its world role with greater economic strength at the present time? In the rise of any new nation, there is always a phase of immaturity that must be overcome before that country can begin to contribute to international progress and stability. America, for instance, was initially reluctant to take on new international obligations that its power amply justified as it moved toward primacy. Today it remains unclear whether

18. See Peter Drucker, *The New Realities: In Government and Politics/ In Economics and Business/ In Society and World View* (New York: Harper & Row, 1989).

Japan is fully ready to assume many of the burdens of world leadership. A weak United States will surely not be able to persuade Japan to do so, and the world could be in for a new interregnum.

Thus there are two major questions. First, does the United States deserve to be revivified, does it have a continuing international vocation? Second, if so, what role should U.S. governmental institutions play in its revival? As to the first, as we have already seen, the United States remains the keystone of the international arch, bridging the gap between Europe and Japan, between the Third World and the First, and between the Soviet Union and the rest of the system. As to the second question, one needs to address the Reagan critique. Essentially President Reagan denied that government should take the taxpayer's money and spend it for him; instead, individuals should make their own financial choices. But this response was too simple. As we have already seen, if expenditure is totally private, there will be few public goods. Police, regulatory, and welfare functions will be neglected or underperformed.

It's true that the record of Congress and the administration in normal times does not lend great confidence that they can be entrusted to solve major national problems, like those of economic growth and equity in the distribution of income and services. But crisis decision making has been much better. In the Depression and again in World War II, an American administration coped with major national and international problems. And today there is no alternative to national leadership in the solution of the greatest problems. The difficulty in the past has not typically been that government did not understand the problems, though that occasionally occurred, as with Hoover's response to the economic slump in 1929–33. Mostly it has been because the President and Congress were afraid to propose the draconian measures that were necessary (spending cuts and higher taxes) for fear of popular opposition. When taxes were mentioned in the 1984 election campaign, it sealed the defeat of Walter Mondale, and Michael Dukakis denied the liberal label until the very end of the 1988 contest.

In a future crisis, however, political leaders will have greater leeway in finding solutions to major social and economic problems. A major recession would certainly stimulate greater social experimentation. An acknowledgment of America's relative decline, already dimly sensed by the electorate, would help justify further action. In addition, the dawning recognition that the Cold War, at least in its old sense, is over could provide much greater support for reductions in the defense budget, providing monies that could be used for needed domestic programs, like education.

Those who believe the state is not the most effective instrument to make important decisions note its limited purview: its lack of jurisdiction to deal with many modern problems that transcend national borders. Yet the instrumentalities that have a broader writ, like the United Nations, have little power. The International Monetary Fund (IMF) has a great deal of authority in its limited field, but again it is dependent on the votes of its membership to undertake new tasks. In the end, the national state comes back as the leading international decision maker because it can make a choice, stick to it, and then negotiate with other states to seek to implement it. Three or four major states, acting together, can in this way accomplish a great deal. Agreement among them underpins the work of international agencies, like the IMF.

In contrast, the multinational corporation is an essentially irresponsible entity. It has no constituency, save that of its shareholders, and even then management has great leeway in its action, so long as it makes a profit. In contrast, the modern state has to strive to please the citizens within its jurisdiction, while the multinational corporation has no territorial jurisdiction at all. Perhaps in fifty or a hundred years there will be international organizations endowed with political, economic, and military power that have independent authority not derived from their member states, but that has not happened yet. Even the countries of the European Economic Community have to agree individually to join the European Monetary System. Nothing forces them to do so. The European Parliament does not yet have real power over the actions of the member states in the Council of Ministers.

Of course, many believe that the state, or at least the American state, cannot act effectively. It is a "weak state" with horrendous problems of coordination both within and between branches of government. It has too many bureaucratic players to reach an effective consensus, and besides Congress always gets into the act. Yet this pessimism does not apply to crisis situations when the different organs of government have proved they can cooperate relatively efficiently. The U.S. government depends upon an effective national will. It can partly formulate that will and influence it, but it is also affected by it. When the country calls for leadership and action, Washington responds. The state of the American economy and society represents a crisis that government must address, a crisis that will gradually unfold over the next several years.

THE SHORT-TERM COMPLEX

Most of the problems America faces derive from its short-term mentality. There is nothing necessary about this temporary aberration; it certainly has not been a historic predisposition. In the past, leaders were able to anticipate some of the major problems that confronted the new society and to deal with them. The westward movement had an imminent logic of its own, and many perceived America's "manifest destiny" to move to the Pacific. From the thirteen original colonies on, settlers knew they would be organizing new territories, and the political and economic system lent flexibility to these endeavors. U.S. institutions and strategies did not, of course, cope with the split that produced the Civil War, but for some years it appeared that the South and the agrarian Middle West might make common cause on the tariff and other issues, averting a clash. Despite the failure in the Civil War, American society and politics adjusted rather well to the incoming tide of foreign immigration in the nineteenth and twentieth centuries, without making fundamental changes in the nature of the American system. In the Depression and World War II, U.S. institutions met the challenge adequately.

But in the 1990s there may be an initial conflict of agendas. Habituated to the Cold War rhetoric and modes of behavior, many will continue to want to spend large amounts on the military, even as Russia's threat recedes. In contrast, the new, broader, and nonmilitary challenge to the United States is less well understood. It can't be encapsulated in slogans like the past "war on poverty." What is necessary is to establish a more "cooperative society" in America. If achieved, "cooperation" represents a continuing state of affairs. Further, it represents a partial turning inward toward uniquely American purposes. It focuses on how Americans should cooperate, not with the outside world (though that is also necessary), but rather with themselves.

Until the Great Depression, most American projects were outward-looking in character: to settle a continent and win a war. After the Second World War the social energy expressed previously in the westward movement was directed overseas. Americans were supposed to carry the torch to Europe and Japan and to keep peace in the world. The U.S. economic system was supposed to be planted abroad. While spreading U.S. economic and military practices internationally, however, America spent little enough time renewing them at home. At the conclusion of this process in 1990, the United States, like the British after 1956, had in its own way lost an empire, but not yet found a role. Reflecting on the Japanese challenge, one Briton said confidentially to an American author: "Why don't you just face the fact that you're second raters, like us?"[19]

The terms of the American debate now are not too different from our oldest ally's traditional uncertainty over which to emphasize: Great Britain or Little England, one stressing the imperial vocation, the other improving life at home. When colonial administrators returned to Britain in the 1940s and 1950s, they often found themselves bereft of an occupation and needing a new livelihood. It was perhaps two generations before Britain's domestic economic role could be resumed, and the fires of economic growth rekindled. America can ill afford such a hiatus today.

The United States has spent too much time responding as an imperial leader should: putting out fires, answering sudden crises, lending assistance to others, as if the founts of national power would never run dry. It has had no leisure to plot long-term or grand strategy for the American economy and nation. The debate between George Kennan and Walter Lippmann, however, foreshadowed our present uncertainties as early as 1947. Kennan favored a functional extension of American interest and power to contain every probe by the Soviet Union toward other states. Lippmann endorsed a much more limited and geographical American

19. James Fallows, *More Like Us: Making America Great Again* (New York: Houghton Mifflin, 1989), p. 10.

role, tightly limited by considerations of cost. Since Lippmann's eloquent argument, however, cost has been a relatively insignificant factor in the decisions made by U.S. foreign policy planners. It has always been assumed that what the United States wanted to do, it could do, at least economically. Now and in future, however, the problem of "opportunity costs"—of opportunities given up as a result of choosing a particular strategy—has to be addressed. Selecting a particular military or foreign policy strategy, we now may have to give up certain economic strategies.

In short, in the recent past U.S. strategy has been short-term in character because America was not constrained to think of the long term: U.S. economic resources would be sufficient to support virtually any course of action. In contrast, long-term strategy in the future will deal precisely with the question of sufficiency. It is not surprising that this is so. Countries on top do not spend time thinking overmuch about longer-term issues. It is countries which are at the bottom or halfway up the ladder that must have long-term strategies. It is not amazing that Japan, Germany, and Korea have all had well-defined long-term strategies: they needed either to reclaim or to achieve a stronger position.

In American history the same has been traditionally true: as a developing and weak nation, the United States had a much more clearly defined idea of what needed to be done than it has today. This correlates at present with the necessary distinction between two functions of entrepreneurship: management and augmentation of resources. Management deals with deploying and attaining maximum returns from existing assets, augmentation with increasing those assets. The one seeks to increase income, the second to amass new capital. Profit is the measure of the first; market share, for many purposes, is the index of the second. For too long American business leaders dealt only with the first of these two goals. That was not surprising because their concerns were fundamentally short term in character. They had little to do with long-term survival of the firm as a competitive entity.

The short-term mentality, of course, was encouraged by our tax laws. Japan has an exemption on capital gains taxes resulting from the sale of securities. In the United States, both corporations and individuals pay full capital gains taxes. President George Bush has suggested a reduction of the tax on capital gains. A better proposal might be to abolish altogether the tax on long-term capital gains (on securities or savings accounts). Here "long term" would be understood as five or six years. This change, though it would occasion a short-term revenue loss, would have a very salutary effect on the tax base and on lengthening investor horizons. In response, it would also reduce chief executive officers' concern over short-term fluctuations in the stock price. Investors would be locked in, their flexibility reduced. At the same time, such a change would be an incredible boon to the stock market and to equity capital in general, and new money would flow in. The U.S. savings rate would increase through the same mechanism employed in Japan.

The short-term mentality also derives from other aspects of U.S. business practice. As long as leveraged buyouts and takeovers are possible within existing tax laws, they will challenge management and force it to adopt a short-term strategy. The revision of the tax code to move to a fully integrated tax system for corporations and individuals would reduce the favorable tax treatment that today rewards debt and punishes equity.[20] But if an integrated tax regime is not formally set up, takeover and buyout artists will create an informal new regime. As Peter Canellos writes: "The net result of all this is that the corporate tax borne by the entity [company] is radically reduced, and whatever was formerly paid out as nondeductible dividends is being paid out as deductible interest."[21] The restructured entity is saddled with an enormous load of debt, though it has few taxes to pay.

Are such takeovers a burden on the body politic and economic? One study by Kohlberg Kravis Roberts (KKR), a not uninterested party, concluded that leveraged buyouts increase employment, augment research and development expenditure, and actually yield higher taxes to the federal government. Other studies have reached opposite conclusions. According to these, after a buyout, employment did not typically rise, but either held steady or declined, as management spun off assets of the new firm. The National Science Foundation studied eight major corporations that had undergone leveraged buyout, buyback, or other nonmerger restructuring. It

20. See particularly Peter Canellos, "Corporate Tax Integration: By Design or Default?" in *Corporate Tax Reform: A Report of the Invitational Conference on Subchapter C,* American Bar Association Section on Taxation (Washington, D.C., 1988).
21. Ibid., p. 157.

demonstrated that research and development expenditure had declined for these an average of 12.8 percent. While the KKR report acknowledges that the new entity paid no taxes after restructuring, it asserts that capital gains tax paid by shareholders and interest income tax by debt holders would more than compensate for the loss in corporate tax revenue. This would depend, however, on the tax status of those holding the debt and owning the corporation. Pension funds and tax-exempt institutions would not pay such taxes.

KKR highlights the presumed effect of takeovers on efficiency, as they would be reflected in operating income and sales. In two other studies, however, investigators found that the sales by the target of the leveraged buyout did not grow as fast as sales in its industry. Even if short-term profits increase, one cannot be sure that they will continue in face of the heavy overload of debt and the need for further asset sales. The KKR study also biased its favorable conclusions by including any improvement in the record as a result of subsequent acquisitions, while neglecting the performance of divested units.[22] Other studies suggest somewhat more unfavorable results.

Overall, the possibility of hostile corporate takeovers enforces short-term thinking on beleaguered management. If profits go down, even for a quarter, the stock price may be affected. If it falls, "raiders" or other corporations may calculate that the value of the underlying assets of the firm is larger than the stock price suggests: they may bid for the company, promising its stockholders vast new profits if the transaction is approved. To fend off the prospective buyer, the company's management will promise higher returns to stockholders and a higher stock price, achieved by borrowing and ruthless cost cutting. Thus the bid, successful or not, leaves the company with much higher debt and a lower cash flow. Less can be spent on new investment and on research and development. To please the stockholders, the company may have become less competitive.

There is also a conflict between stockholders and bondholders.

22. See W. F. Long and D. J. Ravenscraft, "The Record of LBO Performance," paper prepared for the Conference on Corporate Governance, Restructuring and the Market for Corporate Control, Salomon Brothers Center for the Study of Financial Institutions, May 23–24, 1989, p. 7.

Undertaking new debt after restructuring, corporations have to honor new claims on their assets, which in turn devalue the bonds previously issued. These lose quality, and frequently go down in price. Bondholders now lobby to prevent takeovers. If the corporation misses an interest payment they are ready to force it into bankruptcy.

And that may well occur. A recent study by the Brookings Institution concluded that companies are now so leveraged with debt that a recession like that of 1973–74 could put one in ten American companies into bankruptcy. The *New York Times* comments: "Obviously, the most highly leveraged companies will suffer the most. Because of their huge interest payments, they have little room for error in good times—and even less in bad times."[23] Revco is a leading example of a company that did not survive restructuring. It had a debt-to-equity ratio of 512 percent. But one Wall Street firm concluded that the majority of companies that financed their takeovers or buyouts with junk bonds had an even higher ratio. A recession would certainly plunge many of them into receivership.

There is no doubt some advantage to be derived from corporate restructuring in response to takeovers. The companies emerge with a leaner and more efficient management; the corpocracy is trimmed. The prospect of buyouts powerfully concentrates the corporate mind. But it also sops up the resources that the company needs to be an effective long-term competitor. And it makes corporate management even more sensitive to tiny movements in the stock price. It thereby lessens the management's time horizon and compounds the short-term mentality. One management consultant commented: "It has been a wrenching experience for managements. The pressures in the financial marketplace are such now that your incentive as a top manager for operating long term is taken away. If a guy is investing too much in long term activity, he's going to get taken by a raider."[24]

The experience of a leading tire company illustrates these pressures. In 1986 Goodyear was on a roll. It had begun to diversify out of the tire business and had acquired properties in aerospace, motor wheels, and oil pipelines. It had started an ambitious new

23. *New York Times*, August 7, 1988, p. 5.
24. William Dunk, quoted in the *Christian Science Monitor*, August 17, 1987.

project to automate the production of tires. Seeing the tire business plateau, management came to believe that future growth depended upon diversification and was trying to reduce Goodyear's tire operations to 50 percent of its business. Enter Sir James Goldsmith, the British takeover artist, who purchased 11.5 percent of Goodyear stock at the beginning of September 1986. The stock was then selling at 31⅞. When Goldsmith announced his stake in early November, the stock rose to 48⅝. Then Goldsmith capped this performance by offering to buy the entire company for $49 a share.

Management in the person of Robert Mercer, however, would not yield leadership of the firm. He quickly adopted a restructuring plan that would give Goodyear more clout with stockholders. Through loans, asset sales, stringent cost cutting, layoffs, and retirements he raised a $4 billion war chest to fight off the takeover. Most of this was spent on buying Goodyear's stock, in the hope of raising its value above $50. He also got the Ohio legislature into the act with new legislation designed to make Goldsmith's plum unpalatable. Even though Mercer failed, and Goodyear's stock slid back to 41, Sir James agreed to settle for $49.50 a share for his 11.5 percent stake: he pocketed $618 million, nearly a $90 million profit for about eight weeks of work. In the aftermath Goodyear had to cut back on capital spending from $1.3 billion to $500 million. Research and development expenditures were also affected. A Goodyear spokesman explained: "What we were originally trying to do and what Mr. Goldsmith did not like was our program of diversification. Now we have temporarily deemphasized the long range type of R & D and concentrated on things that have a more immediate payout."[25]

Goodyear emerged from this episode with a stronger balance sheet, though without its diversified assets. It was able in 1988 to raise R&D spending. Still, its debt had nearly trebled, and it has fewer assets to carry it. Having to maintain high revenues to service its debt, Goodyear could be vulnerable in a prolonged economic slump. Mercer commented in late 1987: "I don't see the Goodyear of today as a plus. What's the plus? What's the upside? People say we're now concentrating on our core business, but we've always

25. *Christian Science Monitor,* August 17, 1987.

concentrated on it. How else do you get to be No. 1 and increase market share? People have said our restructuring is just doing what Goldsmith would have done. But that's not the case. We cut off an arm and a leg. He would have cut off both arms and both legs."[26]

The prospect of hostile takeovers is, of course, not the only reason for the short-term mentality in American business. The cost of capital is much higher in America than in Japan. Savings rates are low in America and still high in Japan; hence, Japan is awash with capital and has a low interest rate, America a relatively high interest rate. If American firms have to pay back their loans at over 10 percent, they must make 15–20 percent profit for the investment to be worthwhile. With lower interest charges, Japanese companies can earn a profit with a return on investment of 10 percent or less.

But the problem is not only the U.S. money market and deficient savings. While American corporate managers tend to value return on investment more highly than market share, their Japanese colleagues reverse the priorities. Asked to rank their objectives on a scale of ten, U.S. company executives listed return on investment at 8.1 and market share as only 2.4. For their Japanese counterparts, market share was first (4.8), followed by return on investment (4.1) and the development of new products (3.5) For American managers, the development of new products was ranked only 0.7.[27]

Financial returns may be more important in America because of the way corporations are financed. Typically, and at least until the recent buyout craze, U.S. corporations finance themselves through issuing stock. And in any event a much higher proportion of corporate financing is equity than debt. In Japan, with fewer stockholders, management must respond not to stockholder interests or to the share price (or to the need to pay dividends) but to the bank that is providing the loan capital. Banks in Japan, as in Germany, are investment institutions that hold dominant positions in many industries. In Japan Sumitomo Bank will hardly pull the plug on NEC, a member of its group. American banks, on the other hand, tend to lend short-term at relatively high rates, not wishing to be stuck supporting a particular industry for a lengthy period. Again

26. Quoted in the *Akron Beacon Journal,* November 29, 1987, p. A6.
27. Abegglan and Stalk, op. cit., p. 177.

the short-term mentality is reinforced. In Japan even where major companies are not associated with a corporate group, they still manage to find long-term support from banks.

Another problem is the discounted cash-flow criterion as it is applied to new investments by American companies. Many such analyses demand too high rates of return, and investments are postponed as a result. Financial analyst Stewart Myers notes that such analyses frequently underestimate the "option value" of the investment—that is, the future opportunities that will become available if the investment is made; instead companies focus too much on the alternative rewards that can be derived from the money market.

In fact, this method "is less helpful in valuing businesses with substantial growth opportunities or intangible assets. [It] is no help at all for pure research and development. The value of R&D is almost all option value."[28] As Michael Dertouzos and his colleagues on the MIT Commission on Industrial Productivity comment: "When a company invests in a novel technology, the early cash flows are inevitably uncertain, precisely because the potential of the technology is not yet known. The later cash flows are even more uncertain, since everything about the distant future is chancy."[29] Hence conservative management does not take the risk.

But restraint fails to take account of the point made by Hayes, Clark, and Wheelwright, that one's competitors will frequently make those investments, leaving one behind in a new technology sector.[30] Thus investment is not merely a matter of reaping more or less certain future returns; it seeks to prevent an opponent from doing so and gaining the edge in a new branch of industry.

In sum, the present short-term cast of management decisions is not decreed either by the American tradition or by the external environment in which business is situated. Certainly stockholders need to be appeased, but this does not mean that companies cannot aim for the long term, as IBM, Boeing, and Merck have done, and

28. Quoted in Michael Dertouzos, Richard K. Lester, Robert Solow, and the MIT Commission on Industrial Productivity, *Made in America: Regaining the Productive Edge* (Cambridge, Mass.: MIT Press, 1989), p. 65.

29. Ibid., p. 65.

30. Robert Hayes, Steven Wheelwright, and Kim B. Clark, *Dynamic Manufacturing* (New York: Free Press, 1988).

with considerable success. What is necessary is a climate of greater investor understanding of the nature of contemporary worldwide competition, and a greater willingness to wait for results. They do so with start-up companies in biotechnology and other cutting-edge fields; they should learn to do so with established U.S. companies that are trying to regain their feet.

To facilitate a long-term perspective, capital needs to be provided on more favorable terms. Macroeconomically, this certainly means reducing government spending, which is now a primary stimulus to high interest rates. But it also means government initiative to make capital available on freer terms, perhaps the establishment of a new Reconstruction Finance Corporation. Under the leadership of Jesse Jones the RFC invested $10 billion of much-needed capital in America's failing industry during the Great Depression. The creation of a new and well-funded National Technology Foundation to funnel the findings of pure science into new civilian products would also be a great help. The reorganization of our tax code to reduce or eliminate the tax on long-term capital gains and to establish an integrated system for treating debt and equity would also be of prime importance.

But beyond this, business schools need to teach a different form of maximization to their corporate students. Market share has to be given priority along with profit as a criterion for long-term survival. In fact, corporate survival itself has to become an objective beyond that of return to the shareholders and the value of the stock. Businesses also have to recognize that corporate and white-collar bloat impede their efficiency and responsiveness. Too many layers between the top leadership and the consumer only delay and hamper effective service to him. Properly used, the computer can speed this necessary transformation. Taken together, all these changes would begin to obviate the short-term mentality.

EDUCATION, THE WORKING POPULATION, AND IMMIGRATION

The single most salient generalization that one can make about past American decline is that the United States has failed to invest enough in its most important asset: human capital. Taken as a whole, the U.S. primary and secondary educational system turns out students who, compared to those of other countries, are ignorant of many areas of science and of life. It is already well understood that American grade and high school students know less mathematics and science than their counterparts in other industrial countries. Often they know little about their own country, and even less about the outside world. Few understand or can speak foreign languages; they have little familiarity with world history and geography. Compared to students in foreign nations, they have traveled less to other countries and lived less abroad. They have an inadequate knowledge of the economics of world trade, a discipline that will greatly affect their future.

U.S. workers are undereducated. Here the stress must be on education, not training, the latter being a skill that they can develop and refine on the job. A comparison with Japanese education is instructive here. In Japan an equal education is open to all, though the most prestigious universities are difficult to enter. Nonetheless, many workers have the equivalent of two years of college. Their scientific education allows them to adapt to a wide range of tasks once they join the work force. Japanese companies provide on-the-job training as well as access to technical education. An American anthropologist evaluates the differences in the following terms:

> One in ten young Japanese, but one in four Americans, does not finish high school. Equal proportions of students now go on to higher education, but a considerably higher proportion of males is taking a bachelor's degree in Japan than in the United States. More important, the skills and achievements of the average Japanese student are far greater for all levels up through 12th grade. The Japanese go to school one-third more time than do Americans every year; over 12 years, they have had four more years of school. They can accommodate a more accelerated curriculum. They don't lose during summer vacations half of what they have learned the previous year. Elementary education takes them farther in the basics, as well as in art and music, compared with our schools. In high school all students have more required courses in math, sciences, foreign languages, and social studies. The result, I estimate, is that the average Japanese high school graduate has the equivalent basic knowledge of the average American college graduate. The Japanese clearly can-

not speak English well but their knowledge of written English is certainly better than the average foreign language ability of our college graduates. It is not surprising that the Japanese do well in international tests of math and science, or that they now produce twice the number of engineers per capita as we do, or that Japanese literacy as measured by per capita newspaper circulation is higher. If we were to recalculate the costs of education up to 12th grade, comparing them with the results, there is no doubt that the Japanese system would come out at least several times more efficient than our own.

The great accomplishment of Japanese primary and secondary education lies not in its creation of a brilliant elite (Western nations do better with their top students), but in its generation of such a high average level of capability. The profoundly impressive fact is that it is shaping a whole population, workers as well as managers, to a standard inconceivable in the United States, where we are still trying to implement high school graduation competence tests that measure only minimal reading and computing skills.[31]

The answer for the United States lies in better education for all American children, in bringing them up to a higher standard through high school, not more advanced training for the best students, which we already largely provide. Education must be seen as a task for the entire society, and it must address the needs of minority groups and seek to end the inequalities that presently limit their opportunities for employment. Whatever variety of educational reforms and programs are adopted, universities, businesses, and government must become more involved in helping school systems teach to a higher standard and in facilitating the entry of students into the labor force. Crucially, the teaching profession must be given status and importance, and the careers of elementary and secondary teaching must be made more rewarding. Finally, if America is able to improve education in these ways, this needed educational reform will speed the assimilation of present immigrant groups and enhance the very real case that exists to be made for further immigration as a significant step toward a more vital America.

31. Thomas P. Rohlen, *Japan's High Schools* (Berkeley, Calif.: University of California Press, 1983), pp. 321–22.

Inequality remains a major barrier for racial and ethnic minorities. According to Paul Ong and his associates, the Los Angeles metropolitan area, one of the most powerful new and growing regional economies of the nation, is suffering not from lack of economic growth, but from the fruits of inequality.[32] While Los Angeles maintains a higher per capita growth rate than the nation as a whole, it also has a higher poverty rate. Residential segregation is increasing. The national gap in income between the highest 20 percent and the lowest 20 percent of the population is growing (see Table 11). Los Angeles has shown a slight improvement in this ratio since 1979, but its rate of inequality is greater than for the nation as a whole. Also, whereas in 1969 there were fewer Angelenos than members of the national population below the poverty line, in the past two decades Los Angeles has moved two percentage points higher than the national rate.

Furthermore, Los Angeles does not yet confirm the oft-asserted claim that immigrants gradually come to exceed the performance of the native-born population after ten to fifteen years.[33] The Latino population of Los Angeles (including both native-born Chicanos and recent immigrants from Latin America) does not appear to be improving its position. Their black counterparts have

Table 11

Trends in Income Equality

	Los Angeles			United States		
	1969	1979	1987	1969	1979	1987
Income ratio (poorest fifth to richest fifth)	11.8%	9.7%	9.8%	13.8%	12.5%	10.5%
Poverty rate (% below poverty)	11.0%	13.4%	15.6%	12.1%	11.7%	13.5%

Source: Paul Ong et al., *The Widening Divide: Income Inequality and Poverty in Los Angeles* (UCLA Graduate School of Architecture and Urban Planning, June 1989), p. 15.

32. Paul Ong et al., *The Widening Divide: Income Inequality and Poverty in Los Angeles* (Los Angeles: UCLA Graduate School of Architecture and Urban Planning, June 1989).

33. See Barry R. Chiswick, "The Economic Progress of Immigrants: Some Apparently Universal Patterns" in Barry R. Chiswick, ed., *The Gateway: U.S. Immigration Issues and Policies* (Washington, D.C.: American Institute for Public Policy Research, 1982), pp. 119–58.

increasingly been divided into two groups, with one group drop-
ping out of the labor force and suffering extremes of poverty, and
the other improving its position not only in respect to the Latin
community, but also as compared to its previous position in relation to whites. According to Holly Van Houten, black members of
the Los Angeles work force improved their position compared to
whites between 1979 and the present. Over the same period, however, the Chicano and Latino position deteriorated relative to white
workers.[34]

Education does not yet compensate for this inequality. While a
black college graduate improved his earnings as compared to white
graduates, Latino and Chicano degree holders actually lost ground
compared to whites in recent years. The improvement in the performance of black workers may be due in part to the large number
of blacks who dropped out of the labor force. Yet there is evidence
of the beginnings of the development of a black middle class in Los
Angeles. In contrast, the Latin community fared worse in part
because it included a group of new immigrants as well as an established Chicano group. The new arrivals are both younger and less
educated than corresponding Chicanos or blacks. Perhaps we must
wait for the immigrants to adjust to their new surroundings before
any improvement is possible.

But the prospect of economic and educational advance for both
ethnic groups is clouded by the fact that the black and Latin areas
of Los Angeles unquestionably have the worst schools. Cultural
differences between teachers and students are partly responsible
for this situation, but it is also due to understaffing and overcrowd-
ing, which have led to year-round operation of many schools in
south and central Los Angeles. Students attend in different shifts
during the year, and some, starting later, go to school through the
summer. As a result youngsters in the primary grades are often
deprived of a continuous relationship with one teacher over their
nine months as other students come in to displace them in phased
succession. Busing has not helped to solve the problem because the
Anglo community simply moves out, leaving the schools and districts as segregated or more segregated than before. Furthermore,
Los Angeles schools track their students in classes of different

34. Holly Van Houten in Paul Ong et al., op. cit., pp. 89–90.

abilities, and the low level of stimulation offered to the less favored student groups undoubtedly increases the dropout rate. There are sometimes few economic incentives to complete a high school diploma, especially when graduating students may actually perform only at a ninth-grade level and cannot obtain demanding or technical jobs.

A possible remedy for the problems of motivation might lie in a system like the Japanese, in which all students take required courses in mathematics and science to age fifteen, with the better students assisting the less advanced. The virtue of this method would lie in its instilling a sense of corporate as well as individual achievement. This is not to say that Los Angeles or the United States should emulate the Japanese school system in its entirety, for Japanese emphasis on rote memorization and unquestioning obedience inhibits the development of critical thinking and intellectual curiosity. Indeed, Japanese students who have been taught abroad in a more open school environment have to be reeducated and their individuality stifled when they return to Japan. But at least it can be said that American concern for student rights and privileges needs to be balanced by greater support for collective attainment of the class and for the teacher's role.

To rectify the prevailing inequality of racial, ethnic, and immigrant groups in the United States requires an educational system that assists the majority of students, not only the favored few. Giving all the chance to receive a quality education means more required courses. It suggests fewer tracks of students of comparable ability and instead more heterogeneous classes. Most important, it requires more highly skilled teachers and a lower student–teacher ratio. This means America must put education near the top of the national agenda and recruit teachers accordingly, with rewards that enable our best college students to consider teaching careers equally with business and law.

Education should also begin at an earlier stage. Though they are expensive, Headstart programs have been shown to benefit those who participate. Child care, which the Administration and Congress are beginning to take more seriously, should have an educational function, rather than simply serving as nursery or babysitter.

As usual in the United States, it is difficult to suggest a single proper course of reform. The key point is that the American educational system is in such a morass that it can usefully test and accommodate a variety of possible avenues. Different states and school systems may try different methods to achieve a renaissance in state primary and secondary systems, as South Carolina has recently done, for example, with dramatic new progress in test scores, teacher salaries, and parent involvement.

Another avenue of reform lies in national comparison of state educational systems through standardized tests, as former Secretary of Education William Bennett advocates. This method would lead to greater state regimentation and control of the teaching process and would lessen the teacher's role. Such a system can work, however, as the national educational systems of France and Japan prove. Still another approach would allow parents to send their child to any district school they chose. Some would extend this, through the use of vouchers, to private schools as well.

At the opposite end of this spectrum of national control would be schools in which teachers and principals formulated the curriculum, and teachers took considerable initiative in its execution. Greater teacher autonomy and professionalism might pay greater dividends than too much standardization and a lower degree of responsibility. In this realm as in many others, the findings of the Hawthorne experiment may conceivably apply. At the General Electric plant in Schenectady in the 1930s, efficiency experts studied ways in which worker productivity might be increased. They raised the lighting, lowered the lighting, piped in music, and altered the work environment in different ways. They found, surprisingly, that whatever the innovation, output always increased. Psychologists concluded that it was not a particular remedy which helped workers, but rather that others were taking an interest in their tasks and performance, giving them a new status and importance.

Applied to the U.S. educational system, the Hawthorne experiment suggests that lending a much greater national importance to the performance of schools, working with state educational leaders, principals, and teachers, trying different methods of reform—all these initiatives can improve results. No particular solution must be applied nationwide. Some will work better in particular contexts. In inner-city schools, setting higher standards for achievement and graduation may help improve scores on standardized tests. More important than the method, however, is making sure that an education really pays in the labor force after graduation. Thus we would seek to avoid such ironies as the incident in which a Boston insurance company, unimpressed with local high school graduates, who achieved minimal fluency in written English and arithmetic, sent its records to be processed in Ireland, where educational standards were higher and graduates more eager to work.

Government and business need to have a more direct involvement in the processes of education. The Federal Government needs to establish retraining programs for laid-off workers like those in Sweden, to upgrade their technological competence. Businesses should aid local school systems to ensure that their graduates meet professional standards. Companies must establish programs, as the Ford Motor Company has done, to upgrade the training and education of their workers. At Ford every hourly worker receives a $2,000 tuition voucher to study at nearby colleges. Ford plants have learning centers in which workers can improve their skills and even earn a college degree.

Beyond this, schools need an infusion of new talent, from universities, businesses, and government. It is perhaps a paradox of modern American society that we have too many trained white-collar workers in business and government and yet too few teachers to staff our schools. It is not idle today to remember that instruction improved in schools when many young American men, faced with the Vietnam draft, adopted alternative service as teachers in our schools. It is also significant that the Peace Corps continues to attract many U.S. college graduates to teach other nations, but does not funnel our best students into education of our own youth. If, besides the much-needed strengthening of the teaching profession, a program could be adopted that installed business and government servants for two-year tours in the school system, together with recent college graduates, the public school could once again become a place of industry, initiative, and hope.

Universities need to establish and deepen their connections with high schools. Middlebury College sent several of its staff to teach courses at DeWitt Clinton High School, a primarily black school in New York. Clinton's principal observed afterward that the Middlebury faculty let students "see that college professors can be interesting to listen to, and that there's another world of learning out there that they ought to investigate."[35] That successful Americans in many areas would devote such time to education could underscore its importance to otherwise disillusioned students and also help to give them a greater understanding of possible careers when they graduate. For full-time teacher-visitors, this would of course mean that normal requirements for certification would be suspended during the experiment. Neglected for years, the American primary and secondary educational system badly needs an infusion of individuals combining new talent, perspective, experience, and success.

In the final analysis, however, Americans must accord the teaching profession the priority it needs and deserves to accomplish the immense educational task that faces America. If our best graduates are to be attracted to the teaching profession, the rewards for teachers must be much higher than they are now. Teachers need to be paid more, so that many of them will not have to hold second jobs to make ends meet, and can therefore concentrate on their primary profession. Whatever minimal requirements states maintain, individual teachers should be given the initiative to teach at levels well above the levels set by state regents examinations. Given the tax base in some states and school districts, this inevitably means more federal aid. With federal aid to education now languishing at only one-tenth of the current budget of the Department of Defense, it is clear that a substantial change in priorities must occur if the United States is to meet its educational needs and avert continuing decline.

Presuming that education for all (and not just élite education) can be improved, many believe that further immigration is a recipe for a more vital and energetic America. In many respects, immigrants are more pro-American than other citizens. They have made enormous emotional and financial sacrifices to start their new life in the United States. They provide a new element in the labor force and act, as they have done in Los Angeles, to reverse the deindustrialization of America. They take jobs that the native-born neglect or disdain, and work extremely hard. The progress that Cubans and Haitians have made in Florida and Vietnamese and Chinese have

35. Quoted in the *New York Times,* February 8, 1989, p. B9.

made in California are ample testimony to this fact. Yet there is no evidence that they have taken jobs from the local labor force; the number of jobs has simply increased, as it did during the influx of foreign migrants in the nineteenth century. The new foreign workers provide an important justification, aside from the exchange rate of the dollar, for business to return investment to American shores. And many businesses have found that low foreign wages provide no automatic guarantees of profit in investment abroad. Language problems, retraining, and health issues are chronic in some "export platforms" overseas. Foreign governments do not always cooperate, and administrative inefficiencies abound. Partly as a result, in recent years the textile and apparel industry has been given a new lease on life in the United States. High-tech industry is more firmly established than it would have been in the absence of immigration.

This does not mean that immigration is a social panacea. Many, including former Governor Richard Lamm of Colorado, have asked: "Who needs additional people when we cannot employ our own citizens?"[36] In the recession year of 1982 when Lamm made that statement, the idea of a fixed and unexpanding economic pie was quite appropriate. Since then, however, immigration, always presuming that it is linked to greater educational opportunity, has not posed a threat, and the overall size of the pie has increased.

The role of immigrants was central to the process of economic development in early modern Europe. The Spanish Inquisition spread a diaspora of Sephardic Jews throughout Europe; it also forced a migration of Protestants to France and the low countries. With new French restrictions, Protestants were forced to flee again, this time to Holland and England. Even though members of nonconforming Protestant sects were not admitted to the establishment in England, they quickly found work in industrial and manufacturing trades. Elie Halevy's magisterial history of England ultimately attributes the successes of philosophical radicalism and middle-class economic and industrial growth to the burgeoning role of nonconforming and Calvinist Protestants.

Migrants or not, it is not accidental that some of England's leading industrial families were dissenters. Watt, Wedgwood, and Wil-

36. Quoted in Fallows, op. cit., p. 202.

kinson were nonconformists, and Cadbury, the candymaker, was a Quaker. It is estimated that only 7 percent of Englishmen were Protestant nonmembers of the Church of England, yet about 50 percent of the new entrepreneurs were of that religious persuasion. Denied the social status of communicants of conforming religions, they had to find careers in the sometimes denigrated trading occupations. In the United States the odyssey of the Kennedy family shows how long it took before Irish Catholics could move from economic activities to public office on a national scale. This is not to say that impoverished Latino immigrants will soon perform economic and technical skills akin to those of their European Protestant predecessors. Their initial contribution will be in low-wage industries. Given education, however, they will rise as all other immigrant groups have done.

Today immigrant newcomers to America are not likely to be prime candidates for high political and social office. Latinos, Haitians, Vietnamese, and Chinese must, at least for the short term, locate their major occupations in new industries and the developing American economy. Social assimilation will not proceed rapidly enough to give them another alternative. Such new groups give advantages to their new homeland. They work hard, add a stimulus to growth through consumption, and frequently staff industries that might otherwise migrate elsewhere. In Los Angeles, deindustrialization has been partly reversed by the flow of immigration. Under such conditions, investment at home is just as profitable as investment abroad, and it depends less upon a further large depreciation of the dollar.

In the past the stimulative impact of immigration went from the ascendant Great Power to its challengers and followers. The leader's surplus population was sometimes shipped overseas, as in the British case during the nineteenth century. In any event the direction of the historic flow has now been reversed. Instead of migrating from leader to follower, population now returns to the previous leader. Japan takes no immigration and derives little benefit from industrious and intelligent aliens. These now proceed to the United States. Assisted by an improving educational system, the inflow of new migrants offers a bracing stimulus to the native-born and to the national economy.

CONCLUSION

From the need to lessen the bureaucratization of American life and replace the short-term mentality to the crucial reform of education, there is an ample agenda of improvement. The United States cannot reclaim past greatness without larger savings and investment: investment must be derived from a reduction in the trade deficit and an associated cut in government spending, thus increasing the total savings pool of the country. Business must invest more of this pool to increase its productivity to former levels. This means cutting the bureaucracy which has made all our modern institutions—business, the military, government, and education—less productive and responsive. It requires higher government investment (in the sense of creating long-lasting assets) in the people of this country, principally through improving their educational system.

Japan has no natural advantage over the United States. She has no natural resources, having just abandoned her coal industry. She meets her needs—for oil, bauxite, iron ore, and other minerals—by imports. She does not provide all of her own food supply. Her population and territory (about the size of California) are not large. Her only asset is her trained and dedicated population and labor force.

If American business had the same advantage, it would quickly reverse its lag in productivity growth and begin to compete effectively. American business practices have in the recent past (though not in the nineteenth century) emphasized short-term returns. This is in part because of weaknesses in the American tax and investment system, but also because the United States has faced few challenges that forced citizens to rethink typical business-as-usual strategies.

5

Japan and U.S. Resurgence

Japan is an exceptional nation. Few countries have achieved such a high degree of unity in opposition to foreigners. But that sense of unity masks powerful competition among domestic groups, a competition that has in fact been a dominant characteristic of most of Japanese history, with rivalry between shogun (the administrative and military leader) and imperial factions and conflicts among the daimyo (the vassals of the shogun). In fact, while Japan's proximity to the Asian mainland made it fear invasion, its insularity sanctioned domestic strife. When there were no foreign pressures, as for example in the sixteenth century, the country could indulge in civil war. As a result, believes Chie Nakane, the great Japanese anthropologist, Japan is a "frame society" in which the conflict of groups can be held together only by the strong hand of the state.[1] But the state is not the only organ of consensus or compromise. The Japanese tradition emphasizes *wa* (harmony or consensus) as an integrating principle of the social order. According to it, contending groups should moderate their differences, particularly as these are mediated and refereed by the state. This process of

1. She writes: "Competing clusters, in view of the difficulty of reaching agreement or consensus between clusters, have a diminished authority in dealing with the state administration. Competition and hostile relations between the civil powers facilitate the acceptance of state power, and, if that group is organized vertically, once the state's administrative authority is accepted, it can be transmitted without obstruction down the vertical line of a group's organization. In this way the administrative web is woven more thoroughly into Japanese society than perhaps any other in the world." Nakane, *Japanese Society* (Berkeley: University of California Press, 1970), p. 102.

smoothing disagreements, however, does not produce a final unity of society. As Daniel Okimoto points out, the unity of the social order is not buttressed by agreement on universal moral or philosophic principles.[2] The country's mores are Japan-specific, and not for export. Effectively they are rules about how Japanese should behave toward each other, but not toward the citizens of other nations. The distinction between Japanese and *gaijin* (foreigners) remains absolutely fundamental.

It is not surprising that this should be true. Japan grew up as an isolated society, fearful of intrusions from countries near and far. In response to Western pressures for an opening of communications and trade, the shogun initially prescribed exclusion, and that response lasted until Commodore Perry's black ships forced Japan to open up in 1853. In contrast, Western philosophy emerged from an ecumenical environment of Greco-European culture, in which competing city-states were not isolated from one another. They were all thought to be on the same level, morally and politically speaking, and shared a general civilization. The later Roman Empire broadened existing notions of ethnic tolerance and included citizens who might live as far away as Gaul or Britain and still be regarded as Roman. The successor European kings emerged from this overarching framework, in which no nationality or territory enjoyed moral priority over another.

The Japanese centered-ethic was thus very different from European social attitudes, and this has not made it easier for Japan to admit foreigners on an equal basis. For Japanese, it is easier to apply the designation "superior" or "inferior" than to fashion a reciprocal and balanced relationship. This "vertical" character of Japanese society, largely unchanged since the Meiji Restoration in 1868, also affects Japan's attitude toward international affairs. The relationship with Asian countries and with the United States is reflective of this way of viewing the world. From a Japanese standpoint, it is possible to see Japan "above" Asia and still "below" the United States in terms of international influence and power. But the decline of the United States raises confusion among those ha-

2. See D. Okimoto, "Political Inclusivity: The Domestic Structure of Trade," in Takashi Inoguchi and Daniel I. Okimoto, eds., *The Political Economy of Japan, Vol. 2: The Changing International Context* (Stanford, Calif.: Stanford University Press, 1988), p. 312.

bituated to seeing others as either higher or lower than themselves. At one time Japan could view the United States in familial terms as a father or older and stronger brother. Now America remains formally ahead, but it is increasingly regarded as a country declining to Third World status, suffused with violence, drugs, and corruption. To many Japanese, the United States has become a cranky and undisciplined elder with a pronounced drinking problem, who has to be sobered up after repeated binges. Speaking to Americans, the Russians once said: "We will bury you." The Japanese are tempted to say, "We will be your nurse" or (in zoological metaphor) "your keeper."

The notion of superior and inferior,[3] however, can only apply if a country's functions are seen as homogeneous. Many Japanese do not view things this way. For Japan, the United States remains superior militarily but not economically. And some Japanese ask whether Japan should embark on a quest for equality or primacy in both military and economic realms.[4] The debate has been vexed. Like Masataka Kosaka, the distinguished professor at the University of Kyoto, many scholars since World War II thought of their country as a mercantile or trading state, free from military obligations. Japan would leave the latter to the United States, or it would stake its future on a perceived tendency toward a peaceful world order. But others recognized that Japan would have to play her part in carrying the military burden. Prime Minister Nakasone as early as 1983 recommended that Japan build up a military capability large enough to keep the Soviet Union's submarines and naval vessels bottled up in the Sea of Japan in time of war. This, however, would have required a major military buildup and a defense budget much higher than the present one percent of gross national product that Japan spends on arms. For this reason, Nakasone's remarks evoked considerable criticism among Japanese.

3. One well-reputed economist recently asked: "Is it not possible that Japan might be quite different from other countries? Is it not possible that Japan might be quite superior to other countries?" Tsuneo Iida, quoted in Kenneth Pyle, "Japan, the World, and the Twenty-first Century," in ibid., p. 475.

4. One of the new nationalists, Ikutaro Shimizu, wrote recently: "If Japan acquired military power commensurate with its economic power, countries that fully appreciate the meaning of military power would not overlook this. They would defer, they would act with caution; and in time they would show respect." Quoted in ibid., p. 478.

Whether Japan must fulfill military as well as economic international functions can be questioned from another point of view.
Yonosuke Nagai, a distinguished political scientist, has contended
that the nuclear balance between the United States and the Soviet
Union has in fact led to a moratorium on the use of power in world
politics. In the circumstances, military power counts for less and
economic strength for more than it used to. The two need not be
welded together in the policy of a single nation.[5] In fact even in
Japan's history, the functions of samurai and merchant were also
separated, one earning political prestige and influence and the
other economic power. From this point of view, the Tokugawa
Shogunate was created to prevent a homogenization and centrali-
zation of all social functions. So, according to Nagai, it should be
in world politics: some countries will perform different roles than
others, and an interdependent equilibrium among them is possible,
without Japan's assuming new military responsibilities.

Nagai, along with many others, believes that Japan should be
guided only by her own national interests, maneuvering between
blocs and avoiding moral judgments about them. In contrast, his
leading critic, Hisakiko Okazaki, dismisses the notion of Japan as
a neutral state and contends that Tokyo shares not only the strategic position of Western nations but also their moral principles.
Japan should not be neutral in spirit, but committed to individual
and democratic values.

JAPAN AS FREE RIDER

The issue of whether a country should perform all international
functions or only some of them is central to the further evolution
of the role of Japan in the world system and to its relationship with
the United States. As many Japanese know, there are advantages to
adopting a "free rider" stance in respect to a hegemonic power.
The world power provides the essential goods to keep the system
functioning: defense, an open market, and access to capital. It
safeguards the stability of the system so that others can trade their

5. See also Richard Rosecrance, *The Rise of the Trading State: Commerce and Conquest
in the Modern World* (New York: Basic Books, 1986).

goods in peace and tranquillity. The free rider can then save greatly on military expenditures and concentrate on domestic economic growth, sustained by foreign trade. The hegemon will open not only its own market but also those of other countries to the free rider's goods.

As long as the hegemonic power is strong, the smaller trading nation has to think little about diplomacy and less about military preparations. As the hegemon weakens, however, the formerly dependent nation is forced to reconsider its role in the international system. Should it prop up the hegemon to keep him going? Should it shove him aside and itself assume the hegemonic mantle and also the burdens? Should it do neither and rely on others to take up the slack, while continuing its free rider policy? The answers to these questions will determine Japan's role in the longer term and also its relationship to the United States. It will also chart Japan's role in America's renewal. The choice of a long-term Japanese strategy will be influenced by the policy America adopts as well.

Many observers in Japan and elsewhere have tended to see Japan as the primary beneficiary of the international system led by the United States. Despite its growing defense expenditure, Japan has in effect relied on the Pacific power of the United States, represented by American spending of approximately $100 billion per year in that theater alone. Owing to America's influence, markets were opened for Japanese products in the United States and Europe and other countries. Japan received bountiful helpings of U.S. aid in her early industrial revival after the war.

But perhaps more important than any concrete measure of U.S. assistance were the issues that Japan did not have to address, such as formulating a global strategy against the Soviet Union, taking a side in the Middle Eastern conflict, leading or at least abetting the struggle to open up South Africa to democratic and anti-apartheid forces, balancing between China and Russia as well as between India and Pakistan, fighting wars in Korea and Vietnam, maintaining the credibility of the nuclear deterrent, offering sanctuary for helpless refugees from conflicts in Asia, Africa, the Middle East, and Central America, protecting the fish and whale population of the globe, and assisting resistance movements in Communist countries.

It has not just been that Japan, as an ally of the United States, could benefit from the combined force of the Western coalition of nations to further its own purposes. Rather, Japan, more than any other associate of America, has also been able to enjoy the advantages of neutrality. Not having to take a stand between contending forces in different geographical contexts, Japan could work with both of them, usually to her pecuniary benefit. The free rider status thus not only gave access to the collective (or club) good that stemmed from membership on one side, it also left Japan free to negotiate economic arrangements with the other side. Many Japanese, despite the Security Treaty, still do not accept that Japan is an "ally" of the United States. The treaty is still seen as a unilateral pledge by the United States to defend Japan, not one that requires a Japanese commitment in return.

The ultimate result of Japanese free riding, of course, has been that Japan could devote its funds and energies to creating high-technology civilian products, to win markets in the United States and elsewhere. This has frequently been portrayed as a difficult and costly enterprise, and its success a measure of Japan's efficiency and technological superiority. In a narrow sense this is true, but one should remember that selling in the United States is easier and less hemmed in by government restrictions than selling in any other industrial country; certainly it is much easier than selling in Japan. Ultimately Japan came to dominate many American markets, in machine tools, semiconductors, VCRs, and consumer electronics. With the money gained from her export surplus, and given the depreciated dollar, Japan could buy up American assets at bargain-basement prices. Her own banks, flush with cash, could move into international finance in a big way, earning returns in America and abroad, while America devoted some of its monies to protecting Japan.

The situation that resulted was unprecedented. In the words of Clyde Prestowitz, the former U.S. Department of Commerce official and trade negotiator, "This is surely the first time in history that a territory in process of being colonized has actually paid for the right to defend the colonizer."[6] However extreme this formulation may appear, it depicts real aspects of the America–Japan relationship. If Japan strives to render the once proud United States

6. Clyde Prestowitz, *Trading Places* (New York: Basic Books, 1988), p. 311.

into an "economic colony," it can think in such terms because it has been able single-mindedly to concentrate upon one goal and has enjoyed freedom from many other international obligations and responsibilities. This freedom, however, is now coming to an end.

There is no doubt that Japanese industrialists are aware of American political sensitivities about their country's role, and they have not been heavy-handed. Of their investments in the United States they have invested most of their capital in the short-term money market and a lesser though still significant amount in U.S. productive facilities, land, and buildings. At a meeting of leading Japanese industrialists at Keidanren (the federation of business enterprises) in Tokyo in September 1986, Takushin Yamamoto, the president of Fujitsu, counseled, "the strong should walk on tiptoes" in their dealings with the United States.[7] And to date Japan has not engaged in a "hostile" takeover of any American company.

But the problem with continuing the free rider option is that Japanese policy is not allowed to evolve: it remains wedded to a concentration on exports, high savings, and low defense spending. Diplomatic responsibilities are frozen, with Japan pursuing a tentative policy of "niceness" to all countries. Such a policy does not cater to Japan's growing sense of self. Her station in the world deserves more recognition and responsibility. Nor does it respond to the growing criticism that Japan's past role has engendered in the United States, Europe, and East Asia. Japanese officials are aware that the tide of anti-Japanese sentiment is increasing and will rise so long as the trade issue remains unsolved. (In 1989 the trade deficit with the United States will not be much better than it was the year before, amounting to about $50 billion.) The failure to resolve trade disputes led directly to Congress's passing of the Omnibus Trade Act of 1988. Now, some of the most sensitive trade issues, as for instance the failure of Japan to import American rice, will be on the formal agenda, with Congress as the watchdog to see that the issue is dealt with. In other words, the trade imbalance can no longer be finessed by the power brokers in Washington and Tokyo.

Informed Japanese have sometimes thought that the issue could be deflected or avoided altogether. On the one hand, Japanese

7. Quoted in ibid., p. 309.

investments in the U.S. money market have propped up the American dollar, investment, and purchasing power. If Japanese pension funds or banks took their money out of the American market, there would be an immediate run on the dollar, and the Fed would have to jack up interest rates to retain supplies of capital. This might trigger a recession. America would not want this to happen, and thus, some Japanese have believed, the United States doesn't really have enough leverage to force a further opening of the Japanese market. This argument is accurate and might lead some U.S. policy makers to go lightly on Japan. But it neglects the fact that a recession in the United States could be worse for Japan than for America. It would drastically cut the U.S. demand for Japanese goods. Hence, few Americans think Japan would risk such a pullout of funds.

On the other hand, Japanese business has cultivated the U.S. Congress and state governors. Japanese investment in U.S. productive facilities is greatly sought after and competed for in state capitals. Many American law firms have Japanese companies as important clients. Support by Japan can be influential even in congressional races. Americans, some feel, should not risk offending such an important supporter of the national economy.

But if Japanese political influence in the United States were decisive, the Omnibus Trade Act would never have passed; President Reagan would not have signed it; Japan would not have been charged with a violation of the agreement on semiconductors. There would have been no dispute about the sale of a new version of the F-16 (FSX) to Japan. The atmosphere in Congress would still be hospitable to Japanese exports and business practices. In fact, however, the reverse is true. Japan is facing a mounting chorus of criticism in the United States, a criticism that cannot be defused by "business as usual" responses and a continuance of the free rider policy. Along with necessary economic adjustments that the United States must make, Japan also needs to act to reduce the trade friction.

Finally, Japan, as a great nation, must take a role in the international system more suited to its growing strength and power than the essentially negative free rider stance it has adopted in past years. This means more defense spending and greater assistance to the U.S. role in the Pacific and elsewhere. It is worth noting that

Japan offered little support when America was escorting reflagged tankers through the Persian Gulf. This was significant because America was policing a region from which it derives little oil, while Japan is vitally dependent on the flow of oil from the Persian Gulf. As Clyde Prestowitz points out, the amount Japan offered in assistance—$10 million—was "really only symbolic."[8] He continued: "It would be more generous for Japan to pay the whole cost and also to pick up the full tab for U.S. forces stationed in Japan."

But the primary reason for Japan to modify its past free rider role resides in Japanese interest, not U.S. pressure. Summarizing the views of the nationalist Ikutaro Shimizu, Kenneth Pyle writes: "Japan . . . is a 'peculiar' and 'abnormal' country. . . . It has lived for decades under a constitutional order forced on it by occupying military forces. It has abnegated the essential characteristics of a nation-state, military power and the required loyalty of its citizens. Other nations had lost a war, but where was there another that had wholly lost its national consciousness?"[9]

If these sentiments evoked an echo in the Japanese populace, there would be support for a more balanced and symmetrical Japanese policy, a policy not skewed entirely toward economic money making as the be-all and end-all of state activity. It was not lost on the Japanese public that President de Gaulle of France once dubbed a Japanese premier "a transistor salesman." Redressing the balance would mean enhancing Japan's diplomatic and military role in world politics. It would mean sharing some of the diplomatic and military burdens with the United States, and it would entail a considerable increase in Japanese arms. More than this, it would suggest the formulation and expression of clearly defined Japanese policies on Europe, the Soviet Union, China, and the Middle East. These presently do not exist. European nations have not hesitated to express views separate from the United States on these matters. Nor in time will Japan. Even powers, like West Germany, that have largely made their way in world politics through a trading and developmental strategy have not declined to differ with the United States on matters of arms control, deterrence, and relations with the Soviet Union.

8. Ibid., p. 327.
9. Quoted in Pyle, op. cit., pp. 478–79.

As soon, however, as separate Japanese policies are developed on a wide range of matters, there will need to be diplomatic and political resources available to buttress and support them. In providing them, Japan will emerge from the shadow of the United States. In particular, Japan might consider a role as a global problem solver, helping African countries with their economic and marketing problems, Latin Americans with their debts and exports, and Eastern Europeans with their debt, industrial production, and quality-control problems. Japanese defense aid might also be appropriate for some countries in the Middle East and South Asia, and even Southeast Asia. The Philippines desperately needs Japan's economic assistance. If these things are done, Japan's role as the world's paramount free rider will have finally come to an end, and her role as a system stabilizer will have begun. And, of course, Japan will have to pay for her more active participation in the system and will have less left over to devote to pure economic expansion. Japan's status and power demand increased international responsibilities, but costs will also attend her new role.

JAPAN AS HEGEMONIC POWER

Does that mean then that Japan should assume the mantle of hegemonic leadership for the world? Some think so. Yujiro Eguchi of the Nomura Research Institute believes that world leadership in the future will pass to Japan as it passed first to Rome, then to Britain, and finally to the United States.[10] But he then quickly qualifies this idea and contends, unrealistically, that Japan's leadership must be economic, not military, with defense spending limited to about one percent of Japanese GNP. When Japanese were asked recently about the role they believed Japan should play in the community of nations, they stressed that "Japan should contribute to the healthy development of the world economy" and "should cooperate in the economic development of developing countries." Only 7.8 percent believed that "Japan should consolidate its defence capability as a member of the Western camp."[11]

10. See *Japan Echo,* vol. 12, no. 1 (1985), pp. 9–14.
11. Quoted in Takashi Inoguchi, "Four Japanese Scenarios for the Future," *International Affairs,* vol. 65, no. 1 (winter 1988–89), pp. 16–17.

There are other strands in Japanese thinking which, without embracing the fully hegemonic alternative, suggest greater independence from the United States. A more independent and self-reliant Japan might seek a link with the Soviet Union. This would give Japan access to the raw materials that Japan coveted in her Northern Strategy, mooted before the outbreak of the Pacific War. Instead, as we know, in 1940–41 she chose the Southern Strategy and expanded to the south, while attacking Pearl Harbor. But if Russia could provide natural gas, metals, and oil, what could she buy in quantity from Japan? Her market could in no way substitute for the American market. Nor could a defense tie with Russia be anything but claustrophobic for Japan. Russia is too close for Japan's comfort. The advantage of the American connection is that the United States is not geographically poised at an instant to invade Japan. It would be an enormous stretch of American logistics and even global interests to contemplate a reconquest. American interests in Japan grew from the Japanese attack on the United States, and later from the willingness to protect Japan, not from any intrinsic desire to dominate Northeast Asia. Both Tsarist and Soviet Russia, however, have historically expanded to the east, toward Korea and Japan.

Alternatively, Japan might consider an alliance with China. Japan can import corn and other food products from China, if American supplies are unreliable. Eventually, China's market might even be more attractive than Russia's, but it would be a very long time before Chinese consumption would be able, say, to support the Japanese automobile industry. China, however, might not reciprocate Japan's overtures. Beijing would fear too close a Japanese embrace and would distrust long-term Japanese intentions. Nor would China offer the cornucopia of raw materials that Japan needs. Oil would be in short supply. Thus neither imports nor exports from China would solve Japan's problem.

A third possibility for a newly independent and powerful Japan might be the nuclear option. Over past years Japan has frequently considered and then rejected a massive nuclear weapons program. As an addition to U.S. nuclear capabilities, a Japanese deterrent makes about as much sense as British nuclear weapons do today: they would be significant, but still only a marginal addition to the security of the acquiring nation. As a substitute for American nuclear protection, they would contribute little deterrence unless somehow an antimissile shield could be erected over the Japanese islands. America and Russia do not face a problem of the same order of magnitude as Japan's—that of tiny islands populated with a few large cities. For the United States, several incoming missiles would not spell the end of American civilization. But the same number of missiles targeted on Japan's major cities could have a much more shattering impact. This is why Takashi Inoguchi believes a Pax Nipponica depends on "either the removal of the superpowers' strategic arsenals or the development of an antinuclear defence system."[12] If the U.S. nuclear umbrella were withdrawn from Japan, on the other hand, Japan might acquire such weapons as a last resort.

Each of these options—Russia, China, and nuclear weapons—represent palliatives for Japanese insecurity in certain unfavorable conditions. But though individual Japanese have occasionally suggested one or the other of these expedients, nowhere does one find a recommendation that Japan should undertake to shoulder the world's hegemonic burden, with all of the diplomatic, military, and political costs that such a course of action would entail. The Foreign Ministry occasionally veers toward Gaullism; public attitudes sometimes favor Japanese neutralism or isolationism. Individual Japanese are proud of what their country has accomplished. But though other nations attribute greatness and leading-power status to Japan, Japanese tend to think of themselves as "small." They do not want to take on world responsibilities, certainly not alone. Japan does not want to lead a coalition of nations. Assisted by the United States, Japan might focus on a range of important unsolved problems. But it does not want to have to cope with world problems by itself.

Nor is there a parallel with the U.S. rise to preeminence. The United States was forced into world leadership by the weakness of the rest of the world in 1945. Japan faces no similar vacuum of power or compelling necessity to assert sole leadership today. A range of powerful nations already partly fill the vacuum. In addition, a Japanese move to full hegemonic power and responsibility

12. Ibid., p. 23.

would be unlikely to have the support of the Japanese population, and it would be resisted by China and other East Asian nations.

A U.S.–JAPAN G-2

If the free rider stance and Japanese hegemony are both unsustainable and unrealistic options for Japan, a third possibility is a close Japan–America accord to manage world problems. In many respects, Japan and America are the two logical allies of the post–Cold War period. During the Cold War, America wanted and needed only military allies, countries that would make a major contribution to the defeat of Soviet armies. The United States also sought strong ideological allies, nations that would articulate and support a philosophy of anti-Communism. West Germany, Britain, and France volunteered for these tasks and performed them well. As the task evolved to an anti-Russian stance (and not just anti-Communist), China came to play a very important role. Japan, however, stayed on the sidelines.

In the post–Cold War era, however, new kinds of stabilizers are needed. An unequivocal opposition to Communism and all its variants is no longer a sufficient policy for the multifarious world that lies ahead. This is not only because Communism is in the process of metamorphosis toward a more open, less bureaucratic economic system. It is also because Russia is not likely to pose a credible military threat in the next decade. Her preoccupations are now economic. The problem in both the Soviet Union and Eastern Europe is low industrial and agricultural productivity. Both regions are likely to be a net drag on the financial resources of the world economy and are unlikely to be propped up by Western governments and industry acting alone. Also, the "joint ventures" with the West that Russia will permit will be limited by shortages of foreign exchange. Western investors, like the Ford Motor Company, are right to question whether they will be able to repatriate their earnings in hard currency. Western Europe may well find that its investments have not yielded the returns it expected: besides, mooted projects have long turnaround times before Westerners can reap

profits from them. The negative experience Fiat had producing the
Lada in Russia is one cautionary tale.

Without financial, managerial, and technological help from
Japan, Western countries are unlikely to be able to make a structural difference in the evolution of Soviet industry. The United
States sells its agricultural surpluses in the Russian market, but has
limited funds to invest to develop that market. Only Japan has both
the resources and the technological know-how, the staying power,
to invest for the long term in the Soviet economy: to extend, perhaps, its foreign manufacturing processes to the Soviet orbit. Even
then Japan may hesitate. For Japan to be drawn toward investments
in the USSR, Russia would have to permit more than 50 percent
ownership of the facilities involved. The Soviets would have to
allow Japan to direct labor and raw materials to Japanese plants
located in the Russian heartland. Japanese factory managers would
also have to have the ability to discipline labor and lay off employees in overstaffed facilities.

This Japanese role could be extremely important to the future
stability of world politics. Eventually, someone will have to invest
in improving Russian industrial processes. This is not just because
the Soviets want such improvement, although they do. It is because
an ungoverned and ungovernable Soviet Empire would be an enor-
mously destabilizing force in world politics. Today the world does
not need another recalcitrant and failing empire, like the Ottoman
or Austrian—especially one possessing such great conventional
and nuclear power. Prior empires have lost or were in danger of
losing part of their national territory, through fragmentation or
annexation. They sometimes waged war under hopeless conditions
to redeem their patrimony. A bruised, hostile Soviet Union, suffering from the pressures of subject nationalities seeking freedom,
could lurch toward disaster.

If such a beleaguered Russia is to be averted, Japan and the
United States need to concert strategy to find ways of helping the
Soviet Union to improve its performance, but *only* in the context
of strong, indeed unbreakable ties to democratic and industrial
economies and governments. A Soviet Union increasingly open to
democratic and free-market influences would be far less dangerous
than a less strong but more closed society, alienated from the rest
of the world. The United States and Japan could act together to

help make this vision of an outward-looking Soviet Union a reality. Europe could assist as well, but Europe's ability to concert strategy with the two other powerful economies in world politics probably awaits a degree of political and policy integration that will not be attained even when full internal free trade among the twelve nations is achieved in 1992. Britain remains opposed to a common currency and to majority rule in the management of the twelve economies of the EEC.

But picking up America's marbles in policy toward the Soviet Union is not the most important role Japan might play in the America–Japan G-2 (Group of Two) of the future. It is difficult to overestimate the importance of international financial coordination between the two leading economies of the world to avoid a crash. Such coordination, however, has been the exception rather than the rule in past history. Britain and Germany did not coordinate efforts by their central banks to avoid the panic of 1873. It instead became the worldwide depression of 1873–96. More important, Britain and the United States were unable to cooperate to avoid first the financial and later the economic impact of the Great Depression of 1929–38.

As we now know, world trade after 1924 depended on a triangle of payments and receipts: America loaned money to Germany; Germany paid reparations to France and Britain; and Britain and France sent money to America in payment of their war debts. Maintaining each leg of this triangle was central to the stability of the system because there was no other way that Germany could discharge its reparations bill. Britain and France would not concede Germany an export surplus in their home markets, and Germany had no gold or foreign exchange to pay with. As soon, therefore, as New York investors lost their fascination with German bonds and switched money into the U.S. stock market, beginning in June 1927, Germany began to encounter difficulty meeting its reparations payments. When the Crash came in 1929, American investors, desperate to make up their losses, dumped German bonds and took their money home. As foreign money fled, German governments raised interest rates and tried to hold on to capital. They launched a merciless contraction of the German economy to reduce prices and wages, seeking to generate a trade surplus to pay their obligations. But they failed. Ultimately, more than a quarter of the German work force lost their jobs, creating a sullen and resentful electorate that turned to Adolf Hitler for a solution in 1933.

Meanwhile, country after country collapsed under bankruptcies and debt. When the Austrians' largest bank, the Kredit-Anstallt, came under pressure in the spring of 1931, no other country could offer resources large enough to calm depositors. To stem the crisis the Austrians brought their money back from other countries, creating a panic in Germany, which in turn called its deposits home from London. In September, without help from the United States or France, the pound sterling went under. England went off the gold standard and levied high tariffs, exempting only the Commonwealth from her discrimination against the rest of the world. By the end of 1931 world trade had been reduced by two-thirds, and unemployment in Europe and the United States rose to 20 percent.

This result occurred because the two leading creditor countries, the United States and Britain, were not able to rescue the countries in trouble and avoid a panic contraction in one economy after the other. America was largely at fault because she had sought to solve her own problems at the expense of others in "beggar thy neighbor" fashion. Not only did the United States enact the highest tariff in U.S. history in 1930, she pushed to retain her export surplus by devaluing the dollar. In other words, the United States did not act to solve other countries' problems and thus maintain the system; rather, she made them worse. The financial crisis soon produced the worst sustained economic crisis that the modern world has ever seen.

These failures hold a lesson for America and Japan. Today Japan stands in respect to the United States the way the United States stood in respect to Britain in the 1920s and 1930s. Then the United States had already become a major creditor power. But in the 1930s she refused to act like one and behaved rather as a free-riding unilateral maximizer. Japan could follow the fallacious American path today, but only with dire results, both for herself and for the system as a whole. Today America is short of funds and is itself the world's largest debtor nation. It can no longer lend money abroad in large amounts. America, in short, can no longer be the "lender of last resort" for other countries.

If nations come up short, they will increasingly have to get funds from Tokyo, not New York. Japan will need to provide capital on attractive, and perhaps sometimes on concessionary, terms to prevent default or the financial collapse of a leading debtor. Otherwise the trading and financial system could descend into a crisis as it did in 1931–32. When that happened, the world's leading exporter, the United States, lost its foreign markets and plunged into deep depression. Japan is aware of the precedents. Her leaders know that they will have to continue to provide capital and loans, if the system is to remain solvent and open to her goods.

This lesson, however, has not always been taken to heart. In 1984 Japanese fund managers overreacted and took their money out of Continental Illinois, a large American bank, when a Japanese news agency mistranslated the American word "rumors" (about its condition) as "disclosure." The bank was not insolvent; the "rumors" that it needed to be rescued were false, but when on May 10th Japanese investors removed their funds, the "rumors" became a self-fulfilling prophecy. The American Comptroller of the Currency tried to deny the stories, but it was then too late. On May 11th, the Federal Reserve was forced to step in to rescue the bank with $4 billion of new funds.[13] If Japan had withdrawn its investments in the aftermath of the October 19, 1987, New York Stock Exchange collapse, the consequences could have been like those of 1929. Fortunately, Japanese leaders are basically aware of how intimately intertwined the economies of Japan and America are.

The situation is like that in the "Sharks and Fishes" computer game.[14] The objective of the game is to maintain ecological balance among the two species. Obviously, if the sharks eat up all the fish, they also die. For balance to occur, the sharks must eat the fish slowly, allowing them to feed and reproduce. Japan is now in the somewhat unenviable position of "shark" in the international trading system. If it eats up all the fish (that is, saturates the world market with its goods, so that no other country can sustain its own industry) it will ultimately lose, because there will be no one to buy its products.

The United States faced precisely the same quandary in 1947. It

13. See the account in R. Taggart Murphy, "Power without Purpose: The Crisis of Japan's Global Financial Dominance," *Harvard Business Review*, March–April 1989, no. 2, p. 73.
14. A. K. Dewdney, "Computer Recreations," *Scientific American*, vol. 251 (December 1984), no. 6, pp. 14–22.

had won all the financial marbles, and the game of international trade could continue only if America gave some of them back. That is what it did in the Marshall Plan. Thus Japan has three basic choices: (1) to give the marbles back (through aid, investment, or loans), (2) to force much of the rest of the world to default on its obligations, or (3) to allow others to sell in quantity in the Japanese home market. This means facilitating U.S. and Third World economic growth by finding a place for imports in the growing consumer economy of Japan. Tokyo cannot risk default by her customers, for she needs to continue to sell to them. Even with increased home demand, Japan cannot manage without exports. Last year America took 36 percent of Japanese exported products, and the share does not seem to be declining.

In certain respects, Japan has become the balance wheel of the international financial mechanism. If private investment in the United States (from Japanese pension funds and insurance companies, for example) is reduced, the Japanese government may have to make up the difference through central bank intervention, supporting U.S. currency and buying Treasury bonds. If foreign support of the American financial market fades, America would have to raise interest rates to attract capital. This in turn would choke off consumer spending and undercut the market for Japanese exports. As a financial hegemon, then, Japan will have to act benevolently to keep markets open for her goods.[15]

Economists recognize that Japan's traditional problem has been too much saving, too little consumption.[16] This oversaving presented few problems before 1975 because most of it was quickly absorbed in new domestic investment, stimulating a very high rate of economic growth. From 1950 to 1973, Japan's GNP increased at an average rate of more than 10 percent per year, one of the highest sustained growth rates in history. When investment declined as a proportion of GNP in the 1970s, the oversupply of savings again caused no problem because they were easily sopped up by government deficit spending programs through 1983. The basic problem of Japanese foreign trade only emerged in 1984 and after because

15. See Richard Rosecrance and Jennifer Taw, "Japan and the Theory of International Leadership," *World Politics*, January, 1990.
16. See Edward Lincoln, *Japan: Facing Economic Maturity* (Washington, D.C.: Brookings Institution, 1988).

excess saving meant that a large number of goods would be produced that would not be absorbed by consumption, by industry in the form of investment, or by government. These had to be shipped abroad as exports. The growth rate declined, but Japan's dependence on overseas markets greatly increased and will remain so until her savings rate declines.

Will this happen? It has already started, and the 25 percent savings rate of a few years ago has now decreased to 18 percent. Japan's population is aging. Normally this would lead to an excess of consumption over saving, for older citizens do not need to put away funds for their retirement. In Japan's case, however, retirement pensions are not always sufficient, and many workers have to continue employment beyond age sixty-five. Frequently they are forced to rely on their children for support. Nonetheless, as *The Economist* argued recently: "New trends toward nuclear families, higher retirement ages, better pensions and new financial instruments to unlock income from illiquid assets such as houses, should let old people in future spend more and save less than the elderly today."[17]

Even more important, Japan faces a crisis of deficient and crumbling public infrastructure. This will almost certainly lead to significant new government expenditure to break the housing barrier, provide new sewer and water systems, build new roads, and provide other means of transport. Equally, faced with the increase in the elderly population, the Japanese government will have to spend much more on medical care as well as improve the quality of life and provide for greater social welfare and recreation. As *The Economist* points out, "The International Monetary Fund has forecast that by 2010, Japan will be spending one-fifth of its gross domestic product on social welfare, against one-seventh today."

Increasingly, therefore, even if consumers do not spend their savings, the Japanese government will make use of them for social and public works programs, through deficit budgets. Japan will no longer need a large export surplus; it can buy from debtor countries (allowing them to repay their loans and to finance Japan's overseas investments). With the new trend toward lower taxes, Japan may ultimately begin to play a role as market of last resort

17. "Survey of Japanese Finance," *The Economist*, December 10, 1988.

for countries in trouble, particularly for the United States and the debtor countries of Latin America and East Asia. This prospect is enhanced with the passage of tax reform by the Takeshita government. Despite the 3 percent sales tax (which may be modified), the net effect of the reforms is stimulative, through lower income taxes.

Through 1985 world economic growth was pulled by the powerful locomotive of the free-spending American economy. Since then, the burden has shifted to Japan and Europe. As one observer noted: "In Japan imports are expanding significantly. In 1987 imports increased by $23 billion over the previous year. The tempo of expansion is now accelerating: in particular, the import volume of manufactured products is now increasing by 30 to 40 percent annually."[18] Japanese industry is beginning to cultivate the domestic market as well as its foreign customers. It seems likely that Japan is entering an age in which increasing consumption buoys lifestyles and the standard of living.

It is perhaps well to remember that in terms of historic precedents Japan is still in the early stages of her development process. If we use the British example, the abolition of the tariff on imported grain (the repeal of the Corn Laws) came in 1846. This undercut the high-cost British wheat producers, and from then on Britain bought four-fifths of her food overseas. At that stage Britain for the first time became a true consumer society, for only then did the real wages of the British population begin to rise significantly. Today, the average American spends 11 percent of his income on food; in Japan the percentage is more than 20. Housing costs are extravagant even when compared to those in New York and Los Angeles. The Japanese consumer finds that stereos, TVs, VCRs, automobiles, cameras, and computers are all more expensive than those purchased outside Japan.

In other words, Japanese real wages have not yet increased commensurately with the wealth of Japan. In the British case, middle-class consumption sustained British industry even when exports were no longer the primary engine of development. Ultimately, it was the flowering of the British home market that was the true

18. Tetsuo Kondo (member of the Diet and former Minister of State for Economic Planning), "Japan's New Financial Strategy and the International Debt Problem," lecture given at the Wilson Center of the Smithsonian Institution, Washington, D.C., May 3, 1988, p. 10.

measure of modernity in social, economic, and political terms. This stage has not fully been reached in Japan, though it will definitely occur in the years ahead.

There appear to be definite phases in the maturation of an industrial power. In the first stage a high savings rate requires high investment to avoid stagnation. But then home consumption is necessary to buy the goods that have been produced. The country moves to an export stage when new products have been refined and molded in the fires of competition in the home market.[19] In this second stage, which lasts for several decades, domestic tariffs and export-led growth determine production and sales; the home market does not greatly expand. The domestic population does not initially benefit from the worldwide success of export industries.

There comes a point, however, when the general population inevitably comes to share in the great triumphs of an exporting power. Imports burgeon because there is a latent common interest uniting home consumers and the foreign customers of export industry. The latter have to discharge their debts (accumulated through purchases of the home country's goods); the former wish to improve their lives through cheaper food and wider access to the industrial products of the globe. These can be obtained only through foreign trade. They can be luxury goods: art, painting, sculpture, expensive modes of transportation and tourism, fine food and wines, a profusion of fruits and exotic woods, soaps and furniture, elegant consumer delicacies, high-fashion textiles. Tourism, as it is doing in Japan, eventually convinces provincials of the metropolitan power that they lack some of the refinements that other societies enjoy. Today Japan has reached but not yet fully embraced this third stage. It is certain that it will do so soon, for the processes of political development that accompany economic development are irreversible.

No great economic power has been able, for long, to hold out against them. If we take the leading powers of the world successively—Rome, Venice, Spain, Amsterdam-Holland, Great Britain, and the United States—each one went from austerity to richness,

19. See the Staffan Linder thesis in *An Essay on Trade and Transformation* (New York: Wiley, 1961) and *The Pacific Century: Economic and Political Consequences of Asian-Pacific Dynamism* (Stanford: Stanford University Press, 1986).

a richness which, for political as well as economic reasons, had to be shared with all citizens. The capstone—leisure and cultivation—is the longest in coming, but it is the most appreciated when it arrives.

The Japanese transition, for such it can be called, will come in the next few years. That is not only because of historic processes, but because the world financial system will be tipped unstably in one direction if it does not. The U.S.–Japan alliance will become a duopoly to handle many of the world's political and economic problems, and the alliance between the two countries will become closer. That alliance will have three assignments: (1) to revive the United States and American industry; (2) to help solve the world debt problem; and (3) to cope with the illness of the Soviet Union, which if untreated could unleash war, just as Austria's attempt to regain her strength following a period of decline and weakness was the basic cause of the First World War.

Most important, Japan and America must work together to rehabilitate the United States. Americans are beginning to recognize that the maintenance of the United States as a great power and the achievement of higher growth rates now depends greatly on the support the U.S. receives from others. In implementing a new grand strategy, Japan has become the critical ally for the United States. In the past, challengers never assisted the former hegemonic leader. As she took over the reins of power from Holland in the eighteenth century, Britain did not extend help to the Dutch. A century and a half later, thrusting Germany did not assist Britain, the retiring hegemon. But the future prosperity of the world now depends upon a de facto U.S.–Japan alliance to manage the world economy. Since Japan will probably reject the manifold burden of becoming the sole hegemon herself (and emerging as the world's leading military and nuclear power), allies will probably have to help sustain the lessened American Great Power role.

If the United States is to be able to pay its debts, its economy needs to be strengthened. Influential Japanese recognize that America needs help. The U.S. trade deficit cannot long continue as it is at present. Within the next five years it will be ended and reversed. To assist the United States the Japanese strategy has largely been to support the American money market, holding back on direct investments in land, plant, and equipment. In direct investment, Japan ranks third in the United States, behind Britain and the Netherlands. But money-market investments or loans do not solve the long-term problem of the deficit because dividends and interest payments must be transferred back to Japan: to the Japanese pension funds and insurance companies who make them. This means that America must run an export surplus to finance them. Ultimately, therefore, Japanese money investments exacerbate the problem of the trade imbalance.

This would not be true if Japan invested in real facilities: plant and equipment, the profits of whose production would not have to be repatriated to Japan. It is not surprising, thus, that direct investment in the United States is proceeding rapidly. Such industrial investment has another virtue: it produces goods—steel, automotive components, vehicles, and electronic goods, which, as products of Japanese firms, will indubitably be purchased by the Japanese population. These add to the U.S. export ledger, and for some may be seen as the long-term solution to the U.S. trade problem: America will not be able to export enough; the exports of Japanese firms in America will make up the difference. Economically, therefore, Japanese direct investment and exports from U.S. territory seem to help redress the trade imbalance.

Politically, however, such Japanese direct investments do not offer a solution for the United States. They do not rehabilitate American industry; in fact they compete with it. For every dollar of Japanese direct investment in America, U.S. jobs are lost: American factories have to lay off more workers than Japanese companies employ. Of course, there are a number of palliatives that might make Japanese direct investment more acceptable: "domestic content" legislation could guarantee that Japanese companies in America are not mere assembly plants for Japanese components produced abroad. Finally, the United States could insist that Japanese firms in America be vertically integrated, producing raw materials and all components needed for final manufacture in the United States. Even research and development for the new product lines could be done in the United States.

But this would not solve the problem that American industry faces, and though it would employ more American workers, it would still not make up for the jobs that American employees have lost through Japanese competition. It is no comfort to the American auto industry that Japan is gearing up to produce two million cars a year in the United States, some of which will be exported. The number of American jobs will increase only if the exports of American companies increase. This means that American firms have to export more to Japan, or alternatively, be allowed to produce in Japan themselves, with the profits repatriated back to America.

It will not be sufficient for Japanese to buy American grain and food, or U.S. raw materials. High-tech U.S. products will have to be on the export list, including air frames, aircraft engines, computers, semiconductors, microprocessors, medical equipment, and other items. Further, the United States will have to begin, perhaps with the support of the Department of Defense, to manufacture the complicated machines and numerically controlled manufacturing tools, including chip-making machines, that are now so liberally imported from Japan. Cincinnati Milacron and other firms will have to do better in competing with Japanese Fanuc. Like Harley Davidson of a few years ago, they will need financial help and temporary relief from excessive Japanese competition. To guarantee this result, the dollar will probably have to be lowered further, to equal about 100 yen. Only such a change is likely to induce American firms to bring their funds home and to begin quantity production in the United States rather than in Korea, Singapore, or Taiwan.

Some will say this is a lot to ask of Japan. It also poses a challenge to U.S. industry. America must adopt new business practices and world views in preference to traditional ones. American business has been internationally oriented, and all too willing to substitute production overseas for investments in American plant and equipment. U.S. multinationals may hang back. Japan may not be willing to regear its export machine to admit American imports. If both countries cling to outdated practices, the world, Japan, and the United States may have to face a fourth alternative—a breach.

A U.S.–JAPAN BREAKDOWN

Some Americans and some Japanese have believed that ultimately there would be a breakdown of relations between the United States and Japan. According to this view, what sustained the Japan-

America accord was an implicit willingness on the part of the United States to allow Japan to increase its relative international position through free riding. As long as the United States did not ask anything of Japan or impose any systemic burdens, the tie with the United States was tolerable from Japan's point of view. Once America began to demand a less one-sided relationship, however, Japan, the world's most selfish power, could only refuse: politely at first, but then with increasing vehemence. Perhaps Japan's militaristic energies, chained since 1945, will find expression in new quarrels and then a break with the United States.

Influential Japanese have an important grievance as well: America wants Japan to help shoulder the burden of sustaining an open world economy and contributing to the defense task, but Washington is not willing to share decision making with Tokyo. America decides, and then Japan implements; this, many have believed, is the American design. It will not work. Britain tried to exclude Germany from imperial decision making in the 1880s and afterward and Berlin never forgot the slight. Particularly after Bismarck left power in 1890, Britain made little effort to come to terms with the new young monarch, the volatile Kaiser Wilhelm II. Germany then built a fleet to challenge Britain's overseas ascendancy. History displayed the results of that quarrel in 1914.

In certain respects American policy toward Japan has been even more patronizing than Britain's toward Imperial Germany. The slap in the face of the Japanese economic representative who dared to come up with a Third World debt plan not fully identical with the one planned by Secretary of the Treasury Nicholas Brady is merely one example of American arrogance (or possibly thoughtlessness). (The damage in this instance, however, seems to have been largely repaired.) And yet Japan is supposed to be a major contributor to the plan; her participation is critical to its success.

Not that the United States has forgotten how to work with other powers on an equal basis. After 1941, the Americans had to play junior partner to the British in planning for the European war. They briefly learned how to get on with a great nation on equal terms. They can do so again. But the Japanese fear has always been that if they make willing contributions to the American system for the world, they will not be included in the planning about what should be done. Hence, they have hung back and devoted their attention to becoming the world's best trading state, shunning diplomatic, political, and military responsibilities.

The paradoxical point is that America must become more of a trading state, while Japan moves toward a greater role as a political stabilizer. This means that America will not only be doing less in system maintenance terms; it will be less able to dictate how the system should be run. Britain always tried to play "Greece to America's Rome," and that worked so long as British power was sufficient. When it declined, however, America went on its own. As America readjusts, it must share responsibility with others. It cannot simply tell Japan what to do.

Whether there will be a breach between Japan and the United States, thus, is up to the United States to decide as much as to policy-makers in Tokyo. If good sense prevails, the two greatest powers will share the system maintenance task. If it does not, there will be a major world depression, like that of 1929–32, and Japan and America will both lose. When countries cannot pay back, leading lenders and creditors suffer the most.

Maintaining the system is important to Japan for another reason. As the Japanese public receives more benefit from Japan's export-earned wealth, consumption will gradually increase relative to savings. This will be the beginning of a transition to lower economic growth. The rewards given to citizens for years of faithful service will have to be increased. First this will take place at the higher status levels, only later to be extended to the general population. One cannot yet say for sure, but the Recruit-Cosmos scandal, implicating the entourage of two prime ministers, the head of NTT, the Finance Minister, and scores of other officials in illegal insider trading schemes, may have begun the process of undermining public morale and faith in the disinterested leadership of Japanese politics. The enrichment of scores of political leaders makes ordinary Japanese wonder whether they should continue to sacrifice for the nation's benefit. The nation's *gaman* (or perseverance) may be weakening. Along with this, the electoral fortunes of the Liberal Democratic party may decline. Not only do the bribery and sex scandals cause revulsion along with resignation in the public, the 3 percent sales tax has become an affront to already beleaguered Japanese consumers. A consumer as well as a political malaise may be gathering force in Japan.

To add to the growing recognition of conspicuous consumption and indulgence, economic and military historians point out that Japan has already achieved its peak rate of growth relative to that of other nations. That occurred in the 1960s. By some time in the second or third decade of the twenty-first century Japan will have achieved its highest relative position in world politics. Even now, China and India, Korea and Taiwan, Thailand and Pakistan are growing more rapidly, on average, than Japan (see Table 12). And this is without the resurgence that will soon take place in South America. By 2010 the growth of other countries will increase further and begin to reduce Japan's relative lead. In textiles, construction, shipbuilding, steel, machinery, and even television and semiconductors, Japanese industry will become too expensive to compete against all comers. Japan will begin to experience decline. As America is doing now, she will then seek to devise a strategy for an industrial renaissance.

This is not surprising. As hegemonic nations take on new burdens to make the system work, they almost inevitably contribute to their own ultimate demise. We have already seen how Britain and the United States followed that path. The trajectory is quite clear. Initially, hegemons make a great deal of money through domestic production and exports. Their goods win surpluses on world markets because they are the most advanced. The surplus yields financial returns, which can either be reinvested at home or loaned and

Table 12

Comparative Growth Rates
(% Change in GDP)

	1965–80	1980–86
China	6.4	10.5
India	3.7	4.9
Korea	9.5	8.2
Pakistan	5.1	6.7
Taiwan	9.8*	6.7
Thailand	7.4	4.8
Japan	6.3	3.7

*Figure is for 1969–80.

Sources: The World Bank, *World Development Report 1988* (Oxford: Oxford University Press, 1988), Table 2; and Council for Economic Planning and Development, Republic of China, *Taiwan Statistical Data Book 1987* (Hong Kong: Economic Information and Agency, 1984).

invested abroad. Typically, and in the Japanese case as well, the monies are ploughed into rising industrial nations, where high returns can be earned from investment (and in Japan's case large investments have been made in the United States). As the debts of others accumulate, the leading creditor must allow others to sell abroad to pay them off, particularly in the market of the lender country. Thus, in time, export surpluses are conceded to others in the hegemon's home market. This will happen in the Japanese case as Korea, Taiwan, China, and other countries imitate the Japanese example. Latin American debtors will also have to run surpluses, not only in the American market, but also in Japan. In addition the debt crisis will be ameliorated by the transfer of debts into equity (direct investments) in the erstwhile debtor's economy. Those direct investments will be used to augment exports to the lending nation, and once again the hegemon will have to absorb goods produced by others. As we have seen, it cannot do this while stressing savings at the expense of consumption, nor, historically, can the stage of high consumption be avoided.

A U.S.–JAPAN RAPPROCHEMENT

It would, however, be premature to claim that the gravest tensions in the Japan–America alliance are already past. In the last quarter of 1988 and the first quarter of 1989 the trade imbalance worsened, and Japanese savings increased more than consumption. Japan was named by the United States as a country practicing unfair competition in telecommunications and semiconductors. Japan made some modest gestures toward increasing the sales of U.S. semiconductor producers, but essentially the door to the Japanese market for manufactured goods remained open only a crack. Many think that Japan has not fully understood that such halfhearted measures will not reduce the increasing "trade friction" with the United States and other countries. Probably relations with Washington will have to reach a new crisis before Japanese manufacturers will permit any substantial industrial exports from the United States.

Japan has surmounted "shocks" in the past. Nixon's recognition of China; the sudden cutoff of soybean exports from the United States; the oil shock in 1973–74—all these galvanized Japan to respond to a new world situation. In trade, however, many Japanese have assumed that palliatives would be sufficient to assuage American public and governmental opinion. The evidence suggests the opposite: unless Japan accords the United States an export surplus in the Japanese home market in the next five years, it could find itself radically limited in selling to Americans.

The issue will not go away, and Japan's vaunted ability to overcome the high value of the yen will not stand it in good stead in responding to the new American demands. In a world where payments imbalances are vital factors determining employment and growth, it is not sufficient to overcome economic obstacles and free market forces; Japan must respond to the eminently *political* and domestic need for America to regain its economic feet. Unthinking maximization strategies will only undermine the Japan–America accord and put the alliance at risk. At some point in the not-too-distant future Japan will be told to admit American exports or else. There will then be no possibility of finessing the issue, buying off Congressmen, or trotting out old foreign- and defense-policy arguments, suggesting that worldwide containment tasks require American "understanding" of the Japanese position. When these demands occur, Japan will for the first time have to respond to the issue in a forthcoming way. Otherwise there will be a rupture in trade, and perhaps a political break, between Japan and the United States.

The new *shokku* will be salutary, if sharp. As we have seen, the Japanese interest in maintaining a stable and open international trading system is surely as great as that of the United States. Japan is fully aware of the perils that beset the world financial system in 1931–32. No great creditor and trading nation would want to force others to default or to resort to permanent restrictions on trade. Japan therefore will likely respond to the American shocks with responsible policies, and a new balance in trade will be fashioned between the two most important economic powers. In time the U.S.–Japan alliance will take on a new mutuality and reciprocity. For the past ten years, Japan has been relegated to the status of economic giant, political dwarf. During that same period America attained the role of military giant, economic dwarf. Japan contributed little to America's system-maintenance tasks, either politically or economically. The United States did not assist Japan's emergence as a systemic balancer in the economic field, but now that balancing function is central to the continued stability of the world economy and to world economic growth. It is in fact crucial to the fate of Western industrial and democratic nations, to say nothing of the burgeoning, now liberalizing Third World.

Japan's role in helping to manage the international system can avert another crisis like that of the 1930s, and in this sense a Japanese-American duopoly is needed to replace America's outmoded hegemonic role. Japan will adopt her role as a stabilizer not because America suggests it but because it will be in her own interest to do so to avoid a worldwide collapse. Japan's adoption of that role, however, is greatly in America's interest and is pivotal to an American resurgence in the next few years. Despite what naysayers have predicted on both sides, the American-Japanese systemic accord will strengthen and deepen with time.

This accord will consist not only of more American exports to Japan, but also of more direct investment in Japanese industry by American companies. T. Boone Pickens and Mesa Petroleum proved that it was possible to take a large share of Koito, a key component-manufacturer associate of Toyota. Ford has a 25 percent share of Mazda and Chrysler has an important stake in Mitsubishi. The ability of American firms to invest in Japanese concerns and also to set up operating facilities by buying plant and equipment in Japan is extremely significant in political terms. Not too long ago a project at Cornell University investigated the cooperation the members of the Group of Six (America, Japan, Germany, France, Britain, and Canada) contributed and received in international financial negotiations during the period 1961–71. Initially, the investigators thought that success in negotiations would be associated with the size of the trade surplus, growth rates, or the gold stock. Very surprisingly, and despite its superior growth rates, Japan did the worst in these negotiations. Reluctantly the investigators concluded that while America had a very large stake in the success of European economies, like those of Germany, France, and Britain, it had little stake in Japan.[20] Hemmed in by Japanese

20. Brian Healy, *Economic Power Transition in the International System: The Translation of Economic Power into Political Leverage in the International Monetary System* (Ph.D. thesis, Cornell University, 1973) and William Gutowitz, *The Interrelationship of Economic Factors and Political Relations Among Nations—A Quantitative Analysis* (Cornell University, 1978).

government restrictions, U.S. direct investment in Japan was too small and insignificant to make Americans concerned if Japan did not fare well economically. Only a large and reciprocal stake in each other's economies seemed correlated with a high degree of cooperation on both sides.

Since the 1970s, the stake between the United States and Europe has both grown and become more balanced. In that same period the Japanese stake in the United States has increased dramatically, but there has been little reciprocal growth in the U.S. or European stake in the Japanese economy. The yen is not yet a fully international currency, and the size of the Euroyen market is a fraction of the Eurodollar market. Direct investment in Japan is a difficult and time-consuming process. Thus there is no strong or widespread international constituency to support Japan's continuing economic welfare. If it is to increase, Japan must open its financial doors much wider. In this particular respect, U.S. banks and other investors are far more concerned to assure the performance of a variety of indebted Third World economies than they are the economy of Japan. This is another reason why Japan's political clout in the United States has been diminishing with time. This does not mean that the link between Japan and America is of less importance. It simply means that it must be more symmetrical if its political significance is to match its economic potential. In time it will become so.

Finally, one should bear in mind that four or five countries cannot cooperate closely enough to run an international financial system. Even three countries muddy the waters and make durable cooperation difficult, if not impossible. Because France and Britain were competing for economic and financial leadership in Europe, they could not cooperate to prevent the European economy from falling into Depression in 1931. They also disagreed about aid to Germany: Britain was willing to help the still-democratic Weimar Republic, but France was not, except under onerous political conditions. The United States was not ready to assist either. In the aftermath, when Britain and France finally got together, the United States refused to cooperate, as in 1933. When Britain and America were ready with a new plan, France sabotaged it.

In game theoretical terms, with countries having such different interests, the solution "core" was too small. Two countries, if they had been strong enough, perhaps could have cooperated to prevent the crisis. But three made cooperation impossible. For some-what similar reasons today, two countries, not three, need to take the primary leadership of the international economic and financial system. This does not mean that the Japanese-American Group of Two (G-2) should not meet (with Germany) in a G-3 format. Some-times the G-5 nations will be needed (when reforms of interna-tional finance, the level of interest rates, exchange rates, and so on are discussed [then including France and Britain as well as Ger-many, Japan, and the United States]). For most purposes, however, agreement between the G-2 will be necessary to make these larger meetings a success. General international cooperation and collabo-ration are necessary, but that cooperation depends on the prior agreement of the two most powerful economies, Japan and the United States.[21]

Cooperation between the two world economic powers will not only help to keep the international system stable, it will also permit America to devote a larger share of its GNP to economic moderni-zation. This is not just because Japan will take on more of the self-defense task, though she will do so. It is because the U.S. trade balance will improve, and American indebtedness will stop increas-ing. With this change, the United States will not have to send an increasing share of its GNP abroad to discharge its debts, and more will be left for domestic purposes. There will also be savings in defense because of greater Japanese (and European) expenditure, as well as Soviet cuts. Japanese foreign assistance and lending abroad will also take some of the pressure off the U.S. capital market and off government spending for foreign aid. American interest rates could then fall. U.S. resurgence will then have been speeded by essential Japanese help.

21. Takashi Inoguchi considers four scenarios for the future: a continuance of American hegemony; "bigemony" (a U.S.-Japan G-2); "Pax Consortis" (an agree-ment among four or five major powers in which no single power is dominant, with Japan taking the lead for East Asia); and "Pax Nipponica." In the immediate future he finds a continued U.S. hegemony or "bigemony" as the most realistic outcome. Inoguchi, op. cit.

6

Russia and U.S. Resurgence

Historical Russia and now the contemporary Soviet Union have offered a special challenge to their neighbors. In the past, Russia was not a fully accepted member of the European system.[1] A partly Asiatic power, Russia initially sought to exclude itself from European influences and from political and economic interaction with European states. Only in the military field did the gigantic territorial empire participate and excel, and here it was forced to become a skilled practitioner of the military arts because of its exposed position on the Russian steppes. The Ural Mountains do not protect Russia from invasion from the West, and the open plain has been a highway for intruders from Sweden, France, and Germany. Earlier the Mongols had threatened Russia from the east and south. Like their tsarist predecessors, the Russian Communists feared a Western attack after the Second World War and sought to insulate themselves with a chain of buffer states in Eastern Europe.

Russia has no central or economic core; there is only the political and dynastic center of Muscovy (Moscow), a capital largely isolated from the outside world. When Peter the Great moved his capital north to the Baltic (to what is now Leningrad) at the beginning of the eighteenth century, he did so to establish a window on Europe and the world—to bring modernization to Russia. Since then Russian history has always oscillated between modernizing influences

1. See Hajo Holborn, *The Political Collapse of Europe* (New York: Alfred A. Knopf, 1988).

171

and nativist nationalism.[2] The Slavophil and Pan-Slav movements represented the second tradition, Peter the Great, Alexander I, Nikita Khrushchev, and Mikhail Gorbachev the first.

Communism in Russia after 1917 thus represented a strange amalgam of westernizing and yet anti-Western attitudes. Lenin and Stalin learned from capitalist states and from the capitalist world economy, but they also aimed to develop the new USSR without Western help and to oppose Western military intervention. Despite the relatively liberal and open New Economic Policy (NEP) of 1921–28, Stalin reversed course with the vast collectivization and industrialization in the First Five Year Plan (1928–33). This plan was designed to achieve independence of Western-provided food, raw materials, and industrial technology. Soviet industry and agriculture were to stand on their own feet. In addition, the new mechanization of Soviet factories was to lay a foundation for the waging of modern war. Trucks and tractors rolled from Soviet assembly lines, but they were less complicated versions of the tank, the real weapon in the Soviet arsenal and the main counter to Hitler's armies in 1941. Without the industrial and military rearmament achieved by the first two Five Year Plans, Stalin could not have defeated Hitler in the Russian campaign during the Second World War.

Still, after the war the Kremlin leadership had to decide how to respond to the olive branch offered by the West in the Marshall Plan in 1947. To have accepted Marshall's offer would have been to draw the Soviet Union into the Western-dominated international economy. Afraid of Western economic meddling in Russia, the Communist leaders declined the U.S. invitation and tried to maintain Soviet economic momentum by extracting industrial and raw materials from Eastern Europe. For a time the Soviet efforts succeeded, and growth rates of 5 percent or more were recorded in the 1950s and 1960s.[3] On the basis of this success, Khrushchev could predict that Russia would overtake the United States by 1980. What he failed to understand was that the Soviet economy was on

2. See Walter Pintner, "Russian Military Thought: The Western Model and the Shadow of Suvorov," in Peter Paret, ed., *Makers of Modern Strategy from Machiavelli to the Nuclear Age* (Princeton: Princeton University Press, 1986).

3. See Seweryn Bialer, *The Soviet Paradox: External Expansion, Internal Decline* (New York: Alfred A. Knopf, 1986), p. 49.

the threshold of a massive slowdown, clogged by its inability to solve the technological, quality, and information-processing problems of the modern industrial economy.

Not only did the technological gap between Russia and the West not narrow, it widened. The failure of Soviet agriculture imposed limits on Soviet industry. No longer could money be extracted from the peasants or from their successors, the collective farms; instead, agricultural production had to be heavily subsidized. The massive military rearmament also took its toll. Finally, Soviet planners had to set priorities among three competing claimants: consumers, investment, and the military. Through the mid-1970s, armament was increased at a rapid rate, while consumer spending was held roughly steady. But investment in the underlying base of the civilian economy was sacrificed.[4] Under Brezhnev, life improved somewhat. Millions of new low-quality apartments were built. According to Seweryn Bialer, "84% of the population had radios, 83% had television sets, 71% had refrigerators, 58% had washing machines, and 70% had sewing machines."[5] But lagging investment in the civilian economy slowed economic growth, first to 3 and finally to 2 percent per year or less. By the early 1980s Soviet economists admitted that industrial growth had declined approximately to zero. Clearly something had to be done.

Russian history, however, held out more than one option. Even under the tsars, Russia had never been able to keep up with the West. Rather than accepting the full force of Western economic competition, Russia had preferred to develop territorial enclaves on an exclusive basis. Tsarist leaders knew they could not compete with English or German capitalism on equal terms. Thus the Russian empire grew by military acquisitions, not by economic success. Indeed, for most of the nineteenth century the Russian military depended little upon technical advancement: the greatest costs were always for uniforms, food, and fodder for horses. Extending Russian imperialism in China, Moscow sought and received closed zones of occupation. Where England conquered, she opened her

4. See Myron Rush, "Hindsight," *Commentary*, vol. 43, June 1967, pp. 84–86, and Boris Rumer, "Realities of Gorbachev's Economic Program," *Problems of Communism* (May–June 1986).

5. Bialer, op. cit., p. 23.

new colonies to the trade of other countries. Russia instead always sought to substitute military for economic strength and kept her colonies shut, a tendency that lasted well into the post–World War II period.

This historic practice lent support to internal totalitarianism, but it slowed Russia's adjustment to the outside world, to Western industry and culture. In theory, the Russians should have developed their society as a "socialist paradise," which could win adherents by force of economic example, not through military pressure. In the late 1950s, Soviet leader Nikita Khrushchev still believed in the attractions of the Soviet system and hoped ultimately to win an economic victory over the United States and the West. As the Soviet economy began to groan under its military burdens, however, Russian leaders came to realize that the performance of their economic system would win few converts elsewhere.

In response, once again in the 1960s and early 1970s Russia chose military prowess as the emblem of Soviet progress. Brezhnev's henchmen reasoned: if the USSR could not do both things well, she would excel militarily. The invasion of Czechoslovakia (1968) and threatened intervention in Poland in 1970 and 1981 reestablished the myth of Soviet invincibility, and briefly the Russians even persuaded themselves and a few others (most notably the East Germans) that the "correlation of forces" was moving in their direction and against the United States. In strategic and conventional forces, the USSR seemed even to forge ahead of America and the Western alliance.

This "gain," however, was illusory. Russia did not fashion a satisfactory answer to America's development of new strategies for the electronic battlefield, as reflected in precision-guided munitions and electronic surveillance. She did not want to start a new arms race in the field of space weapons and missile defense. The cost of new weapons was bound to mean a further cut in investment and possibly in consumption as well. As her growth rate slowed down, intelligence analysts came to believe that the Russian economy was smaller than they had originally thought. Accordingly, the military proportion of national income had to be larger than they had at first estimated.

In the 1970s CIA analysts concluded that Russian military spending was about 7 to 8 percent of Soviet product. By the early 1980s, the now smaller estimates of the Soviet economy pushed the proportion of military spending to 12 to 14 percent. By 1988, some experts had concluded that Soviet GNP is no more than one-quarter to one-third the U.S. total.[6] If so, defense expenditure was over 25 percent of Russian GNP. The Soviets' own experts contend that the Soviet defense expenditure of $128 billion is 9 percent of Soviet GNP. As William Safire points out, this would indicate a Soviet gross national product of $1.4 trillion, or less than a third of America's current $5.1 trillion economy and well below the $2.1 trillion usually accorded Moscow.

The failure of Russian production to grow even at the fairly low rates of the U.S. economy worried planners in the Kremlin even more. Radical new policies were necessary to achieve acceleration (*uskorenie*). Again, these might be of two kinds: a radical scaling-down of the arms race and much greater cooperation with the United States and the West; or a sudden military lunge to make up territorially for Soviet economic limitations and backwardness. In the past, the consciousness of Russian decline had cut in two different directions. In 1914, a weakened Tsarist regime had finally decided to refuse to accept Austrian and German ultimatums. Influential Russian planners knew that the result of war could well be revolution, but after backing down in 1908, 1909, and 1912–13, they felt Russia had to take a stand if it wished to remain a Great Power. The result was Russia's agreement to mobilize if Austria did not moderate its claims against Serbia. When this decision was conveyed to Belgrade, the Serbians stiffened their response to the Austrian ultimatum. Austria rejected the reply and declared war.

A fragile Russia, losing power and influence in the system, is in this sense perhaps an even more volatile and unstable factor on the world scene than a confident and growing industrial power. The unanswered question is which of these two responses—the peaceful economic or the bellicose military one—is most likely to be encountered in the future. Gorbachev may fail to reform the Soviet economy and be succeeded by a Soviet hardliner. To some degree, it must also be acknowledged, Soviet choices will depend upon the Western and American response to Gorbachev.

6. See the analyses of Charles Wolf, Jr., and Henry Rowen, cited in William Safire, "Is Peace Bullish?" *New York Times*, June 7, 1989, p. A23.

THE DEVELOPMENT OF SOVIET POLICY

Internationally, and regardless of Soviet leadership, the external environment has become progressively more intransigent to Russian purposes. As a result, Soviet objectives have been trimmed. Initially, Russia sought to transform other countries through direct Soviet military involvement (which incidentally was quite successful in 1944–45, and again in 1956 and 1968). This appeared to work on Soviet frontiers, but it was not a feasible strategy for distant countries. To lure these into her web, Russia sought ideological conversion of other nations. This would be achieved by seducing bourgeois governments (like India or Burma) or, if that failed, through resolute support of national liberation movements in Vietnam and Africa. Support of "national liberation" was of course a much less risky policy than direct intervention, and it depended upon finding a movement that had support in a postcolonial population. Since the Soviets would only send economic and military aid (and Cubans), and perhaps some degree of advice, success depended upon others in a fluid local political situation. Further, the USSR had to admit that the prime centers of capitalist power in Europe and Japan were immune to such strategies.

Gradually, therefore, as political solidarity hardened in Europe, the Soviets turned to converts overseas, in the Third World. In the 1970s, the United States appeared to be in a stage of post-Vietnam paralysis and thus was inhibited from stopping Soviet gains in Africa, the Arabian peninsula, and Afghanistan, or so at least the Soviets reasoned. In truth, the United States did nothing, but the fallout from Russian ventures in East Africa and Angola gradually undermined détente and paved the way for a resumption of the arms race under President Carter. When Brezhnev made his Afghan blunder in 1979, the problem of Soviet "overextension" took dramatic new form. RAND Corporation strategists calculated that the "costs of the Soviet Empire" totaled about 2.5 percent of Soviet GNP,[7] and the benefits were far too low.

Footholds in Angola, Mozambique, and Ethiopia did not guarantee long-term Soviet influence, particularly where regimes needed

7. See Charles Wolf, Jr., et al., *The Costs and Benefits of the Soviet Empire* (Santa Monica: RAND Corporation, 1986).

Western economic support. The communization of Afghanistan was a case of "socialism in one city"—Kabul—and will be modified with the Russian departure. Even in the Caribbean, the Kremlin has paid high costs without gaining new converts. Cuba's economy remains completely dependent upon Soviet donations, and it is not clear that the Sandinistas will ultimately be able to resist internal and external pressure to moderate their political system. Arms aid has not bought Russia very much in the Western Hemisphere except American opposition, and that opposition, under the "linkage" doctrine, affects the American and Western position on arms control and conventional force reductions in Europe—topics of great importance to Soviet leaders.

Thus there has been an evolution in Soviet policy: Russia first relied on military invasion and occupation, then on ideological conversion of regimes through the force of economic example; next came support for national liberation through assistance to guerrilla movements. None of these have achieved their goal. Finally, under Gorbachev the Soviets have begun to concentrate upon influencing leading and growing powers in the Third World, like Brazil and Mexico. But this has meant modifying their support for armed struggles of national liberation.

Still, this does not suggest that the USSR has given up all recourse to military force. A beleaguered and encircled Russia might lash out at its tormentors, as Tsar Nicholas II did in 1914. A weak Soviet Union beset by internal strife could be a more dangerous opponent than a confident and relatively satisfied nation.

CAN THE SOVIET UNION REFORM?

Can the Soviets triumph over internal strife and institute economic and political reform? Internally, the dynamics of political change are extremely difficult to specify, and, if in power, difficult to master. To this point no totalitarian single-party state has ever given up control to the democratic masses, and the short-term outcome of the struggle in contemporary China underscores this reality. There have been periods of loosening, as during the New Economic Policy, 1921–28, in the Soviet Union, and in China from 1985–89. Authoritarian regimes in a series of developing countries have been reshaped in a more liberal direction, and Brazil, Argentina, Korea, and Mexico have achieved a new political openness and responsiveness.

Russia under Mikhail Gorbachev has permitted an unparalleled discussion of political and economic subjects, and elections have been held for about a third of the posts in the Congress of Peoples' Deputies, a body that selects the Supreme Soviet. Russians have elected Gorbachev as their paramount leader (with the title of President), but that does not mean that the position of the ruling Communist party is subject to challenge, or that the President would not be the leading Communist party official. In China the Communist leadership has been sacrosanct, and in the short run, at least, there is no suggestion that the strong challenge by students, supported by workers and the middle class, will survive the clampdown of June 4, 1989. In any event it will be some time before liberal democratic political processes can determine political outcomes in Beijing.

Two regimes in Eastern Europe have moved toward much greater political liberalization. In Poland, the once-outlawed Solidarity union has formed the new government jointly with the Communist party. In free elections it won practically all the seats in the Senate and also the proportion of seats it was allocated in the lower house. In Hungary, new parties have been allowed and proliferated, and it is at least theoretically possible that they will outpoll the dominant Hungarian Social Workers (Communist) party in new elections. Political leaders have also dismantled the "iron curtain" fence between Hungary and Austria, allowing exit to many dissatisfied East Germans.

Nonetheless, the change in Eastern Europe, however quickly it comes, does not mean that equivalent change is possible in the two centers of Communist and previous totalitarian strength: Moscow and Beijing. These two have exerted autonomous control of their populations. Unlike them, the Polish and Hungarian Communist parties always depended on the threat of Soviet intervention to survive. There was no full-blown or self-sufficient apparatus of domestic totalitarianism in either case.

In the past, Russian and Chinese centers of power have always reasserted themselves after brief interludes of liberalization or relaxation of control. Stalin reimposed totalitarianism with a vengeance in 1928. The greater openness of the Khrushchev period (1955–64) gave way to Brezhnev's control by the *apparatchiks* and the military in the years that followed. Khrushchev's fumbling attempts to arrange a mutual slowdown in the arms race were succeeded by Brezhnev and Kosygin's effort to win that race.[8] Mao let "many flowers bloom" in the late 1950s and then moved to revolutionary dominance with the Cultural Revolution in 1966. That change unleashed a torrent of revulsion toward the West, which only reversed course with the revival of the Soviet threat to China in 1969. With such volatile swings in Chinese policy, one wonders whether Gorbachev represents permanent or only transitory tendencies in the Soviet leadership. This issue is of fundamental importance because a liberalizing and ultimately a liberal-democratic Soviet Union would be a far more reliable partner in foreign affairs than a Communist regime that had merely shifted from a military to an economic focus.[9]

But even if full political reform is not possible in the Soviet Union, Western observers want to know whether Gorbachev's purely economic reforms will succeed. Here, as well, there are grounds for uncertainty. Suppressed nationalities in the Baltic states, Georgia, and the Ukraine have staked claims for much greater autonomy. Moscow centralists have to prove that adherence to their rule gains economic benefits, such as new consumer goods and imports. Thus far *perestroika* has yielded few dividends to the Soviet purchaser.

In contrast to Moscow's emphasis upon political reform, in China as in the Republic of Korea economic reform came first, spurred by a united political leadership. The creation of special economic zones, a more flexible price system, and enhanced trade with the West represented new experimentation in China. The highly collectivized communes were replaced by peasant proprietorship, and agricultural production spiraled upward. In fact Deng Xiaoping's failure stemmed in part from too much capitalism too soon. The

8. See Albert Wohlstetter, "Is There a Strategic Arms Race?" *Foreign Policy*, Summer and Fall 1974.

9. See Michael Doyle, "Kant, Liberal Legacies, and Foreign Affairs," *Philosophy and Public Affairs*, vol. 12, pp. 205–35.

introduction of price reform led to inflation and corruption, without producing (at least initially) a great upsurge in the supply of needed goods. In the aftermath of the crackdown against students and workers, reform has been set back, perhaps for years. The present regime has apparently lost its "mandate of heaven" and can only rule by brute force. While present Western and Japanese capital may not be repatriated, new investment has for a time been brought to a standstill. Thus the lesson in China appears to be that economic reform unleashed inequalities that the population was not prepared to tolerate. Confronted with the reaction to these, leaders did not move toward political reform, but rather to repression.

In Korea, the pattern was different, but economic reform also preceded political: large trading and industrial companies were set up with the patronage and protection of the state and directed to produce high technological exports for the American market. Success in economics was the essential prerequisite to political reform in Korea. In China the same process is in its early stages: as we have seen, the regime still refused to accord any kind of democratic participation to its opposition of university students and members of the middle and working classes.

The primacy of political reform in Russian policies is therefore harder to understand. Ideally, *glasnost* (political and intellectual openness) should have followed the success of *perestroika* (economic restructuring and reform). It turned out, however, that *perestroika* could not be achieved without *glasnost*. There was no constituency to support economic reform among the *apparatchiks;* only by broadening the political base could Gorbachev create one. But the problem then became whether a more democratized and less centralized Soviet Union could achieve the degree of unity necessary for economic progress. The answer to this question is extremely important, for economic reforms, emphasizing new investment in the industrial base, may make it difficult to increase consumption. It is at least possible that political reforms may at least initially stifle economic growth by using up the surplus to be devoted to investment. As long as economic success is in question, the ultimate fate of Gorbachev's experiment is in doubt. And if Boris Yeltsin is correct, Gorbachev may be running out of time.

THE ROLE OF WESTERN POLICIES IN THE SUCCESS OF SOVIET REFORM

The most controversial aspect of the "Gorbachev Revolution" (distinctly a revolution from above) is what the West and the United States should do about it. Here there are two aspects—economic and military–political. Economically, it appears that the Russian reforms will not succeed without some help from the West, in credits and new technology. Soviet leaders cannot even measurably increase consumer goods without an infusion of Western products, which must, at least in the short term, be purchased on credit. As the leading Soviet economist Abel Aganbegyan has pointed out, the Russians have scored some successes in housing. They have also increased factory wages by 30 percent in the last several years. But the higher wages do little good if there is nothing to buy with them. If the Russians purchase Western goods to allay the consumer bottleneck, they have little leeway to increase their exports in return.

Table 13 suggests that Soviet petroleum exports have probably peaked, and other exports depend upon help from the West in devising and producing goods that sophisticated consumers might want to buy. Raw materials, chromium, leather goods, furs, vodka, and caviar are no longer sufficient to earn the necessary foreign exchange. The Soviet $25 billion gold stock is not large enough to greatly increase Western imports, on which Russia has recently become more dependent (see Table 14). Meanwhile Soviet gross external debt has risen from $18 billion in 1980 to $36 billion in 1986. Thus the pressure to increase Soviet exports grows by leaps and bounds. If they don't increase, the Soviets will ultimately lose their access to Western credit.

This links up with another problem. Russian planners want large Western investments in the Soviet Union. But Western and Japanese firms will be very hesitant to invest (even if they are allotted as much as a 51 percent share in new enterprises) if they cannot take the profits home in hard currency. Inability to repatriate profits led the Ford Motor Company to drop out of the Western consortium of firms seeking to make new direct investments in the USSR. In short, Russian exports confront a "chicken and egg" problem.

Table 13

Soviet Exports
(Billions US $)

	1970	1980	1983	1985
Machinery	2.75	12.08	11.42	11.85
Fuels	1.98	35.90	49.19	45.89
Chemicals	.33	2.02	2.30	2.82
Wood	.83	3.09	2.58	2.63
Consumer goods	1.31	2.67	2.59	2.56

Source: Directorate of Intelligence, *Handbook of Economic Statistics,* 1987, p. 100.

Table 14

Soviet Imports
(Billions US $)

	1970	1980	1983	1985
Machinery	4.16	23.19	30.70	30.82
Chemicals	.49	3.27	3.21	3.70
Consumer Goods	3.97	24.13	24.97	26.52

Source: Directorate of Intelligence, *Handbook of Economic Statistics,* 1987, p. 101.

Russia needs new investment to devise an export strategy. She cannot obtain this investment from the West without a convertible ruble (which can be exchanged for Western currency), and she cannot risk moving to convertibility without already possessing strong export industries. This problem can only be solved if long-term credits are available, and that depends in turn on the state of political relations with the West and Japan. Therefore, Gorbachev's foreign policies must continue to be conciliatory if Russia's economic problems are to be solved. Russian planners remember that funds were available at the height of the détente period in the mid-1970s, only to dry up as the Soviets sought to expand their influence overseas.

Thus a Soviet foreign policy "appeasing" the West is a requirement for many years ahead. But that "appeasement" could be abandoned if the Soviet Empire suddenly begins to crack at the seams, either at home or in Eastern Europe. Democratic relations with the center of Communist power have always presented a dilemma. On the one hand, peace depends upon international stability and the maintenance of nuclear deterrence and the conventional balance. This requires a careful and calculating adversary that will not rush into hasty and provocative moves. On the other hand, America favors liberalizing movements in Communist and other societies and continues to support them. In 1956 American propaganda perhaps even went too far in encouraging the people of Budapest in their struggle for freedom, provoking Russian military intervention in Hungary. Therefore, too much pressure for liberalization of Communist countries may cause a military crisis, possibly undermining the structure of deterrent stability.

This dilemma might, in time, arise again in the Baltic states or Eastern Europe. The Bush Administration has been trying to square the circle by pressing on both levers at once: improving relations with Gorbachev while at the same time encouraging change in Poland, Hungary, and other Eastern European countries. During his June 1989 trip to Europe, President Bush challenged the Soviet Union to tear down the barriers to the unity of Eastern and Western Europe. In future there could be a point at which America and the West could be blamed for fomenting instability in Russia's backyard. If one Eastern European country after another sought to leave the Warsaw Pact (and not merely develop distinct economic and political institutions domestically), a world crisis could arise.[10] The Soviets might be sorely tempted to use force.

How should the West react? One should remember here that Russia needed an East European buffer only because she feared Germany and the West. If there were no danger of Western exploitation of her troubles at home and in Eastern Europe, she might be willing to adjust to the inevitable. Thus, when a series of regimes seek to leave the Soviet camp, the West and the United States should stand ready with maximum reassurance to the Soviet Union: they should be ready to reoffer the military alliance that James F. Byrnes, the U.S. Secretary of State, proposed to Russian Foreign Minister V. M. Molotov in 1946. That pact did not rule out cooperation with other countries: it merely offered the USSR security against a German invasion for a long period of time. Such a pro-

10. Henry Grunwald, American Ambassador to Austria, writes: "Decaying empires can be dangerous. In Eastern Europe, there is a particularly explosive situation. The constant question is how the Soviets would act if liberalization got out of hand and threatened to undo the Warsaw Pact. Even Mr. Gorbachev would not tolerate that." *Wall Street Journal,* June 12, 1989, p. A14.

posal would not be equivalent to admitting the Soviet Union to NATO. That organization would continue as before, its command and military structure intact. Rather, the Soviets would be given a Reinsurance Treaty not unlike the one signed between Germany and Russia in 1884. That pact did not diminish Germany's primary loyalties to the Triple Alliance (NATO in this case), but it did assure that Germany would not support her own allies' military action against Russia. The United States could easily pledge this to the Soviet Union, without conflict with her North Atlantic Treaty obligations.

Such a situation would resemble the state of affairs after the Napoleonic Wars. At that time, a large number of states signed a general guarantee pact in the form of the Holy Alliance. It was accompanied by the more exclusive Quadruple Alliance, which bound Russia, Britain, Austria, and Prussia to stand together against a resurgence of French militarism. After a period of domestic political restructuring, however, France was accorded membership in the European Concert of Great Powers, which met frequently to deal with threats to the peace and to the domestic order of European states. For fifteen years that Concert managed to keep European relations stable and peaceful. It functioned effectively until Britain relapsed into "splendid isolation" and new revolutionary outbursts in 1830 broke the political solidarity that had united the victors in 1815.

As far as contemporary Russia is concerned, a military link with the West should go a long way to allay Soviet fears that the United States or other powers would seek to capitalize on the USSR's weakness at home or in Eastern Europe. If there were no military danger from the United States, Germany, or NATO, the Soviets would be much less worried about political transformations on their borders.

America thus should stand ready to reassure the Soviet Union quickly, to forestall a crisis. But relations with the USSR are likely to improve even if there is no precipitating military crisis in Eastern Europe. The major goals that each nation seeks to accomplish, economic reform and some reduction of the defense burden, require mutual cooperation between the United States and the USSR. A better East–West relationship could be more important in the future, for the links between the two Germanys will inevitably grow.

A more united Germany can be a peaceful factor in world politics. But for some Soviets it will raise the specter of the powerful and militarized Germany of the past. An American guarantee that Germany will not attack could still those fears.

Fortunately, the new liberalizing Soviet Union is unlikely to be as afraid of political change as the traditional Soviet monolith has been. Infection goes both ways: from the USSR to Eastern Europe as well as in the other direction. As the Soviet Union moves to greater openness and political flexibility, it becomes a more attractive partner for Eastern European states, making it less necessary for them to assert their independence. A liberalized USSR also holds greater attractions for capitalist countries, and ideological divisions begin to dissolve in such an atmosphere. Gorbachev is much less likely to worry about a united Germany than he is to see ways in which he could hope to manipulate and use it for Russian diplomatic and political purposes. One can thus overplay Soviet fears in Eastern Europe, but in a sudden crisis in the satellites they could still be very real.

A NEW US–SU RELATIONSHIP?

There still remains the relationship between the United States, the Soviet Union, and the rest of the world. Up to now the postwar bipolar order has largely remained in place, and because of the Soviet–American tension, the bipolar split has largely solidified cooperative relationships within the Western camp. Opposition to the Soviets has caused Western countries and Japan to compromise their economic and political differences. That order, however, is changing. Neither the United States nor the USSR can now afford the high-tension arms race of the past. Some smoothing of past frictions is necessary for economic reasons alone. What will happen to bipolarity and Western economic solidarity as the Cold War ends? In those circumstances, some analysts have predicted a collapse of the world economy and a breakup of the alliances linking Japan, Europe, and the United States. From their standpoint, external opposition is the cement that holds the Western economy together.

External opposition, however, is not required to garner the gains from trade. The West and Japan would still stick together because the Soviet Union offers few immediate prospects of becoming a large consumer market. Its buying power could increase in time. But it could not replace Western Europe or Japan as an American trading partner. As we have already seen, an extremely close American relationship with Japan will still be necessary. Only such an accord would prevent a world economic breakdown and depression. More likely, the greater cordiality between the United States and the Soviet Union will make possible new investment in Russia and in the Soviet Far East, but the USSR will not become a leading commercial power for years to come. Thus, regardless of the decline in East–West hostility, the Western industrial nations and Japan will still have overriding reasons for maintaining their economic and political solidarity with one another.

Until the Soviets solve the problem of lagging agricultural production that has dogged them since collectivization, they will have to rely on military cuts to find funds for domestic development. In addition there will be credits from the West and Japan. If Soviet workers were more educated and efficient, in time the USSR could become an export platform for major Western multinational corporations, but that will not take place in the near future. Changes in worker productivity depend at least in part on factory managers having the right to fire malingerers and to eliminate alcoholism and absenteeism. And as we have also seen, the inconvertibility of the Soviet ruble makes large-scale Western investment much less likely.

While not undermining Western cohesion, a new relationship between the United States and the Soviet Union could exert a broadly stabilizing influence in world politics. As India develops an intermediate-range missile and Israel lofts a satellite, the diffusion of nuclear weapons and delivery systems continues apace. In the 1960s, the spread of nuclear weapons could have been particularly unsettling, for many new states were clients of either the West or the Soviet Union. A local nuclear war in the Middle East or South Asia could have involved the superpowers, as guarantors of allied states on opposing sides. Today and in the future, however, the two Great Powers would act to restrain their clients, or, if that were impossible, to dissociate from them. The United States threatened precisely such a dissociation from Israel in the 1973 war, and the Soviet Union has always been very careful about going too far in supporting India against Pakistan or China. A less revolutionary Russia would be even more hesitant in future to approach the brink of war on behalf of client states. Perhaps paradoxically, the spread of nuclear weapons and delivery technology has brought the United States and the Soviet Union closer together.

Yet international theorists have occasionally argued that the two largest powers in the system must always be major rivals. History offers some support for this view, with tensions in the nineteenth century between Britain and France, in the twentieth between Britain and Germany, and since World War II between the Soviet Union and the United States. But this generalization overlooks the long period of British cooperation with Germany during the Bismarckian period, 1871–90. In the future, in any event, we will not be sure who are the premier leaders. In economics, Japan may become a primary player, aspiring to more general leadership. An emerging U.S.–Soviet link would make that claim less persuasive and successful. In any event Japan's interests are still not defined on a world stage. It is difficult to imagine circumstances in which they would not defer to Soviet-American agreement.

In future, therefore, we might have two sets of collaborative relationships: the United States and Japan in economics; and a growing rapprochement between the United States and Russia in military security. Soviet and American common interests would be greater than before because the two erstwhile superpowers face decline unless they cooperate to reduce the burdens of the arms race. Would this be a stable arrangement? In the 1930s, Britain and America (the economic players) did not buttress military stability (where Germany was the main disruptive power). The key question was whether the United States would use its economic strength to assist political stability; for a long time it refused to do so.

Today we are not sure how Japan will act in similar circumstances, but at least she seeks to maintain an open international economy and the free flow of capital. Militarily, her future role is unknown, but it is not necessary to chart it now. Under these circumstances, the United States and the Soviet Union could occasionally serve as the "two policemen" envisaged by President Franklin Roosevelt. This association should not in any way interfere with the uniting of Europe, or with further links between East and West Germany. It seems, however, that a further thinning of forces in Europe will take place within the borders of those two countries, safeguarding their economic rapprochement.

In future, economic trends suggest that the world will no longer be bipolar, but multipolar, although four or five major powers will not maneuver in an international vacuum. International financial and trading links will prevent anarchy in the economic realm. NATO will not lapse; it will continue and, if anything, be accompanied by arrangements that would take the form of a kind of general guarantee pact, serving as a crucial stabilizing factor as nuclear and missile proliferation continues in the Third World. Even that spread will not necessarily destabilize the extra-European realm. In the Far East and the Pacific Rim, vital trading relationships will dominate, and military force will sound an infrequent discordant note. In Latin America, the resort to force will solve little, and it will not interfere with rising consumer economies there, once the debt crisis has been disposed of. In Africa, the Middle East, and South Asia tensions will continue, but disagreements will not typically be solved by force. Presumably the West, Japan, and the Soviet Union will increasingly agree on measures to prevent arms assistance to active combatants in these areas. China will need to join this group. The U.S.–Russian link will perform a stabilizing function militarily, just as the U.S.–Japan tie will assist economic stability.

CONTAINMENT, ROLLBACK, OR DOMESTIC INVOLVEMENT?

In the past the United States has kept the Soviet Union at bay through an arm's-length relationship that the USSR also favored. Strictly, the United States did not try to influence Russia except in the broadest terms: to persuade it to avoid aggression and war. The well-known policies of containment and deterrence were effective but very crude influence processes to achieve this result. Inevitably, the sanctions were negative, rather than positive. They declared: "If you invade other nations, we will hit you." The only positive incentive the West provided was the absence of punishment. It certainly did not consciously seek to alter Russian policy by offering inducements or reinforcements, and the United States also contrived to exclude Russia from diplomatic participation in the affairs of many areas of the globe, beginning with Latin America, the Middle East, and East Asia.

In contrast, with other countries, like the nations of Europe and North America, the United States sought much greater influence and involvement: it was not content merely to maintain its defense position vis-à-vis its friends. It wanted to strengthen and assist their internal economic and political liberalization and increase their participation in global affairs. The same was true of American policy toward the Third World. Here U.S. policy makers had all sorts of ideas on how less-developed countries could modernize: what products they could produce and sell on the world market, where they could get loans or grants, how international companies could be drawn to make investments in their economies, and so on. In short, the United States expressed positive power toward its friends, negative power toward its adversaries.

Certainly, U.S. and Western influence in reshaping Japan and Europe and even to some degree the developing countries of the Third World was much greater than its impact on the Soviet Union. While occasionally seeking apocalyptic goals like the "rollback" of Communist power from Europe or Asia, the United States acted as if it did not care what happened in the Kremlin so long as the Soviet Union did not expand territorially. The arms race certainly did not always reflect an American response to what the Soviets were doing. For long periods the United States rearmed when the Russians were essentially quiescent, and didn't rearm when they were very active. The Vietnam War and American development of military technology often governed what the United States did.

It was of course easy to understand why America took such a negative and military view of what might be accomplished. She had tried to intervene in the Eastern European satellite states after World War II and had failed to achieve her objectives. Aside from free elections in Hungary (which were later taken back) and Austria in late 1945, the Communists imposed a heavy hand on Eastern Europe and offered little room for political freedom. Besides, the Soviets were preternaturally sensitive to U.S. influence in Eastern Europe and reacted strongly against it. It remains true, however, that aside from the Austrian State Treaty and the Nuclear Test Ban, the United States did little to work out compromises with the Russians and remained content to deter them through military and political containment.

In the future, however, U.S. influence in Eastern Europe and in Soviet Russia could dramatically rise. That is because Russia and Gorbachev are seeking an economic renovation which depends upon American positive power for its success. Only the United States can unlock the market for Russian goods; only Western and Japanese banks can proffer credit; only Western and Japanese economists and policy experts can tell the Soviets how they might cope with their combined problem of too much (suppressed) demand (and inflation) and too little consumer supply. To advise them simply to "open up" and install a free market is not enough. They need to know what to produce, where to get the capital to invest in it, and where to sell it. Thus, effective and helpful relations with the Soviet Union require a much more intrusive American policy than the United States has ever imagined before—one that seeks to manipulate incentives *inside* the Soviet Union and not merely to reshape its external costs and benefits.[11]

Pentagon experts have frequently denounced new credits for the USSR and inveighed against a repeal of the Jackson-Vanik amendment (which restrains trade and links most favored nation treatment to the scope of Soviet emigration). These same analysts have lobbied to keep the U.S.–European restrictions on high-technology exports to the USSR. Whatever the merits of this position on the basis of previous policies, a broader influence strategy in the changed political environment is now required. That is because the United States never had (positive) leverage actually to get the Soviets to do something good; it had only (negative) leverage to prevent them from doing something bad. Soviet success in the future depends upon an economic reform internally. If the United States plays its cards right, it can help the Russians overcome internal blockages to economic change and exercise an influence within Soviet Russia not unlike that of the IMF in developing countries. Successful positive influence makes it less necessary for the United

11. American policy is gradually moving in this direction, with Secretary Baker's speech on October 16, 1989, offering help to perestroika.

States to depend (as in the past) on negative influence. America's movement toward a more comprehensive influence strategy toward Russia could help both nations.

The Soviet Union and the United States need each other. Bellicose Russian policy will ruin the Soviet economy and offend the West. Present Russian leadership needs more from the relationship than the United States does. Gorbachev's economic program is in jeopardy and it cannot function without Western help, and ultimately without joining the Western-dominated world economy. This means eventual membership in the World Bank, the General Agreements on Tariffs and Trade (GATT), and the IMF. It certainly requires that the Soviets move to convertibility of the ruble, or Western corporations will not invest in Russia. For the United States, a scaling-down of the arms race is also essential. Technically a future U.S. president could try to sustain all the imperial burdens of the past through increased taxes, but neither Congress nor the public will sit still for such measures, isolated as they would be from other reforms and necessary defense cuts. Thus America, too, has a great stake in better relations with Russia. Only in this way will she obtain the savings she needs for programs of domestic resurgence.

DEFENSE CUTS AND THE U.S.–SOVIET RELATIONSHIP

The Soviet Union has already agreed to the principle of asymmetric defense cuts in the forces of NATO and the Warsaw Pact, making clear that the Soviets and the pact will accept the greater reductions, in tanks and in armored divisions. In certain respects asymmetric cuts may favor the USSR because a greater proportion of her conventional forces would thereby be demobilized, returning resources and labor power to the Russian economy. American savings from conventional cuts would be considerably less. But still the balance in Europe would not be affected and could even be improved by large cuts in Soviet tank armies.

At the end of the Reagan Administration, Secretary of Defense Frank Carlucci projected a five-year (1990–94) defense plan that would involve real increases of 2 percent per year. Congress, however, would not agree to any such rises in the Defense budget and, on the basis of past experience, will likely enact defense cuts of 2 to 3 percent per year. As of the end of 1987, 524,000 troops were stationed abroad, costing at least $20 billion in pay and another $20 billion plus in the operation and maintenance of their equipment. In addition, unlike forces stationed in the United States, many of these troops incurred foreign-exchange costs, directly contributing to the trade deficit. Since the general-purpose forces comprise 80 percent of the defense budget (the nuclear forces take the other 20 percent), significant savings would have to be found in that category of military strength.

One of the great dilemmas of the arms-control negotiations, however, is that the United States cannot proceed to trim its forces unilaterally. American cuts make it unnecessary for the Soviets to offer reciprocal concessions. Thus, as the Bush Administration enters conventional talks with the USSR, it briefly has to suspend general-purpose force reductions on its own.

Defense expert William Kaufmann believes, however, that savings can still be obtained through postponing or stretching out U.S. force-modernization programs.[12] The five-year defense program allocated an expenditure of $714 billion for procurement and research, development and testing of new weapons systems, from 1990 to 1994. To buy all the weapons in the pipeline and to cover associated maintenance costs would call for additional expenditures of about $200 billion. At the same time, if Congress cuts instead of increases the Defense budget, the amount available will be no more than a little over $500 billion. Thus, $400 billion of savings on modernization will have to be found. Kaufmann proposes deferring procurement of the B-2 (Stealth) bomber, the rail-garrison MX missile, and the Midgetman missile until after 1994. In addition, he suggests cuts in funding the Strategic Defense Initiative (SDI). In land and naval forces, he would hold back on new forward air defense systems and light helicopters, while limiting the Navy to 570 ships. The Air Force, which has been on a spending binge, would make substantial cuts in the Advanced Tactical Fighter program. Overall savings in procurement and Research, Development, Testing, and Evaluation would be $474 billion.

12. William Kaufmann, "A Defense Agenda for Fiscal Years 1990–94," in John Steinbruner, ed., *Restructuring American Foreign Policy* (Washington, D.C.: The Brookings Institution, 1989).

Kaufmann also recommends personnel cuts in the Navy, Air Force, and Marines in order to add strength to the Army but still squeeze out a saving of $20 billion. In total, Kaufmann would spend about $293 billion per year as opposed to Defense program recommendations of $388 billion each year. Even this saving, which Kaufmann claims would not reduce our defense effectiveness and readiness, could be greatly increased if large conventional reductions could be agreed on with the USSR. Since the Soviets announced 14.2 percent cuts in 1989–90 and are looking toward 30 percent cuts in the year afterward, American reductions, once the conventional talks make progress, could be much higher than the Kaufmann figures indicate, perhaps in the neighborhood of $50 to $75 billion per year.

CONCLUSION

As we have seen, the Soviet Union and the United States need each other, but at the present time the Soviets need the U.S. more. What holds the two nations together is the recognition that others are gaining, together with the fear that unless they stick together, chaos could emerge on the periphery of the system. An improvement in U.S.–S.U. relations could also assist in dealing with American allies. When the Cold War was at its height, allies could argue that the United States, the principal protagonist on the Western side, should carry most of the burden of defense and security.[13] They in turn could free ride, contending that security against the Soviet Union was more in U.S. worldwide interests than theirs. Direct ties with the USSR, however, show allies that America has an alternative to large alliance expenditures. If they want to keep the alliance going (and they most assuredly do), they may have to pay more of the total share.

It is difficult to manage relationships between the two primary rivals of any international system. Under bipolar circumstances, the task is thankless and little cooperation will emerge. In the multipolar world of the future, however, relations between the United States and the Soviet Union can greatly improve.

13. See Mancur Olson, Jr., and Richard Zeckhauser, "An Economic Theory of Alliances," *The Review of Economics and Statistics,* vol. 48, no. 3 (August 1966), pp. 266–79.

7

A Multipolar World

Western analysts are familiar with the mechanics of a bipolar international system. Two polar powers, each supported by military and economic allies, strive to maneuver to gain advantage, but they cannot achieve very much. Nuclear deterrence and the likely ineffectiveness of conventional military expansion diminish the likelihood of success and prompt restraint. A cold peace results instead of a hot war.

In the future, however, the world will not witness bipolarity, but a burgeoning multipolarity—with four or five major states at the top of the system. In the year 2010, the leading powers, measured in terms of GNP, will be the United States, closely followed by Japan, with China and the Soviets next in order. If a united Europe emerges, it would also rank above the Soviet Union. Such a multipolar world will not mean, as it has done in the past, several independent great powers jockeying for advantage in an international power vacuum, unconstrained by economic relationships. In contrast, the future multistate world will be highly interdependent. Unlike in the 1930s (from whose disastrous experience we confidently hope and expect nations have learned), most great nations will *accept* the interdependent relation they have forged to other economies and seek to work within it. In the past forty-five years, nations working within existing economic ties and the world economy have done better than nations that have held aloof: Japan has excelled and the Soviet Union has suffered. Even the United States, which did not get heavily involved in the world economy until after World War II, did not perform that well on its own.

There has been a long-standing argument about the relative stability of bipolar and multipolar systems. In a few cases, multipolar systems have been stable; one recalls the basic stability of the Bismarckian international system, from 1871 to 1890. On the other hand, some believe that multipolar systems are more prone to violence than bipolar ones because the identity of a potential enemy—an aggressive power—is sometimes veiled in the activities of other states. As late as the 1890s Britain thought that France was her primary foe, but Germany was the state she should have worried about. In the 1930s, the British Conservative government was, for quite a time, preoccupied with the Bolshevik threat rather than with Nazi Germany.

Also, under conditions of multipolarity, one does not always know the target of the hostile actions of an aggressive state. In 1914 Britain still might have thought that German actions were aimed at Russia and France and not at her. In 1938, Britain believed that Germany was only seeking to acquire former German territory, and was not interested in wholesale expansion on the European continent. Why then should Britain have had to take a leading part against her? In contrast, under bipolar conditions, the two powers know that all actions are aimed at each other. Thus the conventional wisdom is that balancing is easier and clearer in a bipolar than in a multipolar system.

This wisdom is partly valid. But a multipolar system offers the possibility of recruiting new allies, while allies already are fully committed in a bipolar world. Thus multipolarity provides new *balancers* to help face down an aggressive adversary. In contrast, bipolar opponents can mobilize strength only from within their number, and that may not be sufficient to create a solid balance. Still, balancing is difficult under conditions of multipolarity and sometimes occurs too late to deter an aggressive power.

But if the basic objectives and methods of the system are economic and not military in character, multipolarity is far superior to bipolarity. In a strict bipolar system there can be few economic ties or links of interdependence between the two primary opponents. Such a system cannot use the mechanisms of international trade to affect the outcomes of the competition. In a more multipolar order, in contrast, all countries are possible customers, markets, or sources of raw material and technology. The typical pattern of bipolar opposition recedes or vanishes in such a system. Not only that: each country can influence and even "economically deter" others by granting or withholding access to trade and to foreign investment. In an economic multipolar system, warlike countries generally do not prosper. As both Daniel Bell and later Frank Fukuyama saw, the compulsions of ideology are gradually diluted in such a system.[1] Economic reality tempers fervent ideology, as in the ending of the Iran–Iraq war.

Of course, it does not follow that multipolarity must be essentially economic in character: during most of the European state system, economic ties existed among major states, but they did not constrain political and military actions. Further, any major depression in which countries restrict markets and access to raw materials through high tariffs will force nations to reemphasize military and territorial expansion to acquire what they need. But as long as the international economic system remains an open one and countries work within the existing pattern of interdependence, multipolarity serves all participants quite well.

Trading relationships, in and of themselves, do not necessarily inhibit war. As it was in regard to Imperial Germany, the early onset of interdependence may be a force for war, as nations seek to regain their economic independence through territorial expansion. Also, in the past, a high level of trade between two nations did not necessarily dictate political camaraderie and friendship. Britain and Germany were important trading partners in both 1914 and 1939. Since trade could easily be switched to other partners, however, it had no constraining effect on politics or diplomacy.

Economic relationships also can be transitory or relatively permanent. Buying the stocks or bonds issued by another nation involves little long-term commitment to the other's market. In contrast, buying productive assets (real physical facilities like manufacturing plants and real estate) creates a much more substantial commitment. These assets are illiquid and cannot quickly or easily be sold on the open market. Such direct investment involves a larger stake in the economy of another nation than portfolio investment. Typically, foreign investment in 1914 and 1939 was

1. Daniel Bell, *The End of Ideology* (Glencoe, Ill., The Free Press, 1960) and Frank Fukuyama, "The End of History?" *The National Interest* (Summer, 1989).

portfolio, not direct investment. Now investment in other countries is increasingly direct investment—the acquisition of new productive capacity within the other nation.

In such circumstances, there is a new form of deterrence. Nuclear deterrence allows countries to hold as hostage the population of another nation. But that population cannot be pressured or influenced, it can only be destroyed. The threat of destruction or peace (nondestruction) is an on-off switch; it is a very crude instrument of influence. In contrast, foreign direct investment provides a mutual exchange of hostages *within* each other's territory. Those hostages can be influenced through tax and expenditure policy. The productive facilities held by other nations within a country's territory can be restricted or advantaged. In particular, a country with a heavy direct investment stake in the economy of another nation wants that country to do well economically. For only then will its own investment prosper and yield appropriate returns. When the stake is at once high and mutual, both nations acquire an interest in the well-being of the other's economy. And that creates a strong bond of common interest.

Under conditions of high mutual trade and investment, the growth of one nation supports the growth of the other. More generally, increasing trade offers an increasing market. Higher exports stimulate growth, which in turn stimulates imports. A multipolar international trading system also provides multilateral sources of credit and access to raw materials. In such a system, the rising tide of prosperity lifts some boats off the reef. While this would not necessarily improve relations between particular nations, it would make nations generally more satisfied with their circumstances and hence help promote the stability of the international system.

In the multipolar world of the future, there will be at least four major powers: the United States, Japan, Russia, and China. Europe probably will not be united enough to follow a coherent economic and military policy toward other nations, and Germany will emerge as its single strongest state. Outside of Europe, among the indebted economies of the Third World, Mexico and Brazil will be major factors in international economic politics. In East Asia, Korea and Taiwan will play a greater role, and in South Asia, India will begin to spread its wings. To grow, countries have to absorb new investment. But Third World debtors are instead paying out their surplus (which might otherwise be invested at home) in the form of debt repayment. Up to about 1981, the debtors collectively absorbed about $40 billion per year in foreign funds; since then they have had to pay out $30 billion per year to discharge their obligations. To pay back, the borrowers have been forced to adopt austerity, low growth, and domestic privation in country after country. If interest rates rise, the debtors' situation will deteriorate further. Already, their peoples are up in arms at the restrictions on their standards of living.

Until 1980, the Third World non-oil countries were developing rapidly, and they could afford to buy the goods of the first world in substantial amounts. Now many of them have virtually ceased importing. In particular, the United States has lost about $75 billion in exports to Latin America per year. Perhaps strangely, the economies of the United States and the debtor countries of Latin America now have similar interests.[2] If the U.S. position further deteriorates and America is forced to borrow more and more, this will drive up interest rates and hurt the Latin Americans. Each group would like to see the other's debt scaled down, along with its own.

There is in fact coming to be a potential conflict between the creditor group, principally led by Japan, and the debtor group, now increasingly represented but not led by the United States. If stability is to be maintained, the creditors will have to do two things: first, make it possible to scale down Latin American debts. Argentina has not been able to pay anything for a year. Peru is in a condition of economic receivership. U.S. consultants have apparently advised Bolivia to default. Brazil has not been able to meet payments on its debt. Probably U.S. Secretary of the Treasury Nicholas Brady's plan to reduce the debt by 20 percent is too limited. If Latin America is to regain solvency, 30 to 50 percent reductions are necessary. American, Japanese, and European banks will have to set up loan loss reserves to cover the shortfall, once existing commercial paper is sold off in the secondary market. One should bear in mind here that struggles to pay off debts had disastrous consequences for key

2. See also Ronald Muller, *Revitalizing America: Politics for Prosperity* (New York: Simon and Schuster, 1980).

European states in the period 1929 to 1932. Surely the world does not want to repeat this experience in Latin America—forcing an economic and then a political crisis on country after country.

The second requirement is reduction of the U.S. trade deficit (which will ultimately put a cap on American indebtedness). This means not only that U.S. exporters must try harder; it suggests that creditor countries must move to import in large amounts (as the United States did after 1947), reestablishing equilibrium in the world balance of payments. If Japan cannot buy the products of others in sufficient quantity, it will have to give away the money in foreign aid. Essentially, it is now necessary to get the United States out of the borrowing business, and to return interest rates to much lower levels, stimulating investment and growth around the world. If this does *not* happen, the United States could ultimately be forced into a position where it could not pay off foreign holders of its government securities. In practice this would mean default. Such a repudiation by the world's financial Samson could bring the pillars supporting the roof of the international economic system crashing down with him.

But such dire results, for those very reasons, could never transpire. Instead, the bond between America and Japan must and will become the sheet anchor to windward for other countries in turbulent times. The Soviet Union will follow a more moderate role in the years to come, and the most interesting question now concerns how long it will take to reestablish the movement in China toward reform of its economy and political system.

The most likely scenario suggests that domestic developments in China will not greatly affect long-term international political alignments. The international determinants that dictated a Chinese rapprochement with the West and Japan are still in effect. The economic factors that pressed for reform of the Chinese economic system are still present. China has been dependent on the import of Western technology and capital; it will remain so. Foreign trade is already about 20 percent of Chinese GNP, similar to the proportion attained by industrializing Great Britain in the 1840s. In this phase at least, China's development is heavily dependent on exports. Thus the purge in China cannot be too brutal. The current aging Chinese leaders cannot last more than a few more years.

Their successors will have to reestablish their position with the people through accommodation and compromise and not rely heavily on repression. They will need to co-opt some of the student leadership, whose initial demands for reform were moderate and indeed necessary ones. They will also need to root out the corruption that has eaten into the structure of Chinese life, undermining social equality. Individual Chinese understand that people who start new businesses must be allowed to profit from them. But they do not understand why civil servants or party functionaries should benefit from their licensing and franchising functions, or why relatives of the leadership should earn egregious profits. If prices are to be freed for many consumer goods, the Chinese people want to be sure that higher prices will also result in higher production: that supply will rise to meet demand, and not be stifled by bureaucratic bottlenecks. Altogether, Chinese and foreigners are repelled by the inefficiencies of layer upon layer of Chinese officialdom.

This suggests that further political and bureaucratic reform is the ultimate answer to the partial reforms of the period 1981–89. In the long run, it is difficult, perhaps impossible, to maintain an administered price system for one part of the economy and a free price system for the other part. Otherwise raw material and food prices fail to reflect their proper cost of production, and the whole pricing system is thrown off kilter, a problem from which the even more regimented Soviet Union also suffers. In short, if partial reform has its problems, the antidote may be complete reform. In present-day China this is a long way off, but the basic position of China in the international political and economic system has not greatly changed.

Greater uncertainty clouds the position and policy of a more united Europe. The establishment of full internal free trade in 1992 will hurt many local industries in France and other European member countries. In response the European Commission and Council of Ministers will raise protective barriers against outsiders. Domestic-content legislation will exclude many products that are produced abroad or whose European content is less than 50 percent. Television programs and movies will have to be produced in Europe to air there. This will unquestionably stimulate a rush of foreign direct investment to set up new companies within the European 12. Outsiders will find it increasingly difficult to export to the Community. As it becomes more economically self-sufficient, Europe's dependence on external trade may actually decline.

Increasing introversion in Europe will have an ambivalent effect upon international relations. On the one hand, European Community institutions, hampered by the long process of working out an agreement among their members, will find it difficult to negotiate with Japan, East Asian nations, and the United States on matters of trade and services. The process of compromise and adjustment may become more difficult. On the other hand, economic matters could be more and more distinguished from political and diplomatic ones, for it appears unlikely that a common economic and social policy in Europe will easily translate into a common diplomatic or military policy. In those fields the policy of individual states like Britain, France, and Germany will remain distinct. Thus the difficulty may be that a more united Europe will become an increasingly obdurate trading partner in economics, while in political and military fields a disunited Europe will remain relatively weak. Because of this, Europe is likely to remain a theater for continued great-power rivalry.

The relationship among states in a multipolar system is less predictable than in a bipolar system, but it need not be more hostile. In fact, if power polarities are mediated by economic links, the result would be wholly benign. The problem in a political international system is prevailing anarchy; as economic interdependence develops between states, anarchy can no longer be tolerated, because no state wants or can afford a collapse of the system. This means that each must adjust so that the system proceeds and the general prosperity is safeguarded. To avoid a financial crisis, the problems of debtors must be addressed and some solution found that allows them to resume growth and imports. The amount of the debt has to be scaled down and stretched out. It must represent a smaller proportion of total export capacity (the remainder of which would be used to increase imports).

As the Soviet Union fades as the erstwhile number two nation, there will be increasing rivalry between Japan (the new number two nation) and the United States. Under typical conditions in the past, the new competition would eventually take on territorial and military dimensions. It will not do so in the future, however, because Japan and the United States are the two system stabilizers; they can only lose if the system crumbles. Britain and Germany did not share similar interests in 1914 or 1939. Important great powers in the past were prepared to see the international economic and political system founder, if they could then find jewels in the wreckage. In other words, in the past at least one of the contending great powers did not take system maintenance seriously. That is not true today of the United States and Japan. It is not even true of the contemporary Soviet Union, which in the past sought to subvert the system through universal revolution or military takeover.

Why? Is it possible to believe that the USSR now supports the existing international system? To some degree. First, the Soviets have not acted to undercut bourgeois democratic rule, which if anything is spreading, not receding, even in Eastern Europe. Second, the Russians hope to prosper from assistance from the Western capitalist economy, and they cannot have it both ways. Perhaps there are some old Bolsheviks who pray for a world depression, but economies in Eastern Europe could be hit just as hard as those in the West, with potentially revolutionary consequences and anti-Soviet effects. In depression conditions, ethnic and national conflict would bubble to the surface just as fast as class conflict, and perhaps even faster. Soviet unity would suffer. In the present international system, the Soviets are at or near the top; if that system undergoes transformation, they could be shuffled to a much lower rank.

As far as China, India, and Third World states are concerned, undoubtedly some would favor a wholesale toppling of the power structure. Iran still might. Some Latin American states once wanted to "decouple" themselves from the Western world economy. But most states would like to exert greater influence within the existing structure, an influence that can ultimately be exercised only through greater economic power. That power in turn depends upon economies that are sufficiently open to attract new investment and technology from other countries. One cannot, in short, both fight the system and hope to share in its benefits. Under these conditions, the multipolarity of the future will be governed by common economic interests in ways that did not exist in the past. The degree of opposition existing among Great Powers can radically decline, providing a "peace dividend" to the United States and other countries.

The pattern of opposition and alliances has determined a large proportion of U.S. foreign policy behavior in the past. Broadly speaking, America's past leadership met two requisites: (1) to deter and contain the Soviet Union and (2) to reassure allies they were protected. In the 1940s and 1950s, to meet these twin goals, allied appeals often determined U.S. policy, and the United States was led to take a primary part in organizing Western defense. Rarely if at all did America seek to balance between adversaries and allies, differentiating its position from both.

In the future multipolar world, however, the patterns of reassurance and deterrence may occasionally be reversed. That is, the United States may be much more concerned about disputes with its allies, largely economic in nature, than in the past; also, it may offer some reassurance to the Soviet Union, its erstwhile enemy. Few multipolar systems have functioned successfully and stably without multilateral strategies of reward and punishment toward all players.

The stability requirements of the system demand such evenhanded strategies. The question between now and the year 2000 will be whether the world economic system remains in balance or succumbs to a devastating depression like that of the 1930s. To avoid such an outcome, deficit economies like those of the Third World, Eastern Europe, and the Soviet Union need drastic attention. They cannot be expected to participate or to compete effectively in the international marketplace without considerable restructuring, with new flexibility of prices and incentives. Political changes to accommodate new economic methods could cause a crisis in these regimes. It is therefore easy to imagine conditions in which the United States supports the Soviet Union or Poland while criticizing or withdrawing resources from its allies. Such shifts are of the essence of a more multipolar order.

Greater evenhandedness and less demarcation between allies and enemies does not mean a relapse into the amorphous Balance-of-Power system of the past. The focus in the past was hostile bipolarity between the United States and the Soviet Union. In the future it will be growing solidarity between the United States and Japan, whose common efforts will be needed to stabilize the system, economically and politically.

8

The Impending Economic Crisis

The future impact of international relations on the United States is on balance a favorable one. While relations with Japan and the Soviet Union and the context of burgeoning multipolarity will present challenges to the United States, they will also offer important economic benefits and some saving in foreign policy costs. Thus the foreign as well as the domestic sector contains opportunities on which the United States can capitalize in the next few years to rejuvenate its economy. But still lacking is the necessary spark to ignite dormant social energies and forge a new social cooperation.

Recessions creep in on little cat feet. They cannot be seen in advance. An economy, ostensibly in prosperity, succumbs to crisis. The crisis or crash is worse because, beforehand, people do not think it is going to happen. Large numbers of investors and corporation executives have bet their shirts on "more of the same." Investment advisors and economists have proclaimed that there will be no recession, or that it will not come before next year. One typical scenario has the crash occurring on an upward surge that suddenly runs out of gas. Sooner or later, the rate of growth in sales or the Dow-Jones average reaches levels that it cannot sustain. The economy is like an airplane which, while climbing, suddenly stalls in vertical flight. But recession could sneak in another door. An ostensibly smooth and flat road could suddenly drop down off a hill. A motoring car could find itself sliding down into a valley.

How could these events happen? How *will* they happen? The question can be phrased in this way because whatever economic reforms may have been accomplished, they have not abolished the business cycle. The world economy is more integrated than it has ever been, with a twenty-four-hour stock market in continuous play. Countries are heavily indebted to one another; businesses and consumers are in hock up to their ears; many savings-and-loan institutions are insolvent. It just takes one solid blow to the solar plexus to cause the world financial body to double up.

Take the Crash of 1987. That occurred because the market lost confidence that America was capable of reining in its seemingly perpetual deficits. Japan initially took out some funds. Then the rumor spread that Congress was going to remove the tax exemption on interest charges involved in financing takeovers. If takeovers were stopped, the mechanism driving the rise in the Dow-Jones average from 750 (in 1982) to 2720 (in 1987) would also shudder to a halt. On October 16 and 19, 1987, the market poised—then dived. Yet, at the very same time, some investment advisory services were confidently predicting that the Dow would reach 3600. Many thought there would be a "soft landing" for the dollar, for the government deficit, and for the U.S. economy.

In 1989, the optimists predicted a similar scenario. The government deficit would gradually decrease under the impact of Gramm-Rudman cuts. The Social Security surplus would make this reduction even easier. Besides, many argued, the "deficit" was an artifact of the government's accounting procedures. If government spending were divided between "capital" and "consumption" budgets, and only the latter included in the regular accounts, much of the deficit would be "abolished" at one stroke of the pen. The "capital" spending portion would be treated as investment in capital equipment, the way businesses do. Thus we could proclaim to the outside world (and hopefully convince ourselves) that we had "solved" the problem of the deficit. Of course, the fiscal pressure on interest rates and on the supply of monetary capital would continue as before: the net expansionary (and inflationary) tendency would remain unchecked. The trade imbalance would receive no stimulus to improvement. What would happen then? Perhaps unfortunately, the rest of the world would be right to regard this as fiscal and semantic "legerdemain," to be expected from economic conjurors. It would be seen as a way by which the United States could "avoid," not "solve," its problem.

But the difficulty is that the 1987 scenario is probably set to repeat itself. Once again the short term looks good; analysts are telling us that the cap is off the Dow. The dollar has strengthened, and the trade deficit (on current account) in the first quarter of 1989 was only 7 percent worse. Some even forecast a short-term increase in the savings rate, more than compensating for the government's invasion of its citizens' incomes through taxes spent on public consumption. If savings rise, the amount of money available to finance investment increases, and the interest rate falls, stimulating business capital spending. An increase in savings (as a proportion of income) also cuts domestic consumption, perhaps tempering the American public's preternatural tendency to buy foreign goods.

At the same time, however, there has been an ominous rise in the value of the dollar. Some saw the dollar going higher still, perhaps to 170 or 180 yen. In time this would translate into much higher imports and lower exports. Not only this, but world inflation is rising. Even in the United States, the basic rate of inflation moved beyond 5 percent. As the Federal Reserve and Chairman Alan Greenspan strove to control prices, they raised interest rates. But higher interest rates in turn increased the value of the dollar, ultimately making the trade balance even worse.[1] This suggests that the Bank of International Settlements' Lamfalussy report was not extreme in criticizing the United States' "deplorable" failure to cut its government deficit. Monetary policy can accomplish only so much by itself: if it copes with the problem of inflation, it may worsen the trade deficit. Only if fiscal restraint accompanies monetary tightening can the trade and inflation problems be solved together. Again, the issue comes down to the unwillingness of the United States government (the President and Congress) to really cut the budget (or raise taxes). Politicians would apparently rather avoid blame for the disasters that may come than to incur the wrath of special interests by actually confronting the problem through

---

1. Douglas Sease of the *Wall Street Journal* writes: "But there is a dark side to a stronger dollar, especially for investors who have bought stocks in the belief that the high-flying economy is headed for a 'soft landing'—slower economic growth with moderating inflation. The fear among some market strategists—and among government officials trying to cap the dollar's rise—is that a stronger dollar might undermine U.S. industrial competitiveness." June 12, 1989, p. C1.

real cuts in spending or major tax hikes.[2] The sudden fall of the stock market on October 13, 1989 indicated a similar lack of faith that the U.S. can solve its problems. The initial failure of the UAL buyout raised questions about the future of takeovers and the stability of the market for junk bonds. Funds from the Federal Reserve staved off the crisis on October 17, but there was a real question whether leveraged buyouts would continue to drive the market. If not, much lower stock market levels were possible.

SCENARIOS OF CRISIS

At least four different scenarios could trigger a crisis:

First, there could be a sudden collapse in the Japanese stock market, now at all-time highs. Price-earnings ratios of Japanese stocks are in the 70s as compared to American ratios of 7–15. At some point Japanese stocks will peak. Of course, there is much captive capital in Japan, owing to the failure to completely internationalize the yen and to lend it abroad in large amounts. For a period of time Japanese stocks appreciated in response to governmental appeals to national unity and loyalty. Nippon Telephone and Telegraph (NTT) had its problems nonetheless—problems that only foreign investors could help to solve. The Recruit Cosmos scandal touched nearly every member of the Liberal Democratic political élite, except the Premier, Sosuke Uno, who then found himself vulnerable to a sex scandal.

Partly as a result of the political crisis in Japan, the dollar strengthened in comparison to the yen, worsening the U.S. trade imbalance. At the end of 1988, in any case, Japanese exports suddenly surged forward, and many observers predicted that the Japanese surplus would start rising again. This, of course, would likely trigger import restraints in the United States and Europe. Thus, perhaps paradoxically, the weakening of the yen (while improving the Japanese export position) signals a deepening of the trade crisis. Unless Japanese consumer spending rises, Japan will be

2. See Kent Weaver, "The Politics of Blame Avoidance," *Journal of Public Policy*, vol. 6, no. 4, pp. 371–98, and "Generating Blame for Fun and Political Profit," paper delivered at the Annual Meeting of the American Political Science Association, Washington, D.C., September 1–4, 1988.

caught with a large production of consumer goods that it cannot sell at home. The 3 percent sales tax that Japanese housewives protest against is holding back consumer spending.

If there is no movement toward equilibrium in trade between the United States and Japan, relations will get worse and the "trade friction" will magnify. With the crisis in China, Hong Kong money that used to be invested in the mainland will increasingly move to the United States, pushing up the value of the dollar even further, accentuating the crisis between America and Japan. Money may even leave Japan. At some point Japanese stocks will be affected, as they were in 1987. In this case, however, a collapse of confidence, leading to sudden downturn in the Tokyo stock market, could see investors running for cover. Seeking to pay for their losses, Japanese investors would bring funds back from the United States (as they did in 1987), triggering a collapse in the New York market. Any large outflow of capital would force higher interest rates in the United States, leading to both a further fall in stocks and a general recession in the economy.

Another scenario would have its origins in the Third World. Suppose the U.S. trade deficit does not decrease, but stabilizes or even increases. Then America would be forced to borrow the widening difference between its imports and exports. If world inflation has risen (as a result of oil, commodity, or manufacturing price increases), then interest rates will already be climbing. America's borrowing requirements (perhaps at the level of hundreds of billions of dollars per year) would tend to squeeze out Third World debtors, who need more access to funds to postpone and reschedule their loan payments. This could prompt default of one or more of the leading debtor countries. Already there are calls to set up America's Chapter 11 (the bankruptcy statute) on an international basis. In response to widespread default, the world banking system would plunge into crisis as major loans had to be written off, and some large commercial banks would close their doors. Interest rates would go sky high, and (as in 1981–82) the economy would be thrust into a deep recession.

A third scenario would lodge the proximate causes in the United States. What happens if, after a long rise in the value of the dollar, the trade deficit decisively worsens? Then there could be a collapse in the dollar, spurred by market recognition that the United States had not put its own house in order. As the dollar falls, foreign investors, particularly Japanese, could desert the listing vessel, leading to a further fall. Then only extremely high interest rates imposed by the Federal Reserve could reassure investors. But those would in turn throw the economy into a tailspin.

But confidence could be deflated in other ways. As worldwide inflation grows, it will tend to spiral upward in the United States, and interest rates, prompted by Federal Reserve restrictions, will rise. Savings-and-loan institutions, now under acute pressure, could fail to withstand the strain. Bankruptcies could spread. Under those conditions loans would be difficult to get, except at confiscatory rates, and the housing and construction market could decline into a slump. Once business confidence had been shaken, as in 1931, it would be hard to rekindle, and investment would lag, no matter how low interest rates fell.

A fourth scenario would see the United States gradually lapsing into recession. Capacity limits were being approached as U.S. corporations hit 84 percent of utilization. For the G-7 countries as a whole, production is a higher proportion of capacity than at any time since the early 1970s boom. As a result, inflation pushed up on a worldwide basis as businesses failed to hold the line on prices because they no longer could gain market share through increased production and price restraint. If this scenario materializes, the Federal Reserve and other central banks will tighten further, and higher interest rates would lie ahead. The situation is actually worse if growth continues at an unexpectedly high rate, drawing in imports. Fearing inflation, the Fed will raise interest rates. This will lead to a higher-valued dollar, and the trade deficit will ultimately increase as a result. With the dollar going up and the trade balance deteriorating, at some point there will be a sudden loss of confidence, and the dollar will start falling.

If, on the other hand, growth is lower than expected, consumer spending and investment will tail off. Ostensibly nothing dramatic would happen, but confidence (which has been remarkably sustained over a seven-year recovery period) would gradually erode. Unemployment would edge higher and higher. The Fed might miscalculate as it did in 1979. Then, fears of recession led Federal Reserve officers to release new resources to the banking system; inflation rose, and the recession occurred anyway. To avoid this outcome the Fed might go to the opposite extreme, insisting upon price stability without regard to achieving a "soft landing." America's rise in rates, conjoined with higher rates elsewhere, could then combine to produce world recession.

In late 1989 there were many who believed that a recession would be avoided. The Fed was not increasing interest rates; inflation was apparently moderating. Yet, as Alfred Malabre shows, the economic figures at the onset of a recession are often reassuring, so reassuring that economists miss its onset. The worst recession since World War II was that from July 1981 to November 1982. The Fed cut interest rates repeatedly during this year and one-quarter, with the discount rate falling from 14 percent to 9 percent and the prime rate from 21 percent to 11 percent. The year 1981 was also the year of the greatest cut in tax rates in recent history. Yet the ship of state did not immediately turn around but plunged into the worst recession since World War II.[3]

A recession could have two very different effects. On the one hand, it could accelerate America's past decline and replicate the Depression of the 1930s. Much higher levels of government spending would not be an automatic remedy in such a situation for fear of accentuating the trade crisis, precipitating inflation and a free fall of the dollar. The government could do nothing until it saw how consumers were reacting. Unless they held back on imports and domestic consumption, the government would be powerless to run the economy through pump-priming: that would merely further stimulate inflation (though it would be stagflation) and suck in unwanted imports.

In such circumstances the United States would be thrust back into borrowing abroad, a device that ultimately weakened and impoverished seventeenth-century Spain and eighteenth-century France. By the 1680s Spain could command goods from almost any country, but could not pay for them with hard cash. Its temporary eclipse became permanent, and the sun turned its face on rising

3. Alfred Malabre, Jr., *Wall Street Journal,* August 21, 1989.

Great Britain. A century later, French indebtedness and fiscal weakness led to the calling of the Estates General, which brought on the French Revolution of 1789.

Such a gloomy outcome, however, does not await the United States. Instead, the plunge would be brief. First, a sharp recession would cut spending and increase saving. Unemployment would rise steeply and the nations' families could no longer afford "consumption as usual." In October 1987 the stock price fall had no such salutary effect, and Christmas giving in December was little different from that of the previous year. In a more serious economic crisis in the future, however, purchases will be postponed or canceled altogether because of the rise in joblessness.

Tax collections would fall, and the government deficit rise proportionately. As we have seen, the government would then be squeezed between a rock and a hard place: it would want to spend more to stimulate consumption, investment, and growth, but it would also worry about the effect on its international balance of payments. With declining consumption imports would also fall and the balance of payments improve. There would then be less need for large decreases in government spending, and one would also no longer have to achieve the full Gramm-Rudman targets.

At the same time, market and foreign pressures would persuade the United States to stop behaving like a "prodigal son." It would be clear that the deficit would have to be cut to a smaller proportion of the GNP while new tax legislation was passed to stop giving an advantage to transfers financed by debt, rather than equity. In the end an integrated tax system could emerge, which, like that of most other countries, treats the two equally. Consideration should then be given to a tax system that favored exports as compared to production for the domestic market. If new taxes were still required, a VAT (value-added tax), rebated for exports and for the poor, should be imposed. Among the needed cuts in expenditure would be further reductions in defense to finance an increase in the national educational budget, which is after all the most important single investment in capital, the human capital that is currently going to waste.

In short, a sharp recession would present a challenge to the U.S. economic and political system. The crisis would be salutary in that it would permit political leaders to act decisively to reform the system. Nor would the crisis get out of hand or lead to results like those of the 1930s. Whatever might happen in its first days, the challenge would bring forth international support for the American economy, and money would flow back into the system again. The only danger is that it might come back too soon, and that the necessary social lessons might not be learned. Here Japanese capital would play a crucial role. There seems no doubt that the primary reason why the October 19, 1987, crisis did not develop into a crash was that Japanese capital and new resources from the Fed were invested in the weeks immediately following the fall. The same was true after October 13, 1989. In both cases, the stabilization of the stock market occurred almost too rapidly, and the political negotiations between the President and Congress to cut the U.S. government deficit lost their sense of urgency.

Next time, the capital might not come back quite so quickly. The Fed might initially hesitate. Japan has worried for at least five years about how it might persuade the United States to get its fiscal house in order. The progress in that period has been disappointingly slow. In another selloff, the Japanese investors might initially leave the United States to twist in the wind, hoping that the message would finally be heard. There might be no immediate bailout, and the Japanese response might wait on executive and congressional action. Even so, reinvestment of large amounts of foreign capital and new Fed liquidity would turn the tide and buoy the American economy whenever it occurred. Then taxes and expenditure cuts would move America toward new economic goals.

Would this help solve U.S. problems? In the Great Depression, labor strife increased, and America became a divided nation. Those in public employment (whose incomes were not cut) actually benefited in real terms; in the private sector, however, both business and labor suffered grievously. The only unity lay in blaming the Hoover Administration. In a future downturn, those on fixed incomes would not be hurt as much as those dependent on the success of business and industry. Still, in 1933 there was no impetus to unite against the foreigner. No other nation had caused our problems: we were the problem. In the 1990s any administration that wished to remain in power would have to justify the sacrifices Americans would then be asked to make in terms of the worsening American position in the world and the need to work together to reclaim it. There is abundant good will among the American people; it merely needs to be harnessed. In crisis circumstances, for national purposes, it will be.

9

Prospects for Growth and Peace

Historically, as we have seen, societies go up and down. There is no single irrevocable cycle that leads from growth to decay. A nation can rise, decline, and then rise again. The United States rose on the back of unexcelled agricultural exports, to which she rapidly added motorcars produced on the assembly line. Her electric appliances, stimulated by Edison's fertile imagination, soon became the standard of the world. After World War II the rise of Germany and Japan was associated with superior automobiles, high-quality machinery, and electronics. Though Germany has some coal, in both cases the two countries marched forward because of the skills and dedication of their designers and workmen. The catastrophe of World War II undoubtedly spurred much higher levels of social cooperation, which speeded them on their way.

From the 1950s to the 1990s the United States coasted on its previous achievements. After television, the transistor, the long-playing record, the modern computer, America continued to innovate, but not always to develop and market new products. Partly as a result of a largely beneficent foreign policy, she devolved many economic tasks on others, hoping to inoculate them against social despair and the appeals of Communism. She succeeded only too well.

Now it is America's turn to receive a few foreign policy boons. Concentrating upon her economic strength, the United States has a strong hand in developing digital television, advanced computer

chips, software, parallel processing in high-speed computers, syn-
thetic fibers, civil and military aviation, chemicals and plastics, and
new miracle drugs. Her auto industry is reviving, though consumer
electronics still lags. But, however strong individual industries and
firms may be, the macroeconomic environment is critical to their
success. In the political realm the government is beginning to rally
to the aid of hard-pressed industries, facilitating cooperation in
research and consortiums in production. Congress is if anything
ahead of the executive branch in its awareness of the international
economic challenge facing the United States. But if the present
imbalanced structure of world trade and payments does not stabilize, the United States will face grave problems in the future.

Fortunately it will regain equilibrium. Now and for almost the
first time in modern history, international relations—in this case
international economics—offers the stimulus to domestic change,
not the other way around. In past epochs of history, domestic
change has been the major transforming agent, frequently revolu-
tionizing the practice of international relations. The French Revolution injected a new ideological element into international relations, and a new revolutionary militarism into methods of war. As
a result, international politics became as strife- and conflict-ridden
as French politics had been during the Reign of Terror. The Bolshevik Revolution worked a similar transforming effect upon international relations. Unlike the French Revolution, it did not lead
immediately to war with the capitalist system, despite the Allied
interventions in Russia from 1917 to 1920. The tensions between
Russia and the West were so marked, however, that there was no
cooperation between them to restrain the aggressive actions of
Nazi Germany. Hitler's armies rolled into Poland and into France
because there was nothing to bar the way.

After the Second World War the same result temporarily held
sway. The Communization of Eastern Europe together with the
possible export of the Communist system to other countries led to
the Cold War and to military threats in Korea and other places. For
a time it appeared that the new ideology had transformed international relations and diplomacy, and that nations could not talk with
one another over ideological barriers.

When the new ideological regimes proved no more able to solve
their persistent economic and social problems than capitalist coun-

tries, however, the attractions of Communism waned. In time, those regimes began to consider other means besides subversion and revolutionary military expansion to improve their plight. China deserted the Marxist-Leninist model of economic organization, despite the party's belated attempt to stress ideological solidarity against so-called worker and student counterrevolutionary "thugs." The economic opening to the West and the free industrial economies will continue. Under pressure of economic circumstance, Iran's Islamic fundamentalism was diluted. Eastern European economies experimented with new and different methods of economic output.

The rise of Japan and China demonstrated an international economic influence upon domestic policy and strategy. Japan's success provided a model of economic growth that others might try to follow. It also showed that large self-sufficient economies had no monopoly on growth or high technology. The latter were likely to be less interdependent and less advanced in economic technique than their Japanese rivals. Because of Japan's international success, China moved to follow suit after the Cultural Revolution had run its course. China's success with incentives, special economic zones, and new and freer markets challenged Russia to change in order to keep pace.

For perhaps the first time in modern history, therefore, the impulsion to domestic change now stems from international relations. Since the international economic and political system is governing, domestic change ultimately has to fit within its confines or be modified. The stimulus of international relations—the example of Japan—and the rise of the trading state are what challenge the contemporary United States to respond. Without that stimulus and that competition, business would proceed flaccidly, with U.S. production almost wholly devoted to the domestic market and innovation taking a back seat to cost savings. It is the continuing challenge of international competition that will bring a resurgence to U.S. industry. To be sure, an economic setback will force a redirection of effort and thought, but the international system will demand and sustain further change in American economic practice.

This does not mean that international change is the only transforming element. Once greater liberalization takes place domestically, this change sustains the continuing influence of international economics. War among liberal-democratic states virtually never occurs, and competition among them takes place in economic, not territorial, realms. The twin influences thus can proceed to reinforce one another.

At the end of the twentieth century, the domestic economic situation is becoming much more conducive to world trade in many political contexts. Although this does not lead to immediate free trade, as Japan, some of the Pacific Rim nations, France, Australia, and other high-tariff countries have demonstrated, greater capital abundance in a number of countries nevertheless improves the outlook for freer trade. In the American case, experts estimate that it took more than a generation before de facto capital abundance (achieved in 1910) was translated into support for free trade (in the late 1930s and after World War II). One should therefore not expect capital abundance in Japan to have immediate consequences. But given plentiful Japanese labor as well as capital, one can confidently predict a political coalition (whether sustained by the Liberal Democratic party or by a new party alignment) that will win and open the Japanese market. Tokyo consumer interests in such an outcome will be overwhelming. If countries open their markets progressively, economic growth can become the modus operandi of nations in the future.

This would result in a fundamental change in international relations. Always before in past history, nations ultimately sought to capitalize upon their economic strength with a program of military expansion. As long as passive, unmobilized populations existed on the fringes of international politics, they offered temptations to conquest that could not be resisted. In an era of nuclear weapons, guerrilla warfare, a plenitude of modern conventional arms, and the example of the Afghan resistance, however, military expansion does not appear to be the strategy of choice in most future environments.

If economic growth becomes the objective of most powers in world politics, the amount of conflict in the system automatically declines. That is because economic growth is not constant-sum in character; economic growth for one nation does not preclude growth for another; indeed, it encourages it. Nations will still be able to compare growth rates to determine who is doing the best. But countries do not fight about growth rates, for these can endogenously be changed through domestic strategies of savings and investment.

Thus two developments are increasingly beginning to direct world politics. First, international relations are becoming the primary stimulus to domestic change, and not the other way around, although domestic movement toward democratization will further reduce the need for conflict among nations. Second, a nation's means of improving its position in international relations will be through intensive domestic economic processes, not through territorial expansion. If the international economy remains open, the pursuit of economic growth could lead to a new era of peace and stability among nations.

A facilitative foreign environment, however, does not guarantee high performance for the United States. It merely permits it to occur. A more peaceful world helps all countries, but it would particularly assist the United States and the Soviet Union, who in the past have devoted a larger fraction of their national income to defense than other major powers. Recently *Business Week* commissioned a study by DRI/McGraw Hill to estimate the effects of defense cuts on the American economy. Without cuts, the federal budget remains in more than $100 billion deficit and inflation continues at present rates. With 2 to 4 percent cuts in real defense expenditure, however, interest rates fall, inflation moderates, the federal budget sprints into surplus, and growth rebounds to 3 percent of GNP. Housing surges forward.[1] Investment and savings greatly increase.

Of course predictions are no better than the models economists use, and much depends on how the United States spends its peace dividend. Historically, some countries have frittered it away in enhanced consumption. Surplus resources alone do not guarantee growth. What America needs is to shift fundamentally its economic role in world politics from that of paramount leader to that of a leader who extracts certain follower benefits. In the past, economic historians have made a great deal out of the advantages that followers ("latecomers") derive in competing with industrial leaders.[2]

1. *Business Week*, June 12, 1989, pp. 66–67.
2. See Alexander Gerschenkron, *Economic Backwardness in Historical Perspective* (Cambridge, Massachusetts: Harvard University Press, 1962).

They do not have to innovate, but can rapidly implace established and tested technology.

Leaders can continue and extend their growth if they can derive some follower advantages. First, followers tend to slow down when they have to develop their own technology and cannot simply adapt it from off-the-shelf designs provided by others; the competition between leader and followers then becomes more equal. This is also true because consumption increases in the follower nation. Second, the leader can now benefit from innovations occurring elsewhere; it does not have to invent everything itself. Sometimes this means it can overleap a technological generation, as in the move to digital television with fiber-optic cable. It also means that the erstwhile leader can now become a follower in gaining access to foreign capital. It no longer has to finance itself. The trip up the technological ladder affords additional space for competition. In the early stages, the old leader progressively deserts low-cost in-dustries and leaves them to followers. It focuses on high-wage equivalents. As the rising follower emerges to take some of the high-wage and high-value manufacturing, the erstwhile leader can regain some benefits at the lower end while keeping a strong place at the high end.

In the most general terms America's economic resurgence de-pends upon changes in foreign as well as domestic policy. The balance between "internationalization" and "domestic progress" has been skewed in the past. In the 1930s, America was preoc-cupied with the Depression and neglected foreign threats. Its neu-tral status continued far too long to permit it to adopt deterrence and containment policies toward Nazi Germany and imperialist Japan. Since 1945 it has focused almost exclusively on the foreign threat, neglecting the challenge to its domestic economy.

An appropriate balance in world politics depends on Japan and America's European allies adopting a more international stance, as the United States and the Soviet Union renew their domestic economies. This means that Japan will have to become a short-run maximizer, putting out fires in the world economy, while the United States is freed to take a longer-term perspective. Japan and other nations must take more leadership, the United States become a leading follower. Of course, nations do not always play the roles that history has planned for them. The United States refused to act its part in the 1930s. Japan still has the understandable urge to continue as a long-term maximizer and free rider, disdaining international obligations. European nations are preoccupied, constructing their own further integration. A new recession will bring countries to their senses. The United States will regain its lost economic élan, and instead of refashioning the world, in time America will rebuild a successful and just society at home.

Index